D1738848

JOHN F. KENNEDY
AND ISRAEL

JOHN F. KENNEDY
AND ISRAEL

Herbert M. Druks

PRAEGER SECURITY INTERNATIONAL
Westport, Connecticut • London

Library of Congress Cataloging-in-Publication Data

Druks, Herbert.
  John F. Kennedy and Israel / Herbert M. Druks.
      p. cm.
  Includes bibliographical references and index.
  ISBN 0–275–98007–3 (alk. paper)
  1. Kennedy, John F. (John Fitzgerald), 1917–1963—views on Israel. 2. United
States—Foreign relations—Israel. 3. Israel—Foreign relations—United States. 4.
United States—Foreign relations—1961–1963. I. Title.
E842.1.D78   2005
327.7305694—dc22   2005018670

British Library Cataloguing in Publication Data is available.

Library of Congress Catalog Card Number: 2005018670
ISBN: 0–275–98007–3

First published in 2005

Praeger Security International, 88 Post Road West, Westport, CT 06881
An imprint of Greenwood Publishing Group, Inc.
www.praeger.com

Printed in the United States of America

The paper used in this book complies with the
Permanent Paper Standard issued by the National
Information Standards Organization (Z39.48–1984).

10   9   8   7   6   5   4   3   2   1

CONTENTS

A photo essay follows page 98.

PREFACE

> My fellow citizens of the world: ask not what America will do
> for you—ask what together we can do for the freedom of man.

Thus spoke President John F. Kennedy at his inauguration. He hoped to encourage the nations of the world to work with him for the peace of planet Earth so as to save it from man's destructiveness.

As for the Middle East, he hoped that the nations of that part of the world would work for peace. He tried to encourage good relations with all of the nations there, and he changed America's relationship with Israel. Instead of following the trail blazed by FDR and adhered to by Truman and Eisenhower, he strengthened America's friendship and support of Israel. Kennedy made sure that the Arabs knew that he would not permit Israel to be endangered by them or by such major powers as the Soviet Union. Face to face with Golda Meir he firmly declared on December 27, 1962, that America's relationship with Israel was as important as its relationship with Great Britain. He worked with Israel and the Arab states to resolve the Arab refugee issue, and to foster cooperation between Israel and its neighbors in helping to develop and to share the water resources of Israel and its neighbors—however limited those resources may have been. He tried to persuade all the parties concerned to resolve their differences at the meeting halls of the UN rather than the battlefields of the Holy Land.

Kennedy, despite the views of such individuals as Ambassador Adlai Stevenson, Robert Komer, of the National Security Council, and Secretary of State Dean Rusk, realized that Israel would not be able to accept all of the Palestinian refugees and that they would have to be admitted to other states, including various Arab states.

All this was well and good, but it did not go far enough for Israeli leaders like Ben-Gurion. Kennedy's words, ideas and sentiments were good, but the promises and commitments given in private were not backed up with an open and declared alliance or arms that would restore the balance of power in the Middle East. From 1959 to 1962 Ben-Gurion had tried to persuade President Eisenhower and then President Kennedy to make the Hawk anti-aircraft missiles available to Israel. Finally as President Kennedy learned that Egypt would receive missiles and a large number of jet bombers from the Soviet Union he decided to make the Hawk anti-aircraft missiles available to Israel. But the sale of the Hawks to Israel did not establish a balance of power in the Middle East.

Israel faced the combined forces of such Arab states as Egypt, Syria and Iraq. Israel faced certain annihilation unless it could obtain equivalent, if not superior arms and a certain established alliance with the United States. Neither prospect seemed realizable even though President Kennedy was supportive of Israel. But he could not agree to a dual alliance with Israel and possibly lose all chances of good relations with the Arab states. Prime Minister Ben-Gurion realized that Israel could not rely on others to defend Israel, and he chose to develop Israel's best resource: the genius of its own people. Through scientific research it would seek to find the way to secure its existence. One of those scientific paths was its research into nuclear fission. This went counter to President Kennedy's effort to reduce nuclear proliferation. He was "haunted by the feeling" that by 1970 there might be ten nuclear powers instead of four and that by 1975 there might be fifteen or twenty nuclear powers. For Kennedy this was "the greatest possible danger and hazard."[1] Ben-Gurion and later Prime Minister Eshkol pursued their nuclear card. Whether or not Israel worked to develop nuclear energy or nuclear bombs was Israel's secret and it might help discourage Israel's neighbors from trying to annihilate Israel as Hitler had annihilated six million Jews.

Israeli leaders would remind Kennedy again and again that Israel would not permit its enemies to do to Israel what the Nazis had done to the Jews of Europe. Never again!

Most of Israel's leaders and most of its people were, in one way or another, survivors or relatives of survivors of the Holocaust. John Kennedy was well aware of that history. He had lived it while a son of Ambassador Joseph P. Kennedy who preferred a bad peace with Nazi Germany rather than a war. John Kennedy had studied England's unpreparedness and appeasement of the Nazis and he wrote about it in *Why England Slept*.

While he sympathized with and supported Israel, he could not agree to an open alliance with Israel, nor could he promise them a steady source of arms. The arms kept on coming to the Arabs, but not to Israel. Even France changed its pro-Israel policy as President Charles De Gaulle of France tried to reestablish good relations with the Arabs of North Africa and the Middle East.

In effect, Israel was cornered by the diplomatic and military developments in the Middle East during the Kennedy and Johnson years. Ultimately the Arab threat to Israel led to the preemptive action of June 1967 wherein Israel took on Egypt, Syria, Jordan, Iraq, among other Arab states, and defeated them all.

Kennedy provides us with a fascinating study of a president who had the best of aspirations and high ideals. He was a man of great insight and intelligence as well as humour, charm, and charismatic leadership ability, but with all that he could not fulfill his goal of leading America in the direction of a more peaceful and secure time. He realized the awesome responsibilities of the presidency and his was not a thirst for power or glory. He wanted to be president because he wanted to serve his country. He believed that he could lead his country and "his fellow citizens of the world" to a New Frontier of democracy, freedom and equity. He believed that he could lead America to a more responsible diplomacy. He fought for nonproliferation and disarmament, assisting the community of nations in their struggle to keep their independence. But with every passing moment there seemed to be another major confrontation that Kennedy had to deal with in South America, Europe, the Middle East, Africa and Asia. Somehow he had hoped that he could persuade other world leaders to further "the freedom of man," but in the end his primary concern was to keep planet Earth from being destroyed by war and nuclear holocaust. This was especially so after the Cuban missile crisis of October 1962.

Israeli leaders realized how important it was for Kennedy to keep things under control, but uppermost in their mind was the survival of Israel. They could not entrust their survival on private assurances of a well-intentioned urbane American president. They continued their search for an alliance with the United States and to insure their security, but when that seemed unrealizable, they pursued other ways of securing Israel's survival regardless of the obstacles, regardless of the burden and regardless of the cost.

ACKNOWLEDGMENTS

This is a study of the diplomatic relations between the United States and Israel during the 1000 days of John F. Kennedy's administration. It is based upon published works and documents as well as the papers of the John F. Kennedy Library as well as the Harry S Truman, Dwight D. Eisenhower and Lyndon B. Johnson libraries, the Library of Congress, the National Archives, Yale Library and Archives, the Israel State Archives and various private collections including the Zionist Archives of New York and Jerusalem.

In addition to consulting the archives, interviews were conducted with various participants in the making of this history. Among those interviewed were Moshe Arens, Eytan Bentsur, Benjamin V. Cohen, Rodger P. Davies, Simcha Dinitz, Eliahu Elath, Mordechai Gazit, Israel Goldstein, Mordechai Gur, Raymond A. Hare, W. Averell Harriman, Avraham Harman, Dr. Reuben Hecht, Professor Charles Hill, Samuel Katz, Dr. Emanuel Neumann, Richard H. Nolte, Benjamin Netanyahu, Yitzhak Rabin, Gerhard Riegner, Samuel I. Rosenman, Yitzhak Shamir, Ovadiah Soffer, Robert Szold, Harry S Truman and Ezer Weizmann.

I am especially grateful to William Johnson and Sharon Kelly of the Kennedy Library as well as the JFK Library Foundation for its research grants and Joann Nestor of the Joseph P. Kennedy Papers Donor Committee, and Sherry Warman of the Brooklyn College library. Many thanks to my Greenwood editor Dr. Heather Staines.

CHAPTER 1

JPK and His Sons

Joseph P. Kennedy, the father of John F. Kennedy, was not particularly fond of Jews even though some of his business associates may have been Jews. But apparently, when he saw what the German Nazis were doing to the Jews of Europe, he may have tried to help save some Jews. In November 1938, Ambassador Kennedy proposed a settlement plan whereby some 600,000 Jews of Europe were to be admitted to a sparsely inhabited part of Great Britain's African empire, but the idea was rejected by the British, Secretary of State Cordell Hull, and President Roosevelt.[1] At this time such Jewish leaders as Nahum Goldmann and Louis Lipsky found Kennedy interested in the problems of the Jewish people. They heard him express interest in the discussions of the Intergovernmental Committee on Political Refugees (ICPR) as to whether Palestine should be considered as a place of refuge for the Jews.[2] In his report to the Secretary of State on November 14, 1938, Ambassador Kennedy made note of the attacks on the Jewish communities of Germany and the indifference of world public opinion as to the plight of the Jews. This reflected a most critical situation, and he recommended that some sort of presidential initiative had to be taken to help save the Jews. After communicating with representatives from various Latin American republics, the British Dominions and various colonial empires, he concluded that the doors were closed to the Jews. Some governments claimed that they were willing to consider admitting some refugees if Germany would permit them to take property. But they would not even begin to consider admitting refugees if they were without property. Kennedy concluded his report by observing "that there can be no real appeasement as long as large numbers of people are kept in fear of their lives and uncertain as to their fate. . . ."[3]

Some British officials were concerned with Kennedy's approach to the refugee question and British Ambassador Sir Ronald Lindsay went to see Undersecretary of State Sumner Welles to complain. The British ambassador offered to relinquish Britain's portion of its immigration quota to America in favor of the Jewish refugees. Welles explained that quotas granted by Congress were not the property of the nations to whom they were granted. Ambassador Lindsay was concerned with Kennedy's warning that Anglo-American relations would be prejudiced by the refugee question because the feeling in America against the treatment accorded Jews and Catholics in Germany would become so intense as to provoke even more vehement and widespread criticism in America against the policy of appeasement being pursued by Prime Minister Neville Chamberlain. Welles assured the British Ambassador that the United States still relied on the Intergovernmental Committee and it hoped that Britain would open portions of its dominions or colonies for refugee settlement.[4]

Ambassador Kennedy asked Malcolm MacDonald, "why in heaven's name England did not show more interest in intergovernmental relief as she had all the land," and if the British government would offer some of it, the Intergovernmental Committee might then have something to work with. Kennedy observed that it seemed as if every one was feeling sorry for the Jews, but nobody offered any solution or help. British officials claimed that they were helping the refugees, and in confidence they advised Kennedy that they were admitting seventy-five Jews a day. Apparently they did not want the British people to know that because they were afraid that many might object.[5]

Nahum Goldmann and Louis Lipsky believed that the events in Germany had rendered Zionism a "great service," and they were impressed by Kennedy's own determination to bring about British-American cooperation in "an effective solution."[6]

Others were not persuaded that Kennedy was a good friend. One of the skeptics was Justice Louis Dembitz Brandeis, who wrote to his friend Robert Szold that Kennedy and Chamberlain were giving the Evian project and the Jews "the run-around."[7] Brandeis and Kennedy made reference to the Intergovernmental Committee on Political Refugees which had been established by the Evian Conference of July 1938. Only the Dominican Republic offered to rescue some 100,000 Jews. Ultimately only a few hundred Jews found refuge there. There seemed to be no funds available within the American and European coffers to help rescue any more than a few Jewish people. Those individuals who attended the Evian Conference and ran its Intergovernmental Committee on Political Refugees refused to use the word *Jew* in their official statements or documents. They referred to the Jews endangered by the German Nazis as "political refugees." The word Jew was taboo within those so-called "diplomatic" circles. The ICPR was a front used by the states of "western civilization" for doing nothing to help save the Jews.

Various plans of settlement were bandied about, but little came of them. By December 1938, more than fifty such plans or projects had been discussed, but there was no place of refuge for Jews. When the governors of Alaska and the Virgin Islands agreed to offer asylum, Roosevelt opposed. Roosevelt and the State Department insisted that the admission of refugees to those U.S. territorial possessions represented a circumvention of the quota laws and they warned that all kinds of "enemy agents" might enter the country by the back door. FDR apparently said that he sympathized with the refugees but he refused to "do anything which would conceivably hurt the future of present American citizens." He advised that the Jews find other places of refuge.[8]

While Ambassador Kennedy may have had an interest in rescuing Jews, a search through Joseph P. Kennedy's diary for the years 1933 to 1945 reveals hardly any reference to the persecution of European Jews. On November 15, 1938, he wrote that at "King Carol's dinner he had a long talk with the Prime Minister, urging him to do something for Jews."[9]

JOSEPH, THE ELDEST SON

Ambassador Kennedy had hoped that his eldest son, Joseph P. Kennedy Jr., might enter politics and become president of the United States. Joe Jr. was regarded as handsome; he was well liked and shared the conservative views of his father. Ambassador Kennedy hoped that his son could achieve that which he had not been able to achieve: the Presidency.

During a 1934 trip to Europe Joe Jr. saw the Nazis in action. He sympathized with their sterilization program which he saw as a means of "doing away with many of the disgusting specimens of men which inhabit this earth."[10] Joe Kennedy Jr. was about eighteen at the time, and he regarded National Socialism as "a remarkable spirit which can do tremendous good or harm, and whose fate rests with one man alone."[11] In a letter he wrote to his father on April 23, 1934, he observed that the German "dislike of the Jews was well founded." He accepted the Nazi German claim that the "Jews were at the head of all big business, in law etc. It is all to their credit for them to get so far, but their methods had been quite unscrupulous."[12] Apparently in this instance Joe Jr. accepted hearsay as fact:

> A noted man told Sir James the other day that the lawyers and prominent judges were Jews, and if you had a case against a Jew, you were nearly always sure to lose it. It's a sad state of affairs when things like that can take place. It is extremely sad, that noted professors, scientists, artists etc. should have to suffer, but as you can see, it would

be practically impossible to throw out only a part of them, from both the practical and psychological point of view. As far as the brutality is concerned, it must have been necessary to use some, to secure the wholehearted support of the people, which was necessary to put through this present program. It was a horrible thing, but in every revolution you have to expect some bloodshed. Hitler is building a spirit in his men that could be envied in any country. They know he is doing his best for Germany, they have tremendous faith in him and they will do whatever he wishes. This spirit could very quickly be turned into a war spirit, but Hitler has things well under control. The only danger would be if something happened to Hitler, and one of his crazy ministers came into power, which at this time does not seem likely. As you know he has passed the sterilization law which I think is a great thing. I don't know how the Church feels about it, but it will do away with many of the disgusting specimens of men which inhabit this earth. In all, I think it is a remarkable spirit which can do tremendous good or harm, whose fate rests with one man alone.[13]

Joe Kennedy Jr.'s report was that of a youngster influenced by the racism and anti-Semitism of his time and surroundings. In a letter to his Mother and Dad dated August 25, 1942, from the U.S. Naval Air Station, Banana River, Florida, he confided as to how upset he had been by "a red headed Jew, who answers to the name of Greenberg." The young man had brought a saxophone and a trumpet and he fancied "himself as one of Benny Goodman's best. I stood it for about an hour and then we went in, and made known our feelings toward him and his instruments. He hasn't brought them out today, but I've got my fingers crossed."[14]

His father was more circumspect in his evaluation of Hitler. But Joe Sr. still held to his conviction that young Joe had "a very keen sense of perception" and that his "conclusions are very sound." Then he added that it was "still possible that Hitler went far beyond his necessary requirements in his attitude towards the Jews, the evidence of which may be very well covered up from the observer who goes in there at this time." But he was concerned for the fate of the Catholics in Germany. He asked if Hitler wanted to reunite Germany, and he picked on the Jews, why was it "necessary to turn the front of his attack on the Catholics?"[15]

Joseph P. Kennedy realized that the German Nazis used the Jews as a scapegoat; but he could not understand why they attacked the Catholics. Such was the nature of Joseph P. Kennedy and his son Joe Jr.

Joe Kennedy Jr. spent the summer of 1939 traveling throughout Europe and on June 10, 1939, he was in Hungary. He wondered what advantage it would be for the United States to get involved in the European difficulties:

Would the break up of the British Empire in itself be most dangerous for us or could we still retain our trading position to Germany after such a break? Do we want to get frightfully aroused by the treatment of the Jews when Catholics and others were murdered more cruelly in Russia and in Republican Spain and not a word of protest came? Do we want an increasing anti-Semitism in our country brought about by the production of forty thousand Jews and political undesirables in our country from Europe . . . ? Do we want these people when we have eighteen million unemployed and a budget whose relief expenditures have made for a deficit of billions of dollars? I know it is terrible the way the Jews are being persecuted but the Chinese are being bombed and Catholics were killed in Spain, but as far as I am concerned that is none of my business unless my country wants to dominate the world and impose its conditions of justice on all people and be prepared to support its laws at any time so that freedom and justice will be assured.[16]

After the German and Austrian atrocities against the Jews on November 9–10, 1938, known as *Kristallnacht,* Roosevelt recalled the American ambassador to Germany, and America's interests remained protected by its *chargé d'affaires.* Young Joe seemed undisturbed by the German atrocities against the Jews. What disturbed him was that the United States had withdrawn its ambassador from Germany. This did not seem right to young Joe Jr., and he asked:

Why have we kept our ambassador at home when the English have sent theirs back so that he at least may have some influence. Why did we send an Ambassador to Germany a few years ago who did nothing but criticize the country to which he had been accredited to when the real job of the ambassador is to keep his government informed and he must be on good terms with the government and pretend that he likes them?[17]

Ambassador William E. Dodd, an American historian, had protested against German Nazi anti-Jewish pogroms. Joe Jr. believed that America should "stay out of war and that being a rich nation we can live by ourselves. . . ." He thought that America should have "a real policy in Europe entirely fitting for the greatest power in the world rather than a half hearted mamby pamby policy skipping one way then to the other no one knows what will happen if there is a war."[18] Those were some thoughts of Joe Kennedy Jr. in 1938–1939.

Ambassador Kennedy was greatly concerned with the well-being of his children. Even though he would send them to such private schools as Choate and hire tutors for them, he would not always be satisfied with their progress. When he wrote to George St. John, JFK's tutor, on November 21, 1933, he said that "the work (JFK) wants to do he does exceptionally well, but he seems to lack entirely a sense of responsibility" and that "must be developed in him very quickly, or else I am very fearful of the results. . . . The happy-go-lucky manner with a degree of indifference that he shows towards the things that he has no interest in does not portend well for his future development. He has too many fundamentally good qualities" and once he would get "on the right track he would be a really worthwhile citizen."[19] Ambassador Kennedy was concerned with his children's mental and physical well-being. He was especially troubled by the frailness of John F. Kennedy. As he would write to Dr. Sara Jordon on November 4, 1938: "I worry a good deal more about him than I do about international affairs or anything else. . . ."[20] In a letter to Jack he wrote: "After long experience in sizing up people I definitely know you have the goods and you can go a long way. Now aren't you foolish not to get all there is out of what God has given you and what you can do with it yourself."[21]

For a time Ambassador Kennedy seemed to appreciate such Jews as Felix Frankfurter. He believed that his son Joe Jr. would some day show the letters from that "great man Professor Frankfurter, or Judge Frankfurter" to his grandchildren. JPK found that America was in a state of "confusion." He thought that Father Coughlin, the priest from Michigan, was nothing more than a demagogue who had "his own Bishop on his side and the Catholic Hierarchy are unable to do anything with him whatsoever." Roosevelt seemed to be taking all that "criticism smiling."[22] That was December 5, 1933.

JPK did not always reject Coughlin. On August 18, 1936, he wrote a thank you note to Father Coughlin "for all the kind things you are saying about me. I feel like the fellow on his vacation who sends the postal card back to his friends saying, 'Wish you were with us.' "[23] Apparently the *Boston Sunday Post* had reported that Coughlin had described JPK as "a shining star among the dim 'knights' of the present administration's activities."[24]

Joseph P. Kennedy was an isolationist and noninterventionist as many Americans were in the post–World War I era. Some Americans rejected his isolationist views. Former Wisconsin Governor Lafollette observed that Joseph P. Kennedy was too sympathetic to Chamberlain in order to represent America's best interests in Great Britain. From a very personal standpoint JPK did not wish to see the lives of his children sacrificed to war. "I hate to think how much money I would give up rather than sacrifice Joe and Jack in a war."[25] He would note in his diary entry of February 22, 1938, that President Roosevelt "indicated his firm intention of keeping our country out of any and all involvements or commitments abroad." FDR considered "the situation too uncertain for the United States to do anything but mark time until things have settled down." The president "did not seem to resent the position Chamberlain has taken of trying to make deals with Germany and Italy in order to fend off a crisis."[26]

During Kennedy's March 4, 1938, interview with Neville Chamberlain he advised the British prime minister that the "United States must not be counted upon to back Great Britain in any scrape, right or wrong."[27] Chamberlain said that he was "making his plans for pacification or fighting, as things might develop, without counting on us, one way or the other." Kennedy "talked to him quite plainly and he seemed to take it well."[28] He observed that the dictators had gotten their way by mere bluff.

> Nobody is prepared to talk turkey to Messrs. Hitler and Mussolini, and nobody is prepared to face the risk of war by calling their bluffs. The British will not do anything to check either one of them unless they actually fire guns. If that guess is correct, I am sure . . . none of these various moves has any significance for the United States, outside of general interest.[29]

In a private conversation of mid-February 1938, Roosevelt had informed Kennedy that he intended to firmly keep America "out of any and all involvements or commitments abroad." The president "did not seem to resent the position Chamberlain had taken of trying to make deals with Germany and Italy in order to fend off a crisis."[30]

Kennedy was strongly in favor of advising "our British cousins that they must not get into a mess counting on us to bail them out. We might or might not. But it hardly seems fair to let them assume that we will be ready, as last time, to come to their rescue if they get in a jam."[31] As to the situation regarding Hitler's demands on Czechoslovakia, Jan Masaryk had informed Kennedy that "his country will make its deal with Germany, unpalatable as it may be, unless it is assured of British protection. It does not consider the proffered French assistance as valuable enough to justify putting up resistance against Berlin."[32] Ambassador Kennedy believed that there would be no war and Germany would get "whatever it wants in Czechoslovakia without sending a single soldier across the border. The Czechs will go, hat in hand, to Berlin and ask the Fuhrer what he wants done, and it will be done."[33]

But when war seemed inevitable on September 27, 1938, JPK "argued that ships should be made available to get our wives and the wives of men in business here out as soon as possible."[34] That same day the King of England confided with Joe Kennedy that he was rather downcast because of the possibility of war. He found it "inconceivable" that there would be "another war twenty years after the last one."[35] The following day Kennedy was notified that Hitler had called for a meeting the next morning. There would be further negotiations rather than the war Hitler had threatened to undertake because of the Sudetenland. As Joe Kennedy put it: "I never was so thrilled in my life."[36] That night a feeling spread "all over London that this means that war will be averted." Kennedy believed rather naively that "these four men around a table and with the President always willing to negotiate," might mean the "beginning of a new world policy which may mean peace and prosperity once again."[37]

Did Ambassador Kennedy sympathize with Hitler and his ideas? Joe Kennedy denied having any sympathy for Hitler.

> I have no more sympathy with Hitler's ideas than anyone in America, but I asked myself, what am I going to do about it? If I am going to war with them to stop them, fine, that's one thought; if I am going to cut them off economically fine, that's another thought, but, if I am going to stick my tongue out at them, then I am not with it at all.

And he observed that so much of the mail attacking him came from Jews. "Seventy-five percent of the attacks made on me by mail were by Jews and yet, I don't suppose anybody has worked as hard for them as I have or more to their advantage."[38] The German Nazi attacks on the Jews disturbed him insofar as they interfered with "the whole program of saving western civilization." He was

> hopeful that something can be worked out, but this last drive on the Jews in Germany[39] really made the most ardent hopers for peace very sick at heart. Even assuming that the reports from there are colored, isn't there some way to persuade them it is on a situation like this that the whole program of saving western civilization might hinge. It is more and more difficult for those seeking peaceful solutions to advocate any plan when the papers are filled with such horror. So much is lost when so much could be gained.[40]

Kennedy thought that the Germans were doing themselves a disservice by attacking the Jews. Despite the grimness of the situation Joe Kennedy tried to introduce a light note. He observed that FDR had told Bernard Baruch that ". . . if there was a demagogue around the type of Huey Long, who took up the cause of anti-Semitism, there would be more blood running in the streets of New York than there was in Berlin."[41]

Ambassador Kennedy would advocate "getting along with the dictators" and at times he asked permission to enter into peace discussions with high-ranking German Nazis. In June 1938, German Ambassador Herbert von Dirksen would write to his foreign office that he found Kennedy sympathetic to the Reich and to its racial policies. Kennedy's friendship with Charles Lindbergh and his dim view of Allied air power further promoted the impression that Kennedy was pro-Germany and that like Lindbergh, he, was a defeatist. But according to Amanda Smith, JPK's granddaughter and biographer, by mid-1939 "he supported American aid to Great Britain and an end to American neutrality."[42]

England was at war and the Germans were bombarding British cities to demoralize the British people. By March 20, 1940, Kennedy noted that public opinion in Britain had "turned anti-American and anti-Ambassador Kennedy."

> The things they say about me from the fact that I've sent my family home because they were afraid, to the fact that I live in the country because I am afraid of being bombed. . . . All rotten stuff but all the favorite dinner parties at Mayfair go right to work hauling the U.S. Ambassador down.[43]

While Hitler's Nazi armies were invading and conquering Europe, Joseph P. Kennedy believed that "in spite of everything" Hitler would not "make an attempt at an invasion of England unless his own air force is strong enough to knock off the British air force."[44] Up until August 2, 1940, "We have only had small raids and no very great damage has been done."[45]

Walter Lippman was one of the American columnists Ambassador Kennedy greatly disliked. Apparently Lippmann proclaimed that he had not "liked the U.S. Ambassador for the last six months. Of course the fact that he is a Jew has something to do with that. It is all a little annoying, but not very serious."[46]

Why did Ambassador Kennedy have to make reference to the fact that Lippman was a Jew? Did he believe that because Lippman was a Jew he wrote negatively about him?

Amanda Smith tried to decipher the question of whether her grandfather had been an anti-Semite. It had been reported that Joseph P. Kennedy observed that his Hollywood colleagues were "a bunch of pants-pressers."[47] According to Amanda Smith, those were "secondhand or overheard comments recollected by others years later and are for that reason difficult to trace or substantiate."[48] But she observed that his papers and correspondences "record genuine friendships with a number of prominent Jewish figures" such as Bernard Baruch, Felix Frankfurter, Justice Brandeis, and Henry Morgenthau.[49] And yet he would complain that the bad press at home was due to "Jew influence in the papers in Washington." He would note that "seventy-five percent of the attacks made on me by mail were by Jews. . . ."[50] Like anti-Semites before him Joseph P. Kennedy claimed that his dislike for certain Jews did not mean that he hated all Jews. When his friendship for Felix Frankfurter and Henry Morgenthau had soured he wrote, "It is no secret that I have not a high opinion of Felix Frankfurter—or of Henry Morgenthau, Jr., or of a number of Jews in high places, but that doesn't mean that I condemn all Jews because of my personal feelings for some."[51] When he resigned his post as ambassador and FDR did not

appoint him to any further post JPK blamed it all on the Jews that surrounded Roosevelt.

JPK conferred with the top leaders of England and they advised him that
England would not surrender. Nevertheless he did not have much hope for
England. Comments such as "Democracy is finished in England," that he
made during an interview with the *Boston Globe* on November 9, 1940,
would haunt him for years to come.[52] As would his continued opposition
to American involvement in World War II. As the British were being bom-
barded by the Germans and it appeared by September 11, 1940, that the
Germans would invade Great Britain, Joseph P. Kennedy was concerned
that "the whole problem will finally be dropped in the lap of the United
States" and that "we in the U.S. will have to furnish more supplies and
that means that England will have to have more money, and they can't get
more money unless we give it to them. . . ."[53] But he noticed that American public opinion favored American intervention in the war. On June 11,
1940, Churchill had told Ambassador Kennedy, ". . . We will fight to the
end and give Hitler plenty of trouble. Hitler has not won this war until he
conquers us. Nothing else matters. And he is not going to do that."[54] Prime
Minister Churchill believed that the Americans would come in the war once
they would see that English towns and cities had been bombed and destroyed. An American correspondent of an English newspaper noted that
all it would take for American intervention was an incident and JPK believed that "if that were all that was needed, desperate people will do desperate things."[55]

Ultimately Joseph P. Kennedy would note that the Germans had bombed
London without mercy. On September 10, 1940, he wrote:

> The last three nights in London have been simply hell. Last night I
> put on my steel helmet and went up on the roof of the Chancery and
> stayed up there until two o'clock in the morning watching the Ger-
> mans come over in relays every ten minutes and drop bombs, setting
> terrific fires. You could see the dome of St. Paul's silhouetted against
> a blazing inferno that the Germans kept adding to from time to time
> by flying over and dropping more bombs.[56]

But as the world came apart JPK tried to hold on to a sense of normalcy.
He complained that he had been so busy that he had no time to shave.[57]

On December 1, 1940, after consulting with President Roosevelt, he announced his resignation. The essence of his resignation statement was that
he would continue to work to keep America out of the war: "My plan
is . . . to devote my efforts to what seems to me the greatest cause in the
world today . . . to help the President keep the U.S. out of the war."[58]

John F. Kennedy, tried to help his father explain the position he had taken
on "appeasement." John Kennedy's analysis was a balanced presentation

of that quagmire. As to JPK's view on Munich, JFK suggested his father explain that in November 1938, he had believed "England might have been bombed into submission overnight due to her complete lack of defenses and America would have been in an exposed and dangerous position. You might put in here that it was worth any risk for America to have a Europe at peace, and therefore, you supported Chamberlain."[59] Furthermore, John advised, that with complete frankness JPK should admit "I am gloomy and I have been gloomy since September 1938" but the circumstances have been "so fraught with peril and disaster for us [that] we must take the course . . . completely from the point of view of what is best for America."[60] He advised his father to say that he was "not gloomy for gloom's sake." That in the long run he was "interested in what is best for this country."[61] Moreover, he should make it clear that

> you with your background cannot stand the idea personally of dictatorships—you hate them—you have achieved the abundant life under a democratic capitalistic system—you wish to preserve it. But you believe that you can only preserve it by keeping out of Europe's wars. It's not that you hate dictatorship less—but that you love America more.[62]

Personal tragedies did not make JPK's life or disposition any easier. In early August 1943, John F. Kennedy's PT 109 was cut in half by a Japanese destroyer in the Blackett Straight. He was reported missing in action.

At 2:30 a.m. on August 2, four Japanese destroyers came down the Blackett Strait. The crew of PT 109 tried to defend themselves against the Japanese. As John Kennedy recalled, one of the destroyers "turned straight for us. It all happened so fast there wasn't a chance to do a thing."[63] Eleven out of thirteen crew members made it to safety. They swam to shore in the darkness. JFK helped save his crew. His father knew for two weeks that JFK was missing, but he did not tell the rest of the family. By August 13, 1943, the news arrived that John F. Kennedy had survived. Twenty-six year old Lieutenant Kennedy and ten of his men were rescued from a small coral island deep inside the Japanese controlled Solomon Islands.[64] His back had been further injured. He wrote home on August 13, 1943:

> This is just a short note to tell you that I am alive—and not kicking–in spite of any reports that you may happen to hear. It was believed otherwise for a few days—so reports or rumors may have gotten back to you. Fortunately, they misjudged the durability of a Kennedy—and am back at the base now and am O.K. As soon as possible I shall try to give you the whole story.[65]

A year later, on August 4, 1944, Joe Jr. would write: "I am working on something different. It is terribly interesting, and by the time you receive this letter, it will probably be released, but at this point it is quite secret. Don't get worried about it, as there is practically no danger."[66] Joe Kennedy Jr.'s plane was emptied to make room for 22,000 pounds of explosives. He and his copilot were to lock their aircraft on target which were German fortifications along the Belgian coast, and then they were to bail out. But it did not go well. There was an explosion on board. Joe was missing as a result of that explosion.[67] On August 13, 1944, Rose Kennedy was notified by telegram that her son Joe was "missing result explosion operational flight 12 August 1944 in the performance of his duty and service of his country."[68]

Ambassador Kennedy continued working. In his notation concerning the 1944 political campaign he wrote of his talks with vice president-elect Harry S Truman and Bob Hannigan, Chairman of the Democratic National Committee. They all believed that FDR would die soon and that Truman would become president. Joe Kennedy wrote that Truman and Hannigan believed that "Truman will be President and will kick out all these incompetents and Jews . . . and ask fellows like myself and others to come back and run the government. Truman assured me that is what he would do. He said that he disliked Mrs. Roosevelt very much and that she had snubbed him when she was out west."[69] That was what JPK wrote in his diary. Did it happen that way? Did Truman say that he would kick out of Washington "all these incompetents and Jews?" Perhaps that is what Joseph P. Kennedy may have thought he had heard, or perhaps he would have liked to have heard that? Apparently he also thought that Truman might offer him a job, but he much preferred it if Jack would be offered a job as Assistant Secretary of State or Assistant Secretary of the Navy. He thought that Jack was in a better position than he was with "the group around Roosevelt."[70]

In July of 2003 the Truman library released the contents of a "newly" discovered Truman journal that had apparently been misplaced somewhere in the Truman archives that raised the question: After all is said and done was Truman an anti-Semite? One of his best friends and business partners, Eddie Jacobson, was a Jew. Truman had insisted on a Nuremberg Tribunal that would put to trial the Nazis involved in the murder of some six million Jews. Despite all the opposition within his administration to the Jewish state idea Harry S Truman was the first to recognize the State of Israel. In 1949 he made sure that the United States would lend Israel some $100 million. Yet at one point in time, when Eddie Jacobson asked his friend Truman to see Dr. Chaim Weizmann, the future president of Israel, he found a Harry S Truman unwilling to do so. Jacobson noted in his recollection of that March 1948 meeting with Truman that Harry spoke like an anti-Semite. Apparently Truman had been hurt by the way such Zionist leaders as Rabbi Hillel Silver had spoken to him and had banged his fist on the president's desk. Truman considered that disrespectful of the president, not just disrespectful of Harry S Truman. But after a bit of temper and frank expression Harry Truman agreed to meet with Weizmann. During that meeting Truman assured the Zionist leader of his support.[71]

According to the alleged journal entry of July 21, 1947, Truman met with Henry Morgenthau

> about a Jewish ship to Palestine. Told him I would talk to General Marshall about it. . . . He'd no business, whatever to call me. The Jews have no sense of proportion nor do they have any judgment on world affairs.
>
> Henry brought a thousand Jews to New York on a supposedly temporary basis and they stayed. When the country went backward and Republican in the election of 1946, this incident loomed large on the Displaced Persons program.[72]
>
> The Jews I find are very, very selfish. They care not how many Estonians, Latvians, Finns, Poles, Yugoslavs or Greeks get murdered or mistreated as Displaced Persons as long as the Jews get special treatment. Yet when they have power, physical, financial or political neither Hitler nor Stalin has anything on them for cruelty or mistreatment to the underdog. Put an underdog on top and it makes no difference whether his name is Russian, Jewish, Negro, Management, Labor, Mormon, Baptist he goes haywire. I've found very, very few who remember their past condition when prosperity comes.
>
> Look at the Congressional attitude on Displaced Persons and they all come from Displaced Persons.[73]

Truman was no anti-Semite, but his remarks, if they were his remarks, could easily reflect the notions of an anti-Semite. Perhaps Joseph P. Kennedy may have heard one of HST's outbursts. We may never know.

Once JPK retired from his ambassadorial post he found that Roosevelt seemingly was no longer interested in his services and he blamed all his troubles on "Francis Perkins, Sam Rosenman, Harold Ickes and Henry Morgenthau."[74] As he said to Grace Tulley, Roosevelt's secretary, "I think that most of the fellows around the president are a lot of bastards. . . ." In conversation with the president, Joe Kennedy said he believed that the Italian and Irish voters were not with Roosevelt because "they felt that Roosevelt was Jew controlled. Second they felt that the Communists were coming into control." Roosevelt countered by saying that there was "no Communist Party in the United States." That struck Kennedy as "a very weak answer." Furthermore, Kennedy believed that the Irish and Italians "along with many others, felt that there were more incompetents in Roosevelt's cabinet than you could possibly stand in this country." But when Kennedy said that the "Irish and Italians were off," FDR insisted that the English were to blame for the Italian situation. Roosevelt asked him if the

Irish were off because of the "Free State situation." Kennedy said that he was with the group who felt that the "Hopkins, Rosenmans and Frank-furters and the rest of the incompetents would rob Roosevelt of the place in history that he hoped to have—because they would make such a horri-ble mess of it before they got through."[75]

Roosevelt insisted that "lots of the present group working in Washing-ton would be looking up train schedules November eighth."[76] Moreover, "I don't see Frankfurter twice a year." Kennedy had an answer for that as well: "You see him twenty times a day but you don't know it because he works through all these other groups of people without your knowing it."[77]

JPK admitted that he was "sore and indignant" because of the way he had been treated. "The last blow was when Jack was recommended for a medal by all his officers in direct command which was two degrees higher than what he finally received. He was reduced by Halsey's group for rea-sons unknown to me, but which I suspect were because I was *per sona non gratia* to the powers that be in Washington. . . ."[78]

Roosevelt tried to assuage JPK and he recalled that he had a similar com-plaint. "Well, those things happen. In fact. Elliot was recommended for the Congressional Medal of Honor. The board turned it down because they felt it would look as if he had been given it because he was the President's son." The president said that his son Elliot should have been promoted to general, but he was "held up for the same reason."[79]

They talked about Secretary of the Treasury Henry Morgenthau's plan to reduce Germany into a pastureland. JPK seemed shocked by that idea. Roosevelt observed that the plan had caused a good deal of trouble: "I don't know anybody who has less political sense than Henry. That plan of his caused me great trouble throughout the country."[80]

JPK spoke with Jimmy Byrnes "who had discussed the Morgenthau plan with him." Byrnes apparently told him that Generals Eisenhower, Patton, Patch and Holmes had not seen the Morgenthau plan "which he got from a Jew named Bernstein, who used to work in the Treasury Department."[81]

Moreover he believed that Chamberlain would "never be condemned for Munich," although he would be "criticized for being part of a government which did not prepare to meet this menace."[82] He recalled that after the Munich conference Roosevelt had sent Chamberlain a congratulatory mes-sage which read "good man," and that he had personally "delivered the message to Chamberlain."[83]

Roosevelt looked very sick to Kennedy that day in 1944. The president's "face was as gray as his hair," and his hands shook violently when he tried to take a drink of water. He looked so sick that the "terrible realization came to me that the Hopkins, Rosenmans and Frankfurters could run the country now without much of an objection from him."[84]

Through most of World War II Russo-American relations were very poor. The Russians did not trust the Americans, and the Americans did not trust the Russians. They were headed for serious trouble. JPK talked about those developing troubles and saw that Stalin wanted much more than the Baltics, Poland to the Curzon Line and Bessarabia. Speaking with Lord Halifax he asked: "Aren't you in for trouble in Iran already?"[85]

Some of Joe Kennedy's observations and correspondence seem incredible. He wrote J. Edgar Hoover saying that the most wonderful thing would be if J. Edgar Hoover were elected president.

> It would be the most wonderful thing for the United States, and whether you were on a Republican or Democratic ticket, I would guarantee you the largest contribution that you would ever get from anybody and the hardest work by either a Democrat or a Republican. I think the United States deserves you. I only hope it gets you.[86]

Joe Kennedy helped persuade his son John to enter politics and run for Congress. He fought for John's election to Congress, and later to the U.S. Senate and the White House. But when Eleanor Roosevelt spoke of Joe Kennedy's financial and political support, John Kennedy rejected her remarks as "injudicious" and "false" in a letter he wrote to her dated December 11, 1958:

> I note from the press that on last Sunday afternoon, December 7, on the ABC television program 'College News Conference,' you stated, among other things, that Senator Kennedy's "father has been spending oodles of money all over the country and probably has a paid representative in every state by now.
>
> Because I know of your long fight against the injudicious use of false statements, rumors or innuendo as a means of injuring the reputation of an individual, I am certain that you are the victim of misinformation; and I am equally certain that you would want to ask your informant if he would be willing to name one such representative or one such example of any spending by my father around the country on my behalf.
>
> I await your answer, and that of your source, with great interest. Whatever other differences we may have had, I'm certain that we both regret this kind of political practice.[87]

Mrs. Roosevelt responded and insisted that she was not telling any falsehoods.

John F. Kennedy would be elected to the House, then to the Senate and ultimately he would be elected president. His presidency represented one of the most turbulent times in American history. There was one major crisis after another ultimately ending with his assassination on November 22, 1963. Mrs. Rose Kennedy felt that during his presidency her son had been misinformed and misguided by members of his own administration, particularly the CIA and the State Department. But she would continue to encourage her other children and grandchildren to serve their country and to achieve the highest possible office the nation could offer them.

She observed that during the crises over Cuba John Kennedy "felt he had been misinformed by the C.I.A.—which Allen Dulles was the head of."[88] Jackie "had never seen him so depressed except once at the time of his operation."[89] Rose Kennedy thought that her son Bob should become president after Jack:

> It will be good for the country
> And for you
> And especially good for you know who.
> Ever your affectionate and peripatetic
>
> Mother[90]

CHAPTER 2

John F. Kennedy and Israel

John F. Kennedy was born on May 19, 1917, in Brookline, Massachusetts. He was the second of nine children to Rose and Joseph P. Kennedy. His father, a banker, investor, filmmaker and a Democrat was somewhat involved in Massachusetts politics. Along the way he wanted to become president of the United States. But he could not compete with the very popular Franklin D. Roosevelt. Ultimately Roosevelt appointed him ambassador to Great Britain where he served from 1938 to 1940. Joseph P. Kennedy believed that America should stay out of the War and that it should learn to live with the Nazi Germans even though they were barbarians.

While Joseph P. Kennedy, an Irish Catholic, struggled to achieve social and political prominence in Boston, he could never win acceptance from the Protestant Brahmins of that community, and he held some biased views of his own regarding Jews. According to some State Department documents and a number of his own papers, it seems that during the years of the Holocaust he did try to help save some Jews endangered by the Nazis. But in his diaries covering the years 1933 to 1945 there is hardly a mention of the persecution of the Jews of Europe. Arthur Hertzberg in his book *A Jew in America* recalled how in September of 1939 a rabbi had gone to see Ambassador Kennedy at the American embassy in London to seek some help for his American family who were stranded in Nazi occupied Europe. Despite the fact that his wife and children were American citizens, Embassy officials told him that they could not help and that it was "out of their hands." The man "badgered everyone who walked out of the doors of the embassy building until he got an appointment with Ambassador Joseph Kennedy." Kennedy "received him coldly and told him to stop being a pest."[1] The rabbi was disheartened and so outraged that he uttered a curse:

"May God have as much compassion for your children as you have for mine."[2] According to Professor Hertzberg this became known as the "Kennedy curse."[3]

In 1939, for whatever reason, Ambassador Kennedy sent young John Kennedy on a fact-finding mission to Palestine. Perhaps it was to gather information regarding the socioeconomic and political situation of the Land of Israel which at that time was under a British Mandate, supervised by the League of Nations.

John F. Kennedy's maternal grandfather was John A. Fitzgerald, a congressman and mayor of Boston, and his paternal grandfather was Patrick J. Kennedy, a very active Boston Democrat.

In 1940 JFK was graduated from Harvard University, after attending Choate School and the London School of Economics. For his senior thesis he did a study of Great Britain's unpreparedness for World War II. It was published under the title *Why England Slept*.

Three of Joseph P. Kennedy's sons enlisted in the armed services to fight the Nazis. Joe Kennedy Jr. became a pilot. His plane, carrying explosives, blew up during a secret mission over German occupied territory. It was a tragedy from which the family found it most difficult to recover. Joseph P. Kennedy was perhaps hardest hit. He had hoped that his beloved eldest son would enter politics and some day run for the presidency.

John F. Kennedy enlisted in the Navy in 1941, became a lieutenant, and served as commander of PT boat 109 off the Solomon Islands. A Japanese destroyer crashed into his ship and sank it. Despite Kennedy's injuries he helped save members of his crew. He was awarded the Purple Heart, and the Navy and Marine Corps Medal. His act of bravery further injured his back difficulties, which he had acquired while playing football at Harvard. He would never escape from those back injuries and pain. He may have "looked like a movie star,"[4] and before his presidency he may have been part of Frank Sinatra's circle of friends, but he was often in need of medication to alleviate his back pains.

According to Robert Kennedy, Jack thought of getting into politics in 1944 or 1945.[5] Robert Kennedy believed that "truly in many ways he could do some of these things as well or better than my oldest brother Joe." And when there was a vacancy in the 11th Congressional District, John "felt it was natural that he would go in and run for Congress."[6] His father may have been instrumental in persuading him to enter politics. With his father's financial support he won election as a Democratic Congressman from Massachusetts. He served in that capacity from 1946 to 1953. During that time he supported many, but not all, of the policies of Democratic President Harry S Truman. He was one of 435 members of the House but did not particularly distinguish himself.

JFK's VIEWS ON ISRAEL

Some have wondered if Joseph P. Kennedy's anti-semitism had an impact on JFK. From all that has been researched and written about JFK and from the public record it is evident that he had not acquired his father's anti-semitism.

As a young man Kennedy had traveled to the Holy Land in 1939 and reported back to his father some penetrating observations regarding the Land of Israel, the Jews and the Arabs. As he reviewed the history of British policies and the various claims to the desert which was the Land of Israel, Kennedy observed that the "important thing is to try to work out a solution that will work, and not to try to present a solution based on two vague, indefinite and conflicting promises," such as High Commissioner Sir Henry MacMahon's letters to the Arabs, and Foreign Minister Arthur Balfour's Declaration to the Jews. During World War I the British were eager for assistance from the Jews and the Arabs, and to get that assistance they made separate promises to both sides. The MacMahon letters dealt vaguely with the delineation of independent Arab states. The Balfour document, likewise vague, called for the establishment of a Jewish Homeland in Palestine, taking into account the rights of the Arabs. As young Kennedy keenly observed, Foreign Minister Balfour gave with "one hand what he took back with the other." This also was JFK's "objection" to the White Paper of May 1939. It theoretically presented a good solution, but it just would not work.[7]

He noted that "on the Jewish side there is the desire for complete domination, with Jerusalem as the capital of their new land of milk and honey, with the right to colonize in Trans-Jordan." They believed that given sufficient opportunity they could cultivate the land and develop it as they had done in the Western portion. The Arab answer to this was that the Jews had the benefit of capital, and if they had the capital, equal miracles could have been performed by them. Though this was partly true,

> The economic setup of Arabic agricultural progress with its absentee landlords and primitive methods of cultivation, could not under any circumstances probably have competed with the Jews. However, this very fact lies in the background of the Arabic objection to the Jews. They realize their superiority and fear it.[8]

After some Arab rioting in 1936, the British sent another commission to Palestine. They held hearings before which the Arabs refused to testify and the British came up with another partition plan which became known as the Peel plan. The Arabs rejected it. They refused to grant the Jews even ten percent of the land as proposed by the Peel plan. But then most of the Jews likewise rejected the plan because the British kept Jerusalem and the

Jewish people were denied most of the Land of Israel. Ultimately the British came up with another plan, or White Paper, in 1939, which closed Palestine to further Jewish immigration to all but some 75,000 Jews plus some 20,000 in case of need over the next five years.

JFK "saw no hope for the working out of the British policy as laid down by the White Paper." He believed that the land of Israel should be broken up into "two autonomous districts giving them both self-government to the extent that they do not interfere with each other and that British interest is safeguarded. Jerusalem, having the background that it has, should be an independent unit. Though this is a difficult solution yet, it is the only one that I think can work." It was one of the most difficult and troublesome areas, and while he thought Danzig "was a tough problem," he had "never seen two groups more unwilling to try and work out a solution that has some hope of success than these two groups."[9]

Joseph P. Kennedy saw the war in Europe spreading, and he was prepared to pay any price in order to avoid war and thereby save his sons. He asked Roosevelt to "curb our . . . sentimentality and look to our own vital interests . . . in the Western Hemisphere." John Kennedy likewise considered these questions. Some writers claimed JFK wrote articles for the *Harvard Crimson* calling for appeasement, including "Peace in Our Time," dated October 9, 1939, which observed that in order to achieve peace, "concessions" would have to be made to "Hitlerdom," such as a puppet state in Poland, "a free economic hand for the Nazis in eastern Europe, and a redistribution of colonies." Such concessions would inspire Hitler to disarm, "Hitlerism-gangsterism as a diplomatic weapon—would be gone, Europe could once more breathe easy," and America would be "saved from another, more terrible, world war." According to a November 11, 1939 *Crimson* editorial, 78 percent of Harvard's undergraduates were opposed to U.S. participation in the European war. Both editorials were unsigned. Reference archivist Andrea B. Goldstein of the Harvard University Archives noted that "no author was attributed to either article." After further research, Harvard Archives reference assistant Michelle Gachette found that in "a search of related records of the *Harvard Crimson*, the Comment books of the editorial board cited the author of "Peace in Our Time" as GHH. . . . The initials most likely refer to Garfield Henry Horn, AB 1940, who served as editorial chairman." In the personal papers of John F. Kennedy there is an undated letter to his father in which John says, "I am enclosing an editorial I had written in the *Crimson*—the editorial chairman changed it a bit and didn't emphasize some of the things I wanted him to print."[10] The *Crimson* of June 9, 1940, did include a signed letter from John F. Kennedy, which attacked the policy of appeasement and unpreparedness: "The failure to build up her armaments has not saved England from a war, and may cost her one. Are we in America to let that lesson go unlearned?"[11]

It was about this time that John F. Kennedy's senior thesis, *Why England*

Slept, was published and there he was likewise critical of Britain's unpreparedness and appeasement Policies.

According to Hirsh Freed, a Jewish politician from Boston, when John Kennedy entered politics he "did not know any Jews." Hirsh claimed that JFK "never had come to grips with the questions which faced Italians, Negroes, Jews or for that matter, the Irish, in any specific or immediate way as a politician or as a statesman." Hirsh received phone calls from him, and Kennedy would ask, "Who was this guy and who was that organization and should I associate myself publicly with this and so on."[12] Freed arranged for Kennedy to meet with Jewish leaders of Boston in April 1947, so that he could ask them questions regarding Zionism and Israel. The folks at that gathering "were people who were devoted to a cause. They knew they were right and they couldn't help but speak the truth as they saw it."[13]

JFK was a grassroots campaigner. Phil Fine, a Boston lawyer and Kennedy campaign staffer would recall how Kennedy went from community to community, and from district to district to speak with the people. He likewise visited such Boston Jewish communities as Roxbury, Chelsea, and Dorchester. He spoke with the people and told them who he was and that he was running for Congress. Sometimes he would speak on Israel, and at times various democratic congressmen like FDR Jr. would come up to Massachusetts and campaign with him. He knew that some people resented his father and he was straightforward with them: "Look, I am my father's son; I don't disown him, but I have a mind of my own. My father has never told me what to do up till now in a vote, and he's not going to tell me in the future. I'm going to do what I think is right."[14]

Hirsh Freed believed that Joseph P. Kennedy's views did have an impact on John F. Kennedy's campaign for the presidency. He and his staff had to overcome the feeling that Joe Kennedy had "helped Nazi Germany at one point and that he had never been a friend of the Jews." It was believed that JFK had taken on "a little bit of the coloration of his father and should not be supported," but that attitude came to an end as soon as it was found out that Richard M. Nixon was the Republican candidate.[15]

Myer Feldman observed that Jewish folks were "generally liberal" and Kennedy recognized this. As he would tell Feldman, "Jews are liberal just as the Catholics are normally conservative." "Yes," observed Feldman, "but you're a liberal Catholic and I'm a conservative Jew." Kennedy had to contend with the charges that he was not "strongly in favor of civil rights" and that he was pro-McCarthy. All these problems would influence the Jewish voters. But then no liberal could support Nixon. While Kennedy sought the nomination, individuals like Eleanor Roosevelt attacked JFK as having been pro-McCarthy.[16] But once he was nominated and then elected president he got the backing of such individuals as Eleanor Roosevelt and Jackie Robinson.[17]

In 1951 Robert accompanied JFK on a world tour. They stopped off in the Near East "just for a very short period of time." JFK was impressed by the progress which had been made since he had been there last in 1939, with all the construction in Israel; but he was careful not to travel at night on account of Arab terrorists. The "toughness, ruggedness and cockiness" of the Israeli soldiers impressed him. "You can feel a sense of dedication . . . and a willingness to endure hardship." But altogether it was a "very hard" life in Israel. President Chaim Weizmann's wife illustrated the difference between Israel and the Arab world when she took the group to a rooftop in Jerusalem and pointed out the dividing line across Jerusalem between the darkness over the Arab section and the "bright lights of Jewish held Jerusalem."[18]

There they met Congressman Franklin D. Roosevelt Jr., who seemed to get all the attention from people like David Ben-Gurion and Golda Meir. While Robert did not mention who it was that cared more about the son of Roosevelt than the offspring of JPK, and behaved as "if we were not there," he recalled that the Kennedys chose not stay there very long.[19]

In June of 1951 John Kennedy met Jacqueline Lee Bouvier at a dinner party. It took another seven months before they would meet again. At that time she interviewed him for her column in *The Washington Times-Herald*, and he asked her for a date. They dated thereafter, but as his senatorial campaign progressed he had less and less time for dating. Six months after his election to the Senate they got married.

On May 23, 1952, soon after Israel observed its fourth anniversary, Kennedy spoke in favor of a bill for Israel's refugee program. He noted that Israel's accomplishments stood as a "beacon of inspiration to all free men everywhere." Nothing was more admirable than the "tenacity with which Israel maintained its policy of unlimited immigration. They increased their population from 600,000 to more than 1,200,000 in the past three years. "For the peace of the world it is important that the Arab states recognize the reality of the existence of Israel. Israel is here to stay." He repeated what Ben-Gurion had said to him in November of 1951: As liberal, and progressive elements would emerge in the Arab states, progress could be made toward peace. When Ben-Gurion was asked whether certain Arab states might have reason to fear Israel, Ben-Gurion asked, "How could a country like Egypt with a population of over twenty million fear an invasion from a population of less than two million . . . ? Besides we were once in Egypt and have no desire to return." In May 1952, Kennedy concluded that what Israel had accomplished in ancient times and what Israel achieved in recent times "should be a symbol to all men of the invincibility of the human spirit."[20]

In 1952 Kennedy ran for the Senate against Republican Henry Cabot Lodge Jr. and managed to defeat that Boston Brahmin, but Kennedy's career in the Senate was not spectacular, nor was it dominated by party politics. He criticized Truman for getting America involved in the Korean war, and he was a friend of Republican as well as Democratic Senators. He was a friend of Senators Robert A. Taft, Mr. Republican, and Joseph R. McCarthy, head of the anti-Communist investigatory committee in Congress.

One of his first acts as Senator from Massachusetts was to cosponsor a February 1953 Senate resolution condemning Soviet Russia's persecution of its Jews, and he called upon the Eisenhower administration to demand that Russia "remove all cause for the fears that have arisen throughout the world concerning the future security of the Jewish people now residing within the borders of the U.S.S.R."[21]

As the Near East military imbalance favored the Arabs, JFK joined other legislators who asked Eisenhower to lift the arms embargo against Israel. They argued that since Egypt and other Arab states received arms from the Russians, the United States should reconsider an arms policy that worked to Israel's detriment.[22] JFK declared that it was "time that all the nations of the world . . . realized that Israel is here to stay; she will not surrender— she will not retreat—and we will not let her fall."[23]

In the midst of the Arab war against Israel and western influence, Congress became aware that Saudi Arabia would not permit Jewish-Americans to work in that country even if they were U.S. servicemen. Kennedy joined other senators and congressmen in demanding that the government not acquiesce with Saudi Arabia's discriminatory policies. On July 1, 1956, he cosponsored a Senate resolution which called upon the United States to take a firm stand against such discrimination.[24]

In 1956 Kennedy was hospitalized for back surgery. The operation did not improve his situation. But while in hospital, he worked on his book *Profiles in Courage*, a study of U.S. Senators who voted according to their convictions rather than according to party line. It reflected his own political disposition. The book won him a Pulitzer Prize in 1957.

Once out of the hospital he campaigned for the vice-presidential nomination, but the Democrats chose Adlai E. Stevenson as their presidential candidate and Senator Estes Kefauver as the vice-presidential candidate. John Kennedy was greatly disappointed, but in this instance, it may have been a blessing in disguise. Stevenson and Kefauver lost. It was the second time that Stevenson, the former Governor of Illinois, and a favorite of American "liberal" establishment circles, had lost in his bid for the presidency.

When Kennedy was elected president, Stevenson fancied that he would become Secretary of State. Robert Kennedy recalled that President Kennedy did not like Stevenson and he did not want to entrust "the bastard" with such an important job. Ultimately Kennedy appointed him U.S. ambassador to the UN where he would stay out of Washington, D.C. and out of Kennedy's hair.[25]

After the Israelis defeated the Egyptians in October 1956, the UN prepared to condemn Israel because it refused to leave the Sinai and Gaza, and the Eisenhower-Dulles government seemed sympathetic to that condemnation. On February 13, 1957, JFK expressed his opposition to such a one-sided condemnation:

> I am deeply concerned over the possibility that this Government would recommend U.N. sanctions against Israel for her refusal to abide by the resolutions calling for the complete withdrawal of her troops. . . . It is my understanding that Israel asks only that she be given a guarantee of no further raids or blocking of Israeli shipping on the part of Egypt from the territory which Israel will then relinquish. . . .

He firmly supported Israel's right to defend herself "with any means at her disposal."[26]

On February 24, 1957, JFK called for a permanent settlement of the Middle East problems that would be acceptable to all reasonable men. He believed that the Arab refugees who "were sincerely willing to live at peace with their neighbors and to accept the Israeli government should be repatriated," while others who wanted to remain in Arab states should be assisted to make permanent homes there and to live in "peace and dignity."[27]

Kennedy's book *The Strategy of Peace* was published in 1960 just as he was about to leave the Senate for the White House. Therein he wrote of the importance of Israel's survival and success: "Israel is the bright light now shining in the Middle East. The survival and success of Israel and its peaceful acceptance by the other nations of the Middle East is essential."[28]

In 1960 after a hard-fought battle in the presidential preference primaries, and then with Lyndon B. Johnson at the Democratic convention, John Kennedy was nominated for president. In order to win the support of Texas Democrats he reluctantly asked Lyndon Johnson to be his running mate. Robert F. Kennedy helped engineer Kennedy's campaign. On July 15, 1960, John Kennedy gave the American people an idea of what course his presidency might take:

> We stand today on the edge of a New Frontier—the frontier of the 1960's—a frontier of unknown opportunities and perils. . . . The New Frontier of what I speak is not a set of challenges. It sums up, not what I intend to offer the American people, but what I intend to ask of them.[29]

And on April 19, 1961, he defined his New Frontier as expressing

> our feeling that the 1960's—this coming decade—was going to be a period of entirely new material change, that science had brought the means of a much better life for people, not only in the United States, but all around the world and therefore, we were crossing frontiers which involve the struggle for freedom here in the United States, and

around the world. I thought we were moving into a new period, and the new frontier phrase expressed that hope.[30]

On August 25, 1960, Kennedy had spelled out his support for Israel, before a gathering of the Zionist Organization of America as he declared that fifty years after Theodor Herzl, the prophet of Zionism, "proclaimed its inevitability" Israel was a "triumphant reality."[31] He recalled that he had spent two weeks in the Holy Land during 1939 where he witnessed "great neglect and ruin" left by the Turkish Empire. But the Jewish settlers worked to transform the country "under conditions of the utmost difficulty by labor and sacrifice." In 1939 "Palestine was still a land of promise rather than a land of fulfillment." By 1951 Israel had welcomed some 600,000 Jewish people back to their homeland. He observed that the United States had certain moral obligations to Israel. The United States had declared that there should be free transit through the Suez Canal, but it permitted "defiance of our 1956 pledge." Suez was open, but not to Israeli ships and those trading with Israel. Israel "surrendered" its 1956 victory only because of U.S. and UN pressures. Kennedy observed that Washington's policy and that of the UN had "permitted defiance of our 1956 pledge with impunity—indeed, with economic reward."[32]

There was much rhetoric about the arms race in the Middle East. Kennedy recalled that Ben-Gurion had advised him of the dangers of war, and that he had hoped that there would be peace, but there was "only an embittered truce between renewed alarms."[33] Kennedy called for an international conference of the leaders of Israel and the Arab states "to consider privately their common problems, assuming that we support in full their aspirations for peace, unity, independence and a better life; and that we are prepared to back up the moral commitment with economic and technical assistance." Kennedy believed that the White House offer "honestly intended and resolutely pursued, would not be lightly rejected by either side, unless that side was prepared to bear the burden of breaking the peace." Kennedy had promised not to "waste time in taking the initiative for such a conference once in office," but he would be persuaded by his State Department and White House staff not to support direct face-to-face Arab-Israeli negotiations. He yielded to State Department advice that the United States should be the go-between for any Arab-Israeli talks, and eloquently he would say that the Middle East needed "water, not war, . . . tractors, not tanks," and that its peoples needed "bread not bombs."[34]

Kennedy spoke of Zionist leaders who had envisioned a Jewish state which would have "no military power and which would be content with victories of the spirit." Theodor Herzl, the founder of political Zionism, had envisioned Israel as a neutral state, but with a modern army possessed with the most up-to-date equipment. Herzl knew that unless Israel would be well armed it would become the target of its enemies. Kennedy seemed to understand that the "compulsions of a harsh and inescapable necessity" had "compelled Israel to abandon this hope" of a nonmilitary existence. But once again Kennedy inserted his Cambridge idealism and rhetoric: "I cannot believe that anyone in Israel tonight wants to live their lives out in a garrison state," and he thought the Arabs would be better off if they united in an effort to attack their "accumulated social problems" rather than attack Israel.[35] In his three years as president he would try to encourage the Arab states and Israel to progress toward peace, but with little success.

In November 1960, John F. Kennedy defeated Richard M. Nixon. He was the first Catholic to be elected president. He won 303 electoral votes and 34,227,096 popular votes, but he had only one fifth of 1 percent more popular votes than Nixon. Many admired the young president for his vigor, intellect, courage, pursuit of peace and his patronage of the arts. He came to symbolize a new age of progress. As for Israel, he promised to be a man of independence, a man who thought for himself, and believed that peace between Israel and the Arabs could be achieved.

The history of John F. Kennedy and Israel represents a history of an American president who, like Harry S Truman, sympathized and supported Israel; but was primarily concerned with what he came to believe was in the best interest of the United States and in the furtherance of freedom throughout the world. Although he strove to avoid the mistakes of the past, particularly those of the Eisenhower administration, he pursued similar policies such as appeasement of such Arab leaders as Nasser of Egypt and the rulers of Saudi Arabia and Iraq. While he had made a commitment "to bring peace" to that part of the world,[36] it remained beyond his reach for as long as his efforts were interpreted as appeasement by such violators of the peace as Nasser and the rulers of such dictatorships as those of Iraq, Syria and the Arabian peninsula.

Kennedy tried to find a balanced approach. He tried to persuade both Israel and the Arabs that he was a fair president. As he corresponded with the Israeli and Arab officials, the texts went through several drafts before he was satisfied with them because, as Myer Feldman recalled, President Kennedy wanted to establish "a continuing dialogue and that they should feel free to write to him personally and not even through regular State Department channels."[37] He wanted to show the Arabs that he "was sympathetic to all their legitimate aspirations," but he did not want to give the impression that he was "siding with them in their conflict with Israel."[38] He discussed the variations in text of each letter with his advisors including Myer Feldman, so that the Middle Eastern leaders would feel that he was personally interested and concerned. He wanted them to get "involved in the discussions with us."[39] But in the end his efforts to win the support of such Arabs as Nasser were misinterpreted as weakness and appeasement.

The letters were supposed to be private and secret, but President Nasser of Egypt published a portion of a letter that Kennedy had sent him. "The President was fit to be tied at that because there had been no prior con-

sultation with him" regarding the publication of the letter. Kennedy felt
that the publication of his letters was being "used as a propaganda move
by Nasser, and he considered it a breach of faith." This made Kennedy "a
lot more cautious in his dealings with Nasser," but it did not change his
feeling that Nasser was "the key to the settlement of this whole problem."[40]

What did young Congressman Jack Kennedy know about Israel and the
Jews? His contacts with Jews and Israel had been scanty. His father, Joseph
P. Kennedy, was not known as an advocate of the Jewish people.

Did President Kennedy try to make up for Joe Kennedy's reported anti-
Semitism? Some may wish to speculate.

John F. Kennedy loved his father, but he was his own man. Myer Feldman, a pro-Israel Jew, who was one of the president's closest advisors on
the Middle East, recalled that "one of the major handicaps that we had to
overcome, in the Jewish community, was the feeling that Kennedy's father
had never been a friend of the Jews."[41] But people paid less attention to
this matter when Richard Nixon became the Republican standard bearer.
Liberal Jews then rallied to Kennedy. "No liberal could support Nixon."[42]

According to Hirsh Freed, while young JFK may have been familiar with
the "Jewish question" or the "Palestine question" he knew it only as a
young man, who had taken trips through Europe and had done some traveling in the Near East, but he knew all that in "a very academic way."[43]
Hirsh recalled that on April 30, 1946, Kennedy asked if he should lend his
name to a group headed by Ben Hecht in connection with Palestine activities. Hirsh thought that Ben Hecht was "a nice guy," but his group included some "wild-eyed guys who were somewhat irresponsible." Some
were out of touch with the Jewish community, and he advised him to keep
away from that one, and he did.[44]

In 1947 when JFK was in the hospital, he got a letter from Shilcar who
apparently was his only Jewish buddy during the war. Shilcar wrote
Kennedy to encourage him and told him what "a hell of a nice guy he had
been when he was his chief."[45]

Freed realized that Jack Kennedy was an intelligent, reflective and independent thinker, and he helped Kennedy "educate himself" on such issues as the future State of Israel.[46] That's the way Jack was from an early
age. Various JFK biographers observed that he was determined to be himself rather than conform to anybody's mold, including that of his parents.[47]

Freed recalled that Congressman Kennedy thought for himself and would
not support an issue just because it might bring him some votes.

> I knew Kennedy well enough to know that you couldn't con him into
> a position; that he wasn't going to come out and favor partition of
> Palestine or a Jewish state in Palestine or even a Jewish homeland in
> Palestine merely because there were votes in it, or because he was
> going to do me a favor. He wasn't built that way.[48]

After he studied the issues and saw the relevant materials, Congressman Kennedy supported Partition. The first time he addressed this issue publicly was on June 15, 1947, before the 27th annual convention of the New England Zionist Region:

> America's responsibility is to exercise its position of leadership, and give new hope and new heart to the fear-ridden peoples of the world. Today, the United Nations has before it the solution of the Palestine problem. It is my conviction that a just solution requires the establishment of a free and democratic Jewish Commonwealth in Palestine, the opening of the doors of Palestine to Jewish immigration, and the removal of land restrictions, so that those Jews who desire to do so, may work out their destiny under their chosen leaders in the Land of Israel. If the United States is to be true to its own democratic traditions, it will actively and dynamically support this policy.[49]

At that convention he heard Rabbi Abba Hillel Silver, a prominent leader of the American Zionist movement, deliver one of his orations. Apparently Kennedy, Congressman from the 11th Massachusetts congressional district, was somewhat impressed.[50]

On November 14, 1951, John F. Kennedy spoke of the need for cooperation amongst the people of the Middle East to combat communism. He did not believe that communism could be met effectively "by merely the force of arms. . . . The true enemy of the Arab world is poverty and want." The peoples themselves had to be led to reject it, and it was to those peoples that America's policies had to be directed. Without the support and cooperation of the people of that region, a Middle East Command would fail badly. It "would intensify every anti-western force now active in that area" and "from a military standpoint would be doomed to failure." More than that, said Kennedy, "the very sands of the desert would rise to oppose the imposition of an outside control upon the destinies of these proud peoples."[51]

In May of 1952, as Kennedy supported a $76 million appropriation to help Israel absorb its Middle Eastern Jewish immigrants he spoke of Israel as "a beacon of inspiration to all free men everywhere."[52]

In 1957, after Israel defeated the Egyptians in the Sinai war, then Senator John F. Kennedy joined Lyndon B. Johnson and other senators, in an effort to persuade Eisenhower not to impose sanctions against Israel. As Senator Kennedy observed: "Israel asks only that she be given a guarantee of no future raids or of blockading of Israeli shipping."[53]

On October 1, 1959, Kennedy outlined what his Middle East policies might be if elected president. He seemed to understand the complexity which was Israel as he observed that Israel was a "strongly nationalistic and a strongly universalistic state." While it remained well "armed and alert" it formed "close associations with other nations throughout the world." Israel was even able to close the "dark chasm between her nation and Germany." He recalled that on the very day Israel proclaimed its independence on May 14, 1948, the Secretary-General of the Arab League had declared that this would be "a war of extermination and momentous massacre which will be spoken of like the Mongolian massacres and the Crusades." Even though Israel is subject to constant "alarms and invasions" it has maintained its "basic temper," and its "national life has been one of self-restraint and peace." While some claimed that Israel was the cause of turmoil in the Middle East, Kennedy tried to dispel the "myth that without Israel there would somehow be a natural harmony throughout the Middle East and the Arab world. Even by the coldest calculations, the removal of Israel would not alter the basic crisis in the area." Arab rivalries and pressures within the Middle East, "the quarrels over boundaries and the cross pressures of nationalism" would all still be there even if there were no Israel. The United States helped Israel, but it had also been the "beneficiary" of that friendship. "And the strongest army in the Middle East is not a pawn to be lightly cast aside."[54]

Kennedy emphasized that Israel is a democracy and shares with the "West a tradition of civil liberties, of cultural freedom, of parliamentary democracy, of social mobility" and is "almost untouched by Soviet penetration." In most of the Arab states the "leadership class is small, its popular roots tenuous, its problems staggering" and in many of the countries of the Middle East, the Soviet model holds "special attraction" particularly because the Western allies have not developed long-range programs to attack "the real causes of political disintegration and economic backwardness which are the real allies of Arab communism."[55] Kennedy thought that a regional approach to the Middle East lands should be inaugurated. The great rivers of the Middle East are international: the Jordan, the Nile, the Tigris and Euphrates and various western states besides the United States could make important contributions to the economic and technical assistance within a regional approach. He thought that it was time for multilateral programs to resettle the refugees, a food pool to make use of America's agricultural surpluses and a Middle East development authority to pool capital and technical aid to the area. He hoped that "Israel, one of the youngest republics," and the United States, one of the "oldest republics," would strengthen and expand their friendship. "The reward can well be the most precious gift that can be bestowed—peace in a troubled part of the world."[56]

In an address before a college in eastern Oregon on November 9, 1959, Kennedy observed that America's mistakes in the Middle East were due to mistakes in attitude. The United States tended to deal with the area "almost exclusively in the context of the East-West struggle" and its battle against international communism. Policy-makers dismissed nationalism and economic development as of "secondary importance. We were wrong in believing that what was so clear to us could be made equally compelling to other peoples with problems very different from our own. . . ." The Arabs

had never been occupied by Soviet Russia, but they had been ruled by Western powers, and they were not prepared to abandon their nationalism or
their neutrality for an alliance with the West.[57] There were other mistakes.
"We overestimated our own strength and underestimated the force of nationalism." The United States supported unpopular regimes rather than the
people. The question "is not whether we should recognize the force of nationalism, but how we can help to channel it along constructive lines."[58]
The United States should not rely upon the Voice of America or the Sixth
Fleet, the Baghdad Pact or the Eisenhower Doctrine. If the United States
talked with the Arabs "on terms of their problems, not ours," then the
Middle East could become an area of strength and hope. We should make
clear that, "we will never turn our back on our steadfast friends in Israel,
whose adherence to the democratic way must be admired by all friends of
freedom." But the United States should make it clear throughout the Middle
East that the United States wants "friendship, not satellites."[59]

In a letter he wrote to Rabbi Israel Goldstein of New York's Congrega-
tion B'nai Jeshrun in August of 1960, Kennedy called for a Middle East
peace conference that would end the state of war and initiate Arab-Israeli
peace talks and an end to discrimination against Jewish American troops
from serving in Saudi Arabia.[60]

In August 1960 he addressed the ZOA annual conference saying that Israel was a "champion of democracy."[61]

When Kennedy became president he wanted to separate from the foreign
and domestic policies of Dwight D. Eisenhower. His was a New Frontier. He
envisioned taking the lead in making the world a better place in which to
live. He had high hopes and ideals, and Israel represented hope and progress
to him, not just for Jews, but for all of mankind. He believed that it would
be easier to live with an Israel that was secure than an Israel that might undertake unpredictable adventures such as the 1956 Sinai War. Israel might
even become an effective arm against Soviet expansionist ambitions.

But despite Kennedy's good intentions, the State Department held the
same harsh views towards Israel as the State Department officials of previous decades. Their concern was with Arab views and feelings and often
they advocated Arab causes. They insisted that Israel should absorb some
300,000 Arabs who claimed to be refugees from the Holy Land; they were
opposed to Israel's strong retaliatory measures against Arab infiltrators and
terrorists; they opposed Israel's divergence of the Jordan River waters for
its own agricultural programs; they did not support Israel's desire to make
Jerusalem Israel's capital and, most of all, they did not wish to see Israel
become stronger militarily. Throughout the years 1948 to 1960, some elements of the State Department suspected Israel of being more sympathetic
to Russia than to the United States. On July 12, 1962, Secretary of State
Dean Rusk stated that the "United States does not recognize Israel's rights
in Jerusalem as paramount nor does the United States accept Jerusalem as

Israel's national capital."[62] In 1948, Dean Rusk of the State Department's UN desk had called for establishing Palestine as a trusteeship. During Kennedy's administration, Foreign Minister Moshe Sharett observed that Rusk had not changed much since 1947–1948: "Even though so many years had elapsed. Nothing seemed to have changed in Rusk's heart."[63]

As Dean Rusk observed during an interview for the Kennedy library: "There's always a body of opinion outside the Department of State which thinks that the Department of State is pro-Arab and anti-Israeli simply because the Department of State is not always willing to recommend that we put all of our chips in the Middle East on Israel." He thought that "Jewish interest, the Zionist and Israeli interest, has been strongly in support of the Democratic Party. . . . Anything less than an all-out pro-Israeli view in the Department of State is looked upon with considerable suspicion by the Jewish community in this country." U.S. policy "has been based upon the rather simple and general proposition that the United States supports the political independence and territorial integrity of all the states in the Middle East. . . . We have pursued that policy in this postwar period on a rather extraordinarily evenhanded basis—despite our close friendship for Israel and despite the difficulties we've had in the Arab world because of our strong friendship with Israel." Rusk blamed all the difficulties the United States had with the Arabs on Israel and if there was a commitment to Israel he saw it as part of a general commitment to the "political independence and territorial integrity of all the states in the area." The Kennedy administration was involved in "a triangular relationship" in the Middle East. There were the extreme Arabs versus Israel. There was a "bitter contest between the progressive Arabs—Egypt, Syria, Iraq and the so-called moderate and conservative Arabs, such as Lebanon, Jordan, Saudi Arabia, Libya, Tunisia and Morocco." The triangular competition was "a very complicating issue for us during the Kennedy period." Kennedy exerted a great deal of effort to establish a better relationship with some of the extreme Arabs like Nasser of Egypt. He approved a very large three-year food program for Egypt at a cost of several hundred million dollars, but Nasser did not reciprocate. He would make "fiery speeches condemning the U.S." and he made it difficult for the administration to obtain congressional support for aid to Egypt. When Nasser said that the United States should "dump its aid programs into the Red Sea" Congress called for an end to that program. "Nasser had a very unpredictable and difficult personality, and it was very hard to get very far in a basic improvement of our relations with him, despite major efforts we made, including major aid programs for Egypt." Some of the most severe problems during the Kennedy years came as a result of conflict between Arabs, as in the cases of Egypt versus Yemen and Saudi Arabia. Rusk found it rather difficult to talk with the Arabs. If he talked to one Arab individually he found himself talking to "a reasonable man," but if an Arab had "one other Arab as an audience, he tended to go a little crazy because there's so much pressure in the Arab world to take the categorical attitude of hostility toward Israel." The Arabs could not get themselves to say publicly that they would accept Israel for "one reason there is in the Arab world the phenomenon of assassination." Chances were "very high" that the Arab who would accept some of the "moderate proposals" that we put forward would be "assassinated."[64]

President Kennedy listened to various viewpoints. When Myer Feldman had said quite frankly that he "had an emotional sympathy with Israel," and that this would "color" the advice he might give, and that perhaps the president might want somebody else, the president said, "No." Kennedy insisted that he "would expect Feldman to have those sympathies and he would think less of Feldman if he didn't keep him advised of anything that was happening."[65]

President Kennedy often turned to Myer Feldman for advice on "anything dealing with the Middle East." Secretary of State Rusk, at times, resented this. Feldman recalled that on one occasion President Kennedy asked him to call Rusk and advise him of his discussion and what position the United States was taking on a particular matter. Rusk was upset and told Feldman: "I want it clearly understood that I'm running the State Department and not somebody in the White House, and if there's any doubt about that I want to go to the President." The president then told Feldman that Rusk had to be kept fully advised and that he "had to keep him happy." From then on President Kennedy often sent messages to Rusk directly, rather than through Feldman.[66]

Kennedy tried to make the Tripartite Declaration of 1950 more effective by advising both Israel and the Arab states that the United States would "act with whatever force and speed necessary to halt any aggression by any nation." He invited "all like-minded nations to join with the United States in "signing, registering and depositing this declaration with the United Nations." As it was, Kennedy found the Tripartite declaration "too uncertain of execution and effect to be a useful shield for peace." As it was with states "so close to one another in a sensitive tension-ridden area, a delay of only a few days in international reaction to aggression might well be fatal to a nation's freedom and indeed to the peace of the entire world." Ideally Kennedy hoped that once the states of the Middle East had "a firm and precise guarantee," the need to continue the arms race would disappear, and the "easing of tensions inevitably would follow."[67] But who was to grant those guarantees. Throughout Kennedy's few years in the White House, the State Department advised against providing such guarantees, and he went along with their views.

On May 30, 1961, President Kennedy met and talked with Prime Minister Ben-Gurion. The Jewish leader expressed his great concern with the growing disparity of power between Israel and Egypt. In population alone Egypt had some thirty million people while Israel had only two million, and the gap with respect to arms available to Egypt and those available to Israel was growing. Russia had provided the UAR with three times the quantity of what Israel had, and the Russian arms were of a "superior quality." Perhaps Israel had "superior" manpower, but the Egyptians had hundreds of Russian military instructors.[68]

Israel's struggle with Egypt was not just a question of power, said Ben-Gurion, it was a matter of Israel's survival. The Egyptians wanted to wipe out Israel. "If Nasser were to defeat Israel he would do to the people of Israel what Hitler had done to the six million Jews of Europe."[69] Ben-Gurion spoke of Israel's need for air defenses. While the Egyptians had twenty-six airfields, Israel had only three. In order to deal with this situation and to defend its airspace, Israel needed the Hawk anti-aircraft missiles: "If we get the Hawk missile we are more or less safe." Within its arsenal Israel had "nothing against the Mig 19 or the Mig 21."[70]

Kennedy listened to Ben-Gurion and then observed that there would be a danger of escalating the arms race if the United States would provide Israel with the Hawk missiles. Moreover, "the situation would be different if you were to be at a disadvantage which would imperil you." Kennedy observed that Israel was about to get Mirage planes from France and "an electronic system."

But he was "very anxious" that Israel "should not be at a disadvantage." While he could not give Ben-Gurion an affirmative answer "on the Hawks at this time," he wanted Ben-Gurion to provide him with "an understanding on the extent of the danger" that Israel faced. If there was a "danger" that was "one thing," but if there was "parity" that was "quite another thing." John Kennedy realized that "in the last few months the position in the Middle East had become more acute than it was in this respect."[71]

Ben-Gurion informed Kennedy of Egypt's air force strength. It had twenty MiG-19's; ninety-six MiG-17's; thirty MiG-15's and fifty IL 28's. Overall, Egypt alone had at least 300 planes.

Kennedy listened intently and then expressed his concern. He promised to watch the "count very carefully" because "our interests are closely involved with yours. We want to make sure that you will not be open to attack. . . . I want to make it clear that our interests are very in accordance with yours."[72]

Ben-Gurion asked Kennedy to arrange for a U.S.-Soviet declaration to support "the integrity and independence of all the countries in the Middle East."[73]

The president revealed his great concern over America's extensive international commitments. One such area of commitment was Berlin: "We cannot be moved out of Berlin without breaking the Atlantic Alliance. We do not intend to do that. What use would a declaration on our part be to you if we were to get run out of Berlin? I am not sure that our problems are not as great as yours."[74]

One of Kennedy's greatest concerns was nuclear proliferation. He was alerted to the possibility that Israel was working in that field. An earlier intelligence communication dated January 19, 1961, from the U.S. Embassy in Israel, detailed Israel's development of nuclear research:

> With reference to the recent revelation of the existence of a nuclear reactor in Beersheba, the fact that Israel is working in this field should have come as no surprise inasmuch as almost every nuclear scientist who has contributed to the development of nuclear weapons in the U.S. has been a Jew and a great number of prominent nuclear scientists have come to Israel.[75]

Furthermore, the Soviet-Egyptian project for the construction of a nuclear reactor in Egypt had been known for some time. It was also known that the Egyptians, not satisfied with the help they had been getting from the Soviet Union, approached the West Germans with requests for the kind of men whose speciality was the development of nuclear weapons. Israel knew this, and it also knew that the United States was not in a position to bring effective pressure on the Egyptians. Israel could not "prudently wait until Egypt produced atomic weapons before doing something about one of its own."[76]

Before Ben-Gurion's meeting with Kennedy, the National Security Council provided the president with its views of Israel's possible atomic research. The State Department clearly pronounced its opposition to the proliferation of nuclear weapons. Such weapons, the report stipulated, would have "Middle East repercussions" and Arab concerns were "widespread and deep." Inevitably the Arabs would appeal to the Russians. The development of Israeli nuclear capability as far as the National Security Council was concerned, was "contrary to the interests of peace."[77]

On May 30, 1961, President Kennedy tried to find out from Ben-Gurion whether Israel was pursuing the development of nuclear weapons. The United States was preoccupied with the balance of power in the Middle East and elsewhere. Ben-Gurion expressed his deep concern with the growing disparity of power between Israel and Egypt and he reminded Kennedy of Israel's special circumstances: "We are the remnant of a people struggling for its last hold of its existence. Israel is our last stop."[78] As for Israel's development of atomic energy and power, Ben-Gurion made no secret of the fact that it needed atomic power for its peacetime projects and considered atomic energy for defense purposes. Atomic energy was being used for Israel's desalination projects in order to obtain more water for its desert. Israel had no coal or oil of its own and that was why it turned to atomic energy. France had lent Israel some assistance in its efforts to build an atomic reactor and for the "time being the only purposes are for peace. But we will see what happens in the Middle East. It does not depend upon us.

Perhaps Russia won't give bombs to China or Egypt, but maybe Egypt will develop them herself," said Ben-Gurion.[79]

Clearly Israel was outnumbered, and it could not match the quantity of weapons which the Arabs accumulated. It needed superior weapons to match the resources, population and weaponry of the Arab states and such of their supporters and suppliers as the Soviet Union. It needed weapons that could, if necessary, target the Soviet Union as well as its Arab clients.

Kennedy said that the United States did not "want it to appear that Israel was preparing for atomic weapons," for if it seemed that Israel was preparing such weapons, then the UAR "would try to do the same." The president appreciated the report and wanted it published, but he also wanted some neutral scientists to investigate Israel's atomic energy project. Ben-Gurion agreed to have the report published, but he was skeptical about having a "neutral" intervene in this matter and he asked: "What do you mean by neutral?"

Perhaps someone from Switzerland, Sweden or Denmark? "Would you object to our sending such a neutral scientist?" asked Kennedy.[80]

Ben-Gurion seemed not to object.[81]

What Ben-Gurion did not say was as important as what he did say to Kennedy. Israel was outnumbered, and outgunned. It needed superweapons to match those which the Arabs and their supporters, like the Soviet Union, had.

IN SEARCH OF SOLUTIONS

Israel called for direct, face-to-face negotiations with the Arabs. It had tried to persuade the Eisenhower administration to encourage the Egyptians to negotiate directly. The Israelis believed that if Egypt would negotiate and make peace, the other Arab states would likewise make peace. They tried to get Kennedy's support for direct peace negotiations. The Congo Republic in Brazzaville came up with a resolution which some twenty-one UN members supported calling upon the Arabs and Israel to enter into direct peace negotiations. Feldman knew that this "was not just the idea of the Congo, that this had been generated by Israel." The Israelis believed that they had a "good chance of getting the Brazzaville resolution passed if the United States would support it." But when Feldman inquired of the State Department and the UN "people," they informed him that it would not be possible to get sufficient support to pass the resolution.[82] Kennedy had no objection to direct negotiations between Israel and the Arab states, but he was concerned that if the United States "took the position that there should be direct negotiations, all the Arab states would feel that the United States was siding with Israel and it would be a rather futile thing, so why do it."[83] After "considerable soul-searching" the Kennedy administration tried to come up with a "compromise," but it "didn't satisfy anybody."[84] The United States discouraged Israel from seeking direct face-to-face negotiations with the Arabs, and according to available official documents, it seems there were no official direct negotiations between Israel and the Arabs. But there were unofficial discussions between Israeli leaders like Golda Meir and King Hussein.

In his conversation with Ben-Gurion, Kennedy had asked that Israel work with the United Nations on the Palestinian-Arab question. "I would prefer that the responsibility for a failure should not appear to rest on Israel. Let's see what the Arabs say before you reject. We have trouble in the Congress on this problem. We provide seventy percent of the total UNRWA funds; but all we get is animosity against us. I fully recognize the problems but maybe it is worth making a trial."[85]

"It's always good to try," said Ben-Gurion.

"Blessed is the peace maker," replied Kennedy.[86]

According to the State Department's plan, Palestinian Arabs would have to be repatriated to Israel. If this were to happen, estimates were that the United States would assume 60 percent of the costs, which was about $1 billion. President Kennedy preferred to have a trial run of a few thousand Arab refugees returning rather than many thousands. Thus, Israel might be reassured if the number would be limited. Otherwise it would be hard to get Israel to acquiesce because it might fear that all the Arabs might want to come to Israel. Such a "trial might show that only a few would come."[87]

Feldman felt that the refugee plan should in some way be connected with security guarantees to Israel and the sale of Hawk missiles to Israel. Moreover, Ben-Gurion should be notified ahead of time that Israel was to receive the Hawk missiles. As Kennedy tried to establish good relations with Egypt, he felt that the United States should first talk with President Nasser of Egypt about the Hawks, but all of this had to be "carried out with utmost secrecy."[88]

The president was also concerned with the domestic repercussions of an Israeli-Arab deal. "We should find out what Israel will do. I don't want to get into a costly fight for years and years."[89]

Kennedy decided to send Feldman to reassure Ben-Gurion that the United States would use its influence only in support of those proposals which did not involve "serious risks for Israel."[90]

Israeli leaders had worked hard to persuade Kennedy to sell Israel the Hawks, but were they needed for Israel's defense or were they needed to boost Israel's morale? Most likely both. Israel had various needs. American officials like Ambassador Walworth Barbour listened to Golda Meir plead that the United States consider Israel's arms request, particularly the request for the Hawk missiles. Barbour reported that Meir's "principal point" was that this weapon might offer Israel little or no technical advantage, but it would be of "great psychological value to the Israeli people in bolstering their sense of security."[91] She was most grateful for the courtesies extended to Deputy Defense Minister Shimon Peres during his visit to Washington. Since there were differences of opinion between the United States and Israel regarding the dangers that Israel faced, she thought it was most appropriate for someone like Peres, who was closely associated with Israeli security, to partake in such Washington discussions.[92] Peres was sent to Washington to help establish the groundwork for Israel's military concessions. Israel needed assistance to meet its expenditures for increased military supplies. It needed conventional military equipment as well as such more sophisticated weaponry as the Hawk ground-to-air missile. The reason for this was Nasser's goal to strike at Israel. He had obtained such Soviet weapons as the MiG-21 and various naval craft. Moreover, the United States had helped Egypt economically and this enabled Egypt to focus on the purchase of military equipment from Russia. Peres observed that it would only be fair if the United States made a complimentary gesture to Israel. The Kennedy administration made no promises to Peres, but it did express a willingness to study the air defense issue.[93]

When Peres stressed Israel's need for the Hawks in order to defend its air bases and that the United States should gradually get into a more steady military assistance relationship with Israel, McGeorge Bundy asked Peres what he thought about the introduction of nuclear weapons in the Middle East. Peres said it would be better for Israel if they could be kept out of the Middle East, but if others might move in that direction, Israel would have to consider its own position.[94]

Peres called upon the United States to participate in an initiative to help stabilize the Near East situation and "above all to help relieve Israel's isolation." A possible alternative would be for the United States to participate in a tripartite guarantee of Israel's territory. Perhaps it might be the United States in association with Israel or NATO with Israel. If that were not possible, then the United States might take a major role alongside France, as a supplier of such military hardware as the sonar, early warning system and the Hawk system. Israel believed that France, because of its attempt to regain the friendship of the Arab world, would bow out as a supplier of arms to Israel.[95]

Egypt obtained Soviet IL-28 light bombers and MiG-21 fighters. Israeli intelligence had information that Egyptian technicians were learning to operate missiles. Within a short time, the Egyptians would have Soviet Sam-2 surface-to-air missiles. The Hawks could help Israel defend itself against Soviet missiles and planes. The Defense Intelligence Agency had information that the Russians had delivered missiles to Egyptian positions in the Sinai. The Egyptians and Iraqis had surface-to-air as well as surface-to-surface missiles.[96]

In view of such developments, President Kennedy decided to provide Israel with the Hawk missile system. On June 13, 1962, Kennedy advised Ben-Gurion that since he had met with him in May of 1961, there had been several developments concerning the matters they had discussed, both in the "Near East and in other parts of the world." Some of those developments had given rise to "concern and anxiety," while others provided "a basis for hope that our ultimate objective of peace in the Near East can be achieved." Throughout this time, U.S. policy had "consistently included among its objectives the security and progress of Israel." The discussions between Peres and U.S. officials were being "carefully examined." "Israel's integrity and independence and her economic progress" would continue to "engage our full support." Kennedy supported Israel's desire to develop the Jordan-Yarmuk River system and he hoped that development would enable Israel and its neighbors to enjoy the benefit of those waters. The president promised that the United States would work on behalf of the project and support the UN with a view to insuring its peaceful implementation. It was his conviction that the waters of the Jordan-Yarmuk system which had been "flowing to waste for so many centuries" could become a constructive force for the benefit of the people of the Near East and the "ultimate objective of peace."[97]

Ben-Gurion responded to Kennedy on June 24, by confiding that he had often thought of him since their last meeting, and that "people throughout the world and certainly in Israel" had followed with "admiration your courage and steadfastness in the pursuit of peace, human advancement and freedom." He was most happy to see that Israel and the United States "share an identity of approach." Israel's goal is "lasting and permanent peace and good neighborliness between the Arab states and Israel." To achieve this it was essential that the "doctrine of belligerence" should be resisted and that direct face-to-face negotiations for a peaceful settlement should be encouraged.[98] He shared the president's desire for the settlement of border disputes and that UN representatives on the spot could contribute to that settlement. He was most gratified with the president's support of Israel's water project as the president had shown "a deep and sensitive understanding of one of Israel's most vital needs and interests." Israel planned to use its fair share of the water for the benefit of its people, but it did not wish to "deprive its neighbors of their rights."[99]

Once more Ben-Gurion explained Israel's special circumstances. "We have to shoulder tasks which do not exist in other countries. Israel is home to some 10,000 newcomers every month." Most come from "backward and oppressed countries, where education was neglected for centuries." America—a "great and rich country achieved this in the course of several hundred years. We have to do this in the span of a short time." But above all Israel is threatened with extinction. "It is not our democratic system, or our borders and independence alone which are threatened, but our very existence is at stake." What was done to six million Jews at the hands of the Nazis, "with the participation of Palestinian Arab leaders, among them the ex-Grand Mufti and his henchmen, could be done to the two million Jews of Israel, if God forbid, the Israel Defense Forces are defeated." As Ben-Gurion explained, "It is of the utmost importance to provide the Israel Defence Forces with sufficient deterrent strength which will prevent our neighbors from making war on us. As long as the peace of the world is not secure everywhere we have to secure our peace through our strength."[100] Ben-Gurion was glad to report that two Moslem states—Turkey and Iran—whose combined population exceeded by far that of Israel's neighbors—Egypt, Syria, Jordan and Lebanon—"maintain good-neighborly relations and cooperation with Israel for the benefit of all involved."[101]

Once Kennedy had decided to provide Israel with the Hawks, he sent his Special Assistant Myer Feldman to Israel to inform Ben-Gurion of his decision. He arrived in Israel on August 19, 1962. The president wrote Ben-Gurion that he was sending Feldman to talk about the Hawk missiles, Joseph Johnson's mission on the Arab refugees and Israel's request for a security guarantee.[102]

Feldman recalled that when President Kennedy had decided to provide Israel with the Hawks he said that he wanted to get a fair exchange from Israel. "If we're going to give Israel the Hawks and I'm inclined, I think that we have to—let's see what we can get from the Israelis. The State Department has been asking a lot from the Israelis which they won't give us. They want to make sure that the Israelis don't make atomic weapons. They want to make sure that the U.S. has the right to inspect the reactor at Dimona. They want to make sure that the Israelis will settle the Arab refugee problem in a way that it can be settled by taking back a large number of the refugees. And they want the Israelis to give up rights of retaliation. . . . So let's see what we can do about that."[103]

Feldman met with Ben-Gurion, Foreign Minister Golda Meir, and Teddy Kollek of Israel's Foreign Office American Desk. Feldman informed them that President Kennedy had "determined that the Hawk missiles should be made available to Israel," and that it would make Israel's security "much, much better." Feldman recalled that the Israeli leaders were "ecstatic." It was the first time that an American president agreed to provide Israel with arms. Thus Kennedy's assistant had reassured the Israeli leadership of America's concern for Israel's well-being, but he cautioned that this would have to be worked out in later conversations, and, "We want you to cooperate with us in some ways."[104]

Feldman then talked with them about such issues as Israel's nuclear research projects and the Palestinian Arab refugees.

Ben-Gurion wanted to get more specifics. Feldman told him that the United States would sell the missiles to Israel, but under such terms that would not cause Israel economic harm. Feldman added that this was to be a departure from America's position of not being a supplier of arms to the Middle East. While it would be kept secret for the time being, Nasser would be informed, and he would be told that if he stopped getting arms from

Russia, the United States would stop supplying arms to Israel. Ben-Gurion thought this to be the "best thing," but in view of previous attempts, the Egyptian leader would reject any type of disarmament.[105] As Ben-Gurion said that he preferred no weapons and no escalation of the arms race, Feldman introduced the question of Israel's nuclear research. He was told that Israel would agree to join the International Atomic Energy Agency and that it would permit inspection of its facilities provided the Egyptians would not come to inspect the reactor. Israel would permit the Americans to inspect the reactor, and it would not produce any weapons-grade material for the time being, nor did the United States have to be concerned about Israel's producing atomic weapons.[106]

Feldman found that the Israelis were not as forthcoming when it came to the issue of the Arab refugees. The Israelis could not "see what solution there might be," but they agreed to the repatriation of some Arab refugees, if Nasser would agree to resettle Arab refugees in the UAR, if Nasser would agree not to direct propaganda to those refugees who accepted repatriation and if he would not seek to incite them against Israel. Myer Feldman estimated that not more than one in ten would seek resettlement.[107]

Dean Rusk rejected Ben-Gurion's reservations regarding the Arab resettlement, and he observed, "It would be most unfortunate if the Israelis would end up with the Hawks and strengthened security assurances while being responsible for derailing the Johnson Arab refugee plan before it could even be given a good try."[108]

Golda Meir advised Feldman that the United States should first inquire if the Arab governments would accept the Johnson plan because it would be most embarrassing for the United States to offer a proposal, establish an administrator and find that the Arab states would continue their propaganda so that Israel could not accept the refugees and the whole project would then have to be abandoned. Meir then revealed that "she had received concrete evidence that the Egyptians had guided missiles which they had purchased from West German sources at a cost of 250,000,000 pounds sterling. This, she said, indicated their real intentions." Feldman recommended that under the circumstances "we defer final decision on the Johnson plan. . . ."[109]

Rusk felt that Nasser should be advised that the United States agreed to sell the Hawk missiles to Israel "in the light of the U.A.R.'s acquisition of new types of equipment and in the absence of any limitation on the arms race in the area." Moreover, it had to be made clear that the Hawks were purely defensive in nature and that the United States still wanted to limit the arms race.[110]

Feldman found that many State Department officials had an anti-Israel bias. This attitude could be seen throughout the State Department's establishment. They felt that Israel had nothing to offer, while the Arabs had territory and resources. They believed that America had "everything to gain by being pro-Arab." Israel had no oil, it did not control "any large territories so that it could not give them any communication or transportation at the crossroads of the world." Those State Department bureaucrats had a "very cold point of view and they had lots of papers that were based on this. They would send those papers to the White House all the time saying that our policy ought to be shifted towards the Arabs because the Arabs could do so much for us." There seemed to be no room for morality in their thinking.[111]

Once Feldman got back, he conferred with the president on the conversations he had with the Israelis. Feldman also advised the President that Israel had received an offer from Britain to purchase Bloodhound missiles, but that Israel would not purchase them because they were inferior to the Hawks and "for other reasons."[112]

Kennedy was well pleased with Feldman's mission to Israel and he decided to let members of Congress and key public leaders know that the United States would provide Israel with the Hawk anti-aircraft missiles: "Well, we've told the Israeli government, now, before, it gets out in the press let's see that those people who should know it, know about it."[113] Feldman observed that if there was a public announcement the Arabs would all start making speeches at the UN and elsewhere accusing the United States of favoring Israel and of giving Israel advanced weapons. It would have made matters quite uncomfortable for the United States and there were "those in the Congress and in the country generally who just didn't favor supporting Israel." If the matter was gradually leaked, there would not be "this sudden, mass condemnation of that action." Moreover, there was at least some eighteen months between the time the decision was made and the time the first battery of weapons would be sent. Nasser of Egypt was not told in advance of the decision, but he was told before the actual delivery was made.[114]

There would be two meetings in the White House; one with congressmen and senators and the other with leaders of the Jewish community.

Philip Klutznick, one of the Jewish leaders, observed that "without this decision . . . I think we would have been faced with war in the Middle East because of the preponderance of Arabs, their power and strength. And there would be no defense against Arab planes."[115]

President Kennedy walked into the Fish Room where the meeting was taking place and spoke for about five minutes. He summed up his feelings about why this was an "essential" decision and in the best interests of the United States.

The second meeting was with about twenty-five senators and congressmen and Feldman presented the same overview. They were advised not to go public. It would be best not to make a big announcement about this thing. In any case it would take some eighteen months to get the missiles and to train an Israeli battalion on how to use them.[116] The presumption was that they would keep quiet. Did they?

But how was Israel to pay for these very expensive weapons? Australia had been offered the Hawks on a ten-year loan and 3.5 percent interest. Feldman pointed that out to the president and urged that the same terms should be provided the Israelis, especially since they could not afford such expensive weapons. Feldman checked with Defense Secretary McNamara who verified that Australia got those special conditions, but it was the only state that got such good terms. Everyone else had three years at 6 percent or cash payment.

"Well," said Kennedy, "this nation [Israel] can't afford to pay cash, and twenty-five million dollars isn't much in a hundred billion dollar budget." On his desk there was a document from State that claimed Israel could afford to pay in cash. Feldman thought that was funny, and he informed the president as to who had prepared that document.[117]

Kennedy decided to sell the missiles to Israel on the same terms as the Australians had obtained. Kennedy had broken the "dam." In the years to come Israel would purchase tanks and planes on the same basis.[118]

On August 27, at 5 p.m., Kennedy met with Dean Rusk, McGeorge Bundy, Myer Feldman, Walworth Barbour, Robert Strong and Phillips Talbot. Dean Rusk observed that Egypt had the aircraft to which the Hawk missiles were a defense. Kennedy remembered that Israel had "a comparable aircraft—in comparable quantity. . . ."[119] Feldman disagreed.

Ambassador Barbour thought that Israel claimed it did not have the bombers. Kennedy wanted to know "what the UAR had gotten in the way of bombers lately."[120]

Kennedy concluded that linking the Johnson refugee plan with the Hawk sale would necessitate a presidential commitment, and he was not prepared to invest the full weight of the presidency on such an exercise in futility.[121]

By mid-September, Feldman reported that the Johnson plan did not have a prayer since Johnson had inserted a provision that the United Nations would have authority to arbitrate any conflict over the admissibility of refugees. The Israelis rejected this as interfering with their sovereignty. Some administration officials, like Robert W. Komer of the National Security Council, thought that Israel should not be the one to turn down the American baby, but that Israel should wait until the Arabs turned it down.[122]

President Kennedy did not wish to press Israel on the Johnson plan, especially since there was an off-year election coming up. McGeorge Bundy advised the president that the State Department "should not shower the Middle East with telegrams in praise of the Johnson plan."[123] As far as the Israeli government was concerned, the Johnson plan lacked "integrity and realism." It offered contradictory things to each side—free choice to the Arabs and a final say to Israel. When the Syrians rejected the Johnson plan, they put an end to it. Lebanon, Trans-Jordan and Egypt had been ready to go along with the Johnson plan, but they would not do so as Syria rejected it.

On September 26, 1962, Foreign Minister Golda Meir talked with Secretary of State Dean Rusk on a variety of world issues including the Middle East, the Far East and Africa. Meir thought that India was very much concerned about its relationship with China. Rusk was likewise concerned and felt that the relationship between India and China was "worse than India was letting on."[124] Rusk confided that President Kennedy "was very much concerned about Israel's security as is the whole country and we have to be for a variety of reasons." Kennedy was concerned about the arms race in the Middle East, but he knew that Israel was not responsible for it, and that was why "we have taken this new look." He observed that the arms buildup in Egypt was as much against some of its Arab neighbors as it was against Israel.[125]

Meir said that Israel was prepared for disarmament and that it did not wish to "spend all this money on defense."[126]

Rusk asked Meir if Israel owned a villa in Geneva. "We have some little hole in the wall that we use as an office," said Meir.

"Well, I put my eye on a villa there which I thought we should buy but when I cabled over to the State Department, I received a reply that there was just no money for it. Just a day or two later, an announcement was made of the U.S. Aid Program to India in the amount of about one billion dollars and shortly thereafter India bought the villa."

Israeli Ambassador Gideon Raphael suggested that Rusk ask the Indians if the United States could "rent it" to the United States.[127]

Mordechai Gazit observed that the State Department might have been regarded as a "Fortress of Evil" by those who favored Israel, but "it was possible to change that situation" and that it was even possible to "neutralize" some of those who were opposed to Israel. Gazit held "more than ten lunch meetings each week" in order to provide American officials with information and guidance about Israel. When he was once asked by a State Department official what he thought of State officials he said, "The State Department officials are doing their job and a good diplomat has to be even-handed." Apparently Gazit's response was very much appreciated by that official.[128]

On September 26, 1962, the sale of the Hawks to Israel became public knowledge. The United States officially disclosed that the Hawks were "purely defensive short-range ground to air interceptor missiles" and they would assist Israel to overcome "a growing need for Israel's air defense." The initial Israeli request had been made in 1959 during the Eisenhower

administration, and when Ben-Gurion approached Kennedy on the matter
on May 30, 1961, the president said, "You raised it with President Eisenhower and then it tapered off. I'll look into it."[129]

According to the *New York Times* Kennedy decided to sell the Hawks
to Israel in order to offset Soviet bloc weapons which had been sent to Israel's Arab neighbors. Kennedy's decision reversed the official U.S. policy
that America should not be a major source of weapons for the Middle East.
The Department of Defense had feared that the Middle East arms imbalance would lead to war. The Hawk missiles, which could be used against
aircraft, and three types of offensive missiles were to help offset the large
number of Soviet MiGs and TU-16 bombers and the surface-to-surface missiles supplied by the Soviets to Egypt and Iraq.[130]

A SPECIAL RELATIONSHIP

President Kennedy established a new and "special relationship" with Israel. He was the first president to sell Israel a defense system and the first
to guarantee Israel's security, not just once, but on several different occasions.[131]

When on December 27, 1962, the president met with Foreign Minister
Golda Meir, he said that "the United States has a special relationship with
Israel in the Middle East really comparable only to that which it has with
Britain over a wide range of world affairs." But at the same time he advised her that the United States had to maintain its friendship and ties with
Arab countries throughout the world, and if the United States "pulled out
of the Arab Middle East and maintained our ties only with Israel this would
not be in Israel's interest."[132] Kennedy reminded Meir of America's world-
wide responsibilities and obligations. Israel was only one of those responsibilities. No other country carried the same sort of responsibilities for so
many distant areas such as "Korea, South Vietnam, India, Pakistan, the
Middle East, Africa, Latin America and elsewhere. Our concern is in main-
taining the balance of power in the interest of the free world. This is why
we find ourselves involved in issues between the Somalis and Ethiopians,
Indians and Pakistanis, Cambodians and Thais, and so many other disputes
which are not part of what we see as the central struggle, the struggle of
free peoples against the Communist Bloc." Kennedy realized that Israel had
security problems, but so did the United States. The United States "came
almost to a direct confrontation with the Soviet Union last spring and again
recently in Cuba." There had been almost four direct collisions with the
Soviet Union and China.[133]

Foreign Minister Meir praised President Kennedy for the way he had
handled the Cuban crisis. Israel had regarded the Cuban crisis not just as
a Cuban-American issue, but as a major problem facing the world, and Israel was "delighted at the way it came out." She advised Kennedy that Is-

rael considered itself as part of the free world and it appreciated U.S. policies and actions. Israel gained much encouragement from America's concern with Israel's security and from American friendship. Meir stressed that Israel was not anti-Arab, and that from the start it sought to live in peace with the Arabs. While Israel had always been prepared to have direct talks with the Arabs, there had been no reciprocation on their part. Egypt had been provided with great quantities of arms from the Soviet Union, especially since Egypt's intervention in Yemen. Israel observed that the Soviet TU-16s had flown from Egypt to Yemen, dropped bombs and flown back to Egypt. "If they can do that, what could they do to Israel?" Moreover, Israel knew that Egypt had worked on missile systems with the help of German scientists since 1960, and that Israel had considerable problems along its sea frontiers since Egypt acquired a considerable number of submarines. The "Egyptians say that Israel breathes through only one border—the sea border—since the land borders are taken care of. Maybe this is only Arab talk, but that talk could mean something."[134]

Meir tried to help Kennedy understand what Nasser's ambitions were. It was Egypt that had forced Syria into a union, and since Nasser's intervention in the war in Yemen, Nasser obtained even more weapons from the Russians. Egypt likewise intervened in the Congo and Ghana.[135]

As for the Arab refugees, Meir informed Kennedy that Israel had tried to help solve this problem. In 1949 it offered to "take up to 100,000 refugees back," and even though there was no peace, close to 40,000 were accepted back. Moreover there were some "230,000 to 240,000 Arabs living in Israel, and that constituted about eleven percent of Israel's population. Not all of them are peaceful citizens."[136] President Kennedy conceded that "obviously Israel cannot accept a flood of refugees," and that the Arabs had their troubles too. Perhaps no compromises were possible. But he did not wish to give up on the refugees. Moreover, the Arab refugees were costing the U.S. money and the issue was causing great damage to the prospects of peace. In the judgment of U.S. officials, it seemed that the great majority of refugees would prefer to be resettled outside of Israel. No progress was made on the Johnson refugee plan, and "that is gone." But the president thought that "we should keep trying," and he was not convinced that a solution was impossible. He thought it was like the dispute involving Kashmir, and that it was not possible "to let this dispute run on and blow up."[137]

President Kennedy noted that the United States was as interested in Israel as he was personally. "We are interested that Israel should keep up its sensitive, tremendous, historic task. What we want from Israel arises because our relationship is a two-way street. Israel's security in the long run depends, in part, on what it does with the Arabs, but also on us." He asked that Israel consider "our problems on this atomic reactor. We are opposed to nuclear proliferation. Our interest here is not in prying into Israel's affairs but we have to be concerned because of the over-all situation in the Middle East."[138]

Meir tried to reassure Kennedy that there would be no difficulty between Israel and the United States on the Israeli nuclear reactor.[139] Kennedy expressed his concern regarding Israel's retaliatory raids. "Whether right or wrong, those actions involved not just Israel, but also the United States,"[140] and he asked Israel to restrain those measures.[141]

GROWING DEFENSE CONCERNS

As Egypt expanded its activities in Yemen and the Arabian Peninsula, it seemed that Egypt would likewise try to gain control over Jordan. Israel regarded Egypt's moves against Jordan as most provocative and dangerous to its security and future. The United States kept a close eye on those developments. President Kennedy advised the British to move into Jordan in case of war, and he prepared to send a U.S. air squadron to Saudi Arabia as an indirect warning to Nasser.[142]

Under Secretary of State George W. Ball advised the American Embassy in Israel that a coup in Jordan was very likely and that it was "being planned by the Army and other groups in Jordan, probably with Nasser's assistance." The prospect existed that if the coup succeeded, then Egypt's influence there would be predominant. In that case, Israel might decide to undertake military intervention in Jordan or Egypt or both. Dean Rusk advised the American Ambassador in Israel that if a coup did take place, "You should at once strongly advise Ben-Gurion to take no military action," and that the United States will use its full weight and influence to make sure that the situation on the Jordanian-Israeli border would remain unchanged. The United States likewise advised the Syrians and the Iraqis to stay out of the conflict, and Egypt was warned not to risk war.[143]

Myer Feldman recalled that President Kennedy kept in very close touch with these developments. He met with McGeorge Bundy, Feldman and McNamara and received "the best intelligence reports from Israel" to find out whether Israel would move into the West Bank if Hussein were overthrown. It appeared as if Israel would take over the West Bank, and that presented the United States with a difficult predicament. What were Kennedy's choices at that time? To send troops into the area and drive Israel away from the West Bank? Or would the United States help carve up Jordan? Feldman recalled, "We never decided that issue." But Kennedy did move the Sixth Fleet towards Israel. "It was on its way to Israel when we got word that Hussein was reasonably secure, and they didn't have to go all the way. Instead of going to Haifa the Fleet was ordered to put in at Malta." It had been a tense time and "the President devoted full attention to that because it looked like the beginning of the possibility of a real war."[144] Only the president "knew what action he would have taken if Hussein had been assassinated or had fled the country."[145]

Acting Secretary of State James P. Grant had advised Israeli Ambassador Avraham Harman and Minister Mordechai Gazit, "Something might happen in Jordan," and that there was "a chance of something happening within a few hours or days." It was likely that if Israel moved militarily, Egypt would not sit still, nor would the Soviet Union.[146]

The anticipated coup in Jordan did not materialize. The UAR did not attempt to take over Jordan.

In helping to prepare the 1962 budget, the State Department officials felt that Israel should not get any development loan money since Israel had attained self-sufficiency. Fowler Hamilton, Administrator, Agency for International Development, recommended that Israel should not get anything. The ambassador from Israel advised Feldman that Israel had been promised $30 million in development money, but it received only $15 million. Under Secretary of State Douglas Dillon of the Eisenhower administration had promised that an additional $15 million would be forthcoming. Israel required $45 million, and the basis for the request was the benefits Israel had provided the United States. Israel assisted and maintained good relations with African and Latin American states which was very useful to the United States. If Israel would not receive some assistance, it would have to discontinue its overseas aid programs and that would not be in the best interest of the United States. Moreover, Israel did not receive any grant money for military assistance, while Jordan and other states did get that kind of help. It had always been understood that some of the development loan money was a substitute for grant money.

After further consultations, Fowler Hamilton and Assistant Secretary of State Phil Talbot agreed to recommend that no more than $10 million would be provided to Israel. Support for the aid legislation had come from those who advanced Israel's cause, and they anticipated that Israel would receive some aid.

Feldman went to see President Kennedy about this situation. The president said that he knew all about it. He knew that $10 million was what State and the aid administrator had recommended. "What do you think they ought to have?" asked the president.

"Forty-five million dollars," said Feldman. And he presented Kennedy with the views advocated by the Israeli ambassador, adding that it was worthy of the United States to support Israel.

After ten minutes of conversation, the president said, "Okay, forty five million dollars. You tell them." That was how the decision was made. Feldman called up Mr. Hamilton and told him, "The President said, it's forty-five million for Israel."[147]

"Where are we going to get it?"

"That's not my problem."[148]

On May 4, 1963, Kennedy wrote to Ben-Gurion: "This nation's actions will fully sustain its long and particular friendship for Israel and its attachment to the security and well-being of your country." And then on October 2, 1963, Kennedy reaffirmed that friendship in a letter to Prime Minister Eshkol who had succeeded Ben-Gurion as prime minister:

> Our policies have given concrete proof of our determination to see a prosperous Israel securely established. . . . There is no Near Eastern leader today, whatever his attitude toward your nation who does not fully understand the import of our public national commitment. . . . Our capabilities to carry out this commitment are, and will remain, more than adequate to deter or halt swiftly any aggression against Israel or its neighbors.[149]

Although President Kennedy's words of support were more specific and reassuring than those of Dulles and Eisenhower, they were not specific enough for Prime Minister Ben-Gurion. Israeli leaders wanted a more concrete understanding and military commitments.

Feldman found that "all" the State Department boys had an anti-Israel bias. Assistant Secretary Phil Talbot was an anti-Israel character, and he reflected the bias of the people he consulted like William Crawford, "whose reasoning was that the United States had nothing to gain by being pro-Israel and that it had everything to gain by being pro-Arab." Israel had no oil and lacked vast lands that could be used for communication or transportation at the crossroads of the world. Israel did not have a large population, and it only had one vote at the UN and other international gatherings. The Arabs could give the United States all that Israel lacked. Feldman recalled that the State Department boys would send lots of their study papers to the White House advocating a shift of U.S. policy in favor of the Arabs. "Morality didn't play much of a part in their thinking."[150]

President Kennedy provided the Hawks to Israel but Egypt and other Arab states accumulated even more weapons. Egypt obtained help from German scientists to build missiles and other weapons systems. The West Germans had sold weapons to Egypt as far back as 1949. But this was something new. In the 1960s the Germans were helping the Egyptians develop missile systems and according to some reports available to Israel, the Germans were helping Egypt develop atomic weapons.

Israel protested this German incursion. Some United States senators tried to encourage the Kennedy administration to stop the spread of sophisticated weapons in the Middle East. Senators Hugh Scott, Jacob Javits, William L. Prouty, Kenneth Keating and Thomas H. Kuchel wrote to President Kennedy asking him to intervene with West Germany and other European states in order to discourage the participation of their scientists in the development and construction of missiles as well as other offensive weapons in the UAR. But the United States did not make a major effort to get the Germans out, perhaps because the United States may have preferred to see German rather than Russian scientists in Egypt.[151]

President Kennedy was concerned about the presence of some three hundred German technicians and scientists in Egypt. Even though the CIA reported that only a few of the German scientists in Egypt knew anything about atomic warheads and those scientists could not function effectively because they did not have able technicians. They could provide Egypt with some propaganda device, but they could never give Egypt atomic warheads or missiles.[152] Feldman believed that three Weizmann Institute scientists were of better caliber than all three hundred German technicians and scientists in Egypt.[153] Israeli officials didn't share that opinion. They were more guarded and wanted the United States to "exert every possible pressure to get the Germans out of Egypt. Feldman and the president sided with the Israelis."[154]

The Kennedy administration did intervene with the Germans regarding their scientists and technicians in Egypt, and the German government reportedly did make it more difficult for its nationals to go abroad and work on military projects.

In April of 1963, W. Averell Harriman responded to Israel's protests and the concern of U.S. senators over the German scientists in Egypt. While determining its foreign policy, the United States could not "consider the UAR. action alone. Israel has its missile programs and other aspects must also be given consideration." He insisted that there were only a few Germans working on the UAR missile program and that "they might well be replaced by Soviet bloc personnel, again forcing the UAR. into greater reliance on the U.S.S.R." Harriman insisted that the United States would seek "to deal evenhandedly with all states concerned and to protect American interests."[155]

Harriman's evaluation of Israel's defense situation was unacceptable and offensive to some Israeli leaders. As Foreign Minister Meir saw it, Harriman equated Israel's "defensive" arms program with Nasser's "avowedly offensive" military buildup. She found Harriman's comparison inappropriate and "very unfortunate." Israel, said Foreign Minister Meir, never threatened Egypt with obliteration, and Israel was prepared to proceed to "complete, and total disarmament." But Meir asked how the United States government knew about the "quantity and role of German scientists in the UAR. and that Egyptian rockets had only conventional warheads. Did the United States have American observers in the Egyptian arms factories and their missile sites?" She found no "solace" in the argument that the withdrawal of German scientists would open the door for the Soviets. Said Meir, "Dying is not sweeter with western rockets than Russian ones."[156]

President Kennedy worked to build a relationship of trust with President Nasser of Egypt, but Nasser's ambitions in the Middle East and Africa

stood in the way of better relations with the United States. President
Kennedy tried to get Nasser to reduce Egyptian troops in Yemen, and yet
every time Nasser promised to reduce his forces, he increased them. As
Feldman recalled, "We did get constant assurances from Nasser or from
people representing Nasser . . . that if so and so were done, he would reduce his commitment to Yemen, or 'just wait another thirty days and I'll
let the Yeminis rule themselves. I won't support them.' "[157] Feldman recalled
that Kennedy "just felt that what Nasser was saying bore no relationship
to what he was thinking." The Yemen incident alerted the president as to
Nasser's credibility. Kennedy "knew from then on that there was no basis
for believing anything he said." The State Department tried to persuade
President Kennedy to be more trusting of Nasser. "Don't pay any attention
to what he's saying publicly. He really is going to reduce his troop commitments." Or, "He's just making those noises toward Saudi Arabia, Israel
and other nations because that's good politics in Egypt." But according to
Feldman, "The complete lack of honesty in what Nasser said during the
Yemen discussions convinced Kennedy that he would just have to judge
Nasser on the basis of his actions and not on the basis of what somebody
was telling him Nasser really thought."[158]

Threats against Jordan's sovereignty from the UAR were apparent in
April-May 1963, and the United States was greatly concerned. The
Kennedy administration called for close contact between Israel and the
United States on this matter. "It is equally important that both our nations
refrain from precipitous actions or reactions, which could well exacerbate
rather than improve the situation, and also provide the Soviet Union with
a further opportunity to extend its influence in the area. . . . I continue to
believe deeply that the efforts of the United States to develop effective relations with the Arab states are in fact in the long-term interest of Israel at
least as much as of the United States or the Arab countries themselves."[159]
Moreover, Kennedy was to advise Ben-Gurion on May 4, 1963:

> [America's actions would] fully sustain its long and particular friend-
> ship for Israel and its attachment to the security and well-being of
> your country. On this we stand firm, as I was glad to be able to reaf-
> firm to Mrs. Meir during our talk of last December. And as I also
> said to Mrs. Meir, we count deeply on your Government for under-
> standing and recognition of the purposes and responsibilities which
> inescapably fall to us in the effort to prevent aggression and sustain
> the peace in the Middle East.[160]

The question was what to do if King Hussein should fall. Secretary of
Defense McNamara advised that Israel should rely on U.S. guarantees and
that the United States could prove to Israel that the guarantees were effective by keeping American forces ready to help. He suggested that the United

States move the Sixth Fleet from Gibraltar to the eastern Mediterranean. The president agreed and he gave orders to move the fleet. Kennedy decided that American planes should be made available in case of military need. But the Sixth Fleet got "as far as Italy when the crisis seemed to be over."[161]

The Kennedy administration tried to persuade Israeli officials that they could depend upon the United States, that, "It wasn't the Israeli army that would have to defend itself but it was the planes of the Sixth Fleet that were there and would form an air cover." Feldman recalled that there were at least nineteen incidents during the Kennedy years where Kennedy made good on American commitments to Israel. President Kennedy advised the Israeli officials that they could not possibly defend themselves "against a hundred million Arabs. You just have to rely on the United States. We'll always keep the Sixth Fleet there."[162]

Israeli officials like Deputy Minister of Defense Shimon Peres were not persuaded. "No, the United States would never come to the defense of Israel. We have to defend ourselves and we know it. We're not asking you to do that, we just ask that you keep out of it and try to keep Russia out of it." Feldman believed that after everything was said and done, the Israeli point of view was correct.[163]

Ben-Gurion was not pleased with Kennedy's May 4, 1963, reassurances. Ambassador Barbour reported that he had delivered Kennedy's letter at 4:30 p.m. and that at Ben-Gurion's first reading his reaction "did not appear very favorable." The Israeli Premier reviewed the world situation as it impacted on Israel. He reiterated Israel's request for a joint United States-Soviet declaration to the effect that neither would supply Nasser with aid and assistance unless Nasser recognized Israel's right to exist. Such a declaration would deter Nasser from his warlike intentions.

Ben-Gurion's suggestion that he might approach Soviet Premier Khrushchev directly seemed to irritate members of the Kennedy administration. Barbour said that Khrushchev would probably not respond at all, and he added that Israel represented everything that the Soviets disliked in the Middle East. Israel was "a democratic, progressive, and stable state." It was well known to the United States that Soviet policy did not seek to promote stability in the Middle East.[164]

Nevertheless, Israel tried to achieve more specific understandings and guarantees from Kennedy. Israeli leaders felt that they needed greater United States reassurances in order to forestall an Egyptian attack.

On May 15, 1963, Robert W. Komer of the National Security Council suggested that there should be a quiet dialogue between the United States and Israel rather than public confrontations. Among the issues to be examined were: (1) The implications and repercussions of a regime change in Jordan; (2) An Arab-Israeli arms balance and prospective changes; and (3) the introduction of advanced weapons into the Middle East.

Komer suggested that there should be some ground rules for this dialogue: (1) All discussions would be private and secret; (2) There would be a moratorium on propaganda; (3) During the moratorium on public debate neither side would take actions that would put the other side on the spot; and (4) All issues that either side wanted to bring up would be discussed. One of Komer's prime concerns was the possibility of nuclear proliferation. He wondered whether statements made by Ben-Gurion, Moshe Dayan and other Israeli leaders regarding the need to strengthen Israel's defenses and Israel's campaign against German Nazi scientists were all part of a campaign to justify Israel's nuclear development projects or to threaten to develop it "as an alternative if the United States did not come through with a security pact." Minister Mordechai Gazit grinned in response, but said nothing.[165]

Kennedy continued in his efforts to maintain good relations with the Arab states. Diplomats like W. A. Harriman were concerned with Israel's brand of diplomacy. He conceded that Israel had a right to be concerned over the Egyptian missiles even though they had not as yet developed a "guidance system" for the missiles. "The United States Government would support Israel if it were attacked," said Harriman. He believed that Kennedy had done well in developing better relations with Egypt and other Arab states, and he advised Israel to "be cautious about driving the Arabs in the direction of the Soviets."[166]

Israel continued to ask for specific and detailed bilateral commitments from the United States. General Yitzhak Rabin, one of Israel's emissaries to Washington, asked the Kennedy administration to, at least, arrange for military or staff coordination with Israel. In case the Egyptians attacked Israel, would the United States come to Israel's assistance? And what would happen if American and Israeli forces would fly over Cairo without having established any military coordination? The United States, in its alliances such as NATO, had made provision for such coordination and planning. Rabin called for similar understandings and coordination between Israel and the United States.[167]

Rabin was distrustful of U.S. commitments. "I have a long memory," and he recalled that from 1947 to 1948, when the Arab armies invaded Israeli territory, "no major power helped Israel, and the U.S. embargoed arms shipments" to Israel. If Israel had managed to beat back the Arab invaders, it was only because of the arms it received from Czechoslovakia.[168] Rabin did not mention Israel's dreadful experiences with the Eisenhower administration in 1956 and 1957, and how the United States had abandoned Israel during the crisis that had brought on the Sinai War. Nor did he mention America's failure to help rescue the Jews during the Holocaust. But Rabin concluded, "Israel could not depend solely upon assurances of outside support. It must be able to defend itself come what may."[169]

Robert Komer agreed with Rabin that Israel should not "rely solely upon outside assurances," but then the United States did recognize Israel's need for "a reasonable deterrent posture," and that the United States had in fact "helped subsidize it and even directly contributed to it, most recently via the Hawk sale." Israel is strong and it has United States "assurances," all that should "fill the bill."[170]

Gazit observed, "that while Israel felt it could depend on the U.S. it could not let its own margin of safety become too thin. Because of the increasing threat, Israel needed either stronger security guarantees or a stronger deterrent posture."[171] Stationed in Washington during the Kennedy administration, he found President Kennedy to be "an impressive man who did not act rashly or quickly, but considered the long range implications of policy." His administration was "open minded" to matters that were important to Israel. "Whatever was suggested to the Kennedy administration they were prepared to consider seriously. They approached propositions regarding Israel, positively."[172] Ambassador Gazit recalled that Kennedy told the story of the farmer who had worked hard to plant some trees that took some twenty years to grow. "But why do you work so hard and feverishly, after all, it takes some twenty years for the tree to grow?" "That's why I must work in haste," answered the farmer. This approach was also reflected in Kennedy's quote of a Chinese proverb that the "Journey of 1,000 miles begins with the first step."[173]

While some members of Israel's governmental establishment worked under the premise that America's main interests lay with the Arab countries, Gazit advised the Israeli leadership that Israel's interests were not contradictory to U.S. interests. Ambassador Gazit was one of those who believed that the United States was sympathetic to Israel's needs, but he was concerned that the United States might impose sanctions against Israel unless it would abide by its wishes and goals. He sensed in April 1962 that "John F. Kennedy leaned in favor of Israel," and that he was a "visible" ally. And as far as the State Department was concerned, Gazit observed, "It might have been a Fortress of Evil," but it was possible to change that situation. "It was even possible to neutralize those State Department officials who were against Israel."[174]

President Kennedy wrote a letter to Israel agreeing to its diversion of Jordan River waters for its agricultural and basic needs. Originally the State Department was to draft that letter, but Ambassador Harman preferred that the letter come from the president: "I would rather have a letter from the President." It was Feldman who intervened and got the Kennedy letter for Israel.[175] Kennedy wrote to Ben-Gurion on June 13, 1962:

My attention has recently been directed toward the advanced state of the program for the full development of water resources in the Near

East. This program offers both agriculture and industry exciting
prospects. It is dependent upon the implementation of Israel's plan to
draw from the Jordan-Yarmuk River System those waters to which
she is entitled under the plan drafted by former U.S. Ambassador Eric
Johnston. This project is one which can and should be carried out as
scheduled, both by Israel and by its neighbors. Each can use her fair
share of the water system to improve her economy and advance the
general welfare of her people.[176]

The president believed the Jordan River development project could provide a basis for understanding between the Arabs and Israel. He felt that
if the Arabs and Israelis worked together on the water project, they would
work together on other things as well, and that gradually peace would come
to the area. He believed that the United States could best perform its function by trying to build a bridge between the Arabs and the Israelis. He believed that the more that was done the "better it would be for peace in the
Middle East."[177]

Whatever Kennedy may have done for Israel did not seem to be sufficient for such Israeli leaders as Ben-Gurion, Golda Meir, Levi Eshkol, and
Yitzhak Rabin. By early October 1963, President Kennedy spelled out more
clearly his support for Israel: "The Arabs know full well that the United
States would support Israel and the United States would come to Israel's
assistance in case of Arab aggression." But such private assurances seemed
inadequate for Israel's leaders. They were greatly concerned with the massive Arab buildup of weapons and their plans to destroy Israel. Israel
needed more specific commitments and weaponry to meet the Arab challenges. Kennedy would not agree to such openly declared commitments for
fear of alienating the Arab world. The Israeli government did not appreciate U.S. "even-handed" policies or its diplomatic efforts to secure the balance of power in the Middle East. For Israel it was a matter of survival
and not a matter of theoretical diplomatic or military maneuvers. From
1933 to 1945 the Jewish community had lost over six million of its people
to Nazi murderers and an indifferent world. Israel's leaders would not stand
idly by as Israel and its citizens were faced with annihilation at the hands
of the Arabs and their new-found Soviet Russian allies. As Israel could not
obtain necessary weaponry from the United States and the West and it
could not obtain an alliance from the United States, it had to find roads to
security. In the course of its struggle for survival and its search for security, Israel developed expertise in the field of nuclear technology. The Eisenhower and Kennedy administrations, concerned lest this would encourage
a greater and an even more dangerous arms race, adamantly opposed Israel's acquisition of nuclear weapons. Nevertheless, Ben-Gurion held to his
conviction that the development of nuclear science in Israel might enable
his country to find a means of preventing the Arabs and the Soviet Rus-

sians from seeking Israel's destruction. A matter of greatest concern to John F. Kennedy was the danger of nuclear proliferation and consequently nuclear war. Israel was part of this concern as it began to develop its own nuclear research facilities in response to what appeared to be the threat of another Holocaust. While he appreciated Israel's dilemma he was concerned that nuclear weapons in Israel's hands might ultimately bring a Soviet-American nuclear confrontation, even more menacing than the missile crisis of October 1962.

Winston Churchill had once described Israel as "invincibly established" but Ben-Gurion did not see it that way at all, and he wrote "some fifty-five letters to heads of state describing the dangers Israel had to face." He wanted to see Israel securely established. "Nuclear research was one way he hoped to promote that security."[178]

Despite the advice of such establishment individuals as Adlai Stevenson, Robert Komer of the National Security Council and Secretary Dean Rusk, Kennedy was persuaded that the Johnson refugee plan could not work, and he would not support the State Department view that Israel should be pressed into accepting that plan. He envisioned that most of the Arab refugees would have to be transferred to other Arab states. He also sought to bring about cooperation between Israel and Jordan in sharing the Jordan River waters.

He abandoned a Truman-Eisenhower policy of not selling arms to Israel. On at least two occasions he explicitly tried to reassure Israel that the United States would come to Israel's aid in case it were attacked. In early October 1963, President Kennedy reiterated American support for Israel. Said Kennedy: "the Arabs know full well that the United States would support Israel and the United States would come to Israel's assistance in case of Arab aggression." Israeli leaders wanted the same sort of alliance that the United States had established with NATO. Ben-Gurion could ill afford to rely upon U.S. "even-handedness" policies or efforts to secure the balance of power in the Middle East. For Israel it was a matter of survival and not a matter of theoretical diplomatic military maneuvers. While some State, CIA and NSC officials tried to keep Israel in harness, Kennedy had a greater understanding and appreciation for Israel's position and its desire and need for security, but he insisted that the United States could not be limited to an Israeli-American dual alliance in the Middle East. It was vitally important to maintain the friendship of the Arab states in order to keep the Russians out. Kennedy and his administration could not condone its nuclear and other military-scientific researches. They believed that such endeavors not only endangered the balance of power, but helped jeopardize the future of the planet. Some in the Kennedy administration feared that Israel's possession of such weapons might ultimately bring about a Soviet-American nuclear showdown. Nevertheless, Israeli political, diplomatic and military leaders worked to achieve greater Israeli strength and independence and were determined to achieve an alliance with the United States. They did not seem to realize that these two aspects of their policies were at times incompatible and contradictory. An Israeli independent foreign policy would ultimately have to be modified in return for an "alliance" or greater reliance on the good will of an American president and his staff.

CHAPTER 3

Dimona, January 1961 to May 1963

Israel was isolated and very much alone amidst a sea of Arab nations. On December 16, 1954, Ben-Gurion warned that the seven Arab states that fought Israel in 1948 would attack Israel again. Since Israel could not match Arab population numbers or arms, it would have to develop its human and scientific resources—for ultimately Israel's continued existence and security would depend on that. During a cabinet session of April 24, 1955, Ben-Gurion spoke of Nasser's determination to destroy Israel. There was an imbalance of military power between Israel and its neighbors, and Israel could depend only upon its own strength rather than major power guarantees. He announced that one of his major goals was Israel's "Atomic research."[1] Israel's security needs could be resolved in one of two ways: through "political guarantees" or self-reliance. Guarantees or treaties of alliance were not up to Israel, and they were uncertain and seemingly unattainable. But what depended upon Israel "we must invest all our power." It must develop "weapons superiority" and whatever has to be done with science "we must do."[2]

What persuaded Ben-Gurion more than anything else was Israel's experience during the Sinai-Suez crisis of 1956 to 1957. For it was during that time that Russia threatened to annihilate Israel. On November 6, 1956, after Israel defeated Egypt in the Sinai War in a matter of 100 hours and after the Anglo-French intervention to separate the victorious Israeli and the defeated Egyptians in the Suez, the Russians issued an ultimatum to Israel, France and Britain demanding that they stop their campaign against Egypt or face dire consequences. The Russians accused the Israeli government of "criminally and irresponsibly playing with the fate of its own people. . . . and of jeopardizing the very existence of Israel as a State." In a separate letter to Ben-Gurion, Soviet Prime Minister Nikolai Bulganin warned that Russia would attack Israel with missiles. At the same time U.S. President Eisenhower pressured Israel to withdraw from the Sinai and that Britain and France leave the Suez area. The British and French continued to support Israel, but they could not match the power and influence of the United States and the U.S.S.R. The French Foreign Minister urged Israel to withdraw as the Americans and the Russians had demanded.[3] All this helped persuade Ben-Gurion that Israel needed powerful weapons with which, not only, to face up to the challenges of the Arab states, but, if necessary, such powers as the Soviet Union. As in years gone by so in late 1956 and early 1957, Ben-Gurion realized the validity of the Hebrew saying, "Do not depend upon the word of Princes." If anything, Israel might be able to depend upon its own talents and abilities to defend itself. The ingenuity of the people, the scientists and technicians of Israel would develop systems of defense that would help ensure Israel's survival. It would have to seek the most modern and powerful weapons to counterbalance the vast armament arsenals sold to the Arabs by the West as well as the Soviet bloc. And what were the most powerful earthly weapons at that time? The atomic and hydrogen bombs. If the Russians the Americans, the British and French could develop such weapons, so could Israel, and it had to develop such weapons for the sake of its survival. "If I am not for myself, then who will be, and if not now, then when?" This was from the "Sayings of the Fathers." This was at the heart of Israel's teaching throughout the ages. This was embedded in their tradition and faith. They believed in God, but they were also taught from the time of the Exodus that they had also to rely upon themselves. When the Israelites faced the Red Sea and realized that Pharaoh's armies were in pursuit, they protested to Moses, "Why did you bring us here? Weren't there enough cemeteries in Egypt?" Moses turned to God. And God asked Moses, "Wherefore criest thou unto me? Use your powers. Speak unto the children of Israel, that they journey onwards: But lift up thy staff, and stretch out thine hand over the sea and divide it." And Moses did so, and God parted the sea. The people of Israel crossed the sea, and they were saved from Pharaoh's army.

The people of Israel learned that lesson time and time again. They were to learn it again during the time of the Holocaust. Few, if any, countries gave Jews asylum as the Nazis methodically rounded up and slaughtered over six million Jews—one third of the Jewish people. How could any Jew forget the refusal of the Allies—the Americans, the British and the Russians—to rescue the Jews, or their refusal to bomb the railroad lines that led to the camps? They refused to bomb the gas chambers and crematoriums. Their excuse? The Anglo-Americans claimed that their planes could not reach those targets. But their planes went beyond those targets and dropped a number of bombs in the town of Auschwitz and the slave labor factories near Auschwitz. They refused to bomb those concentration camp targets for fear that their war against the German Nazis would be termed a war to save the Jews. The Russians were situated a few miles from that particular death camp of Auschwitz, but they waited weeks before they sent their paratroopers to liberate the Jews. If ever the Jews learned that they could not rely on earthly princes and powers, it was during the years of the Holocaust. Ben-Gurion and most other Israeli leaders were survivors or relatives of survivors of the Holocaust and could not forget that time. Ben-Gurion would often make reference to the torturous years of the Holocaust. But that terrible time had not come to an end in 1945. The 500,000 surviving Jews living in western Europe had no home. When they tried to go to the Land of Israel they were prevented from doing so by the British who kept the gates of Palestine closed to Jews, but not closed to Moslems or Christians. Nevertheless under the leadership of such figures as David Ben-Gurion and Menachem Begin, the Jews fought and defeated the British and their Arab allies. The Jews now called themselves Israelis as they had been known in ancient times, and they responded to the calling: "If I am not for myself who will be, and if not now, then when?"

But independence did not resolve their difficulties. A Jewish State was reestablished in the Holy Land and the Arab states continued to seek its destruction. They purchased better and more sophisticated planes, tanks, naval craft and missiles, and they prepared for the next round, the next war in which to destroy the State of Israel and its people. In 1956 Israel responded to the threat of massive Soviet arms and equipment in Egypt by preempting against Egypt. This time France and Britain had sided with Israel because their interests had been jeopardized by Egypt and the Soviet Union. The United States had chosen to ignore the British and French interests in North Africa despite the fact that they were allies of NATO. But when the Soviets threatened to annihilate Israel unless it withdrew from Egypt, and when Eisenhower likewise threatened to penalize Israel unless it withdrew from the Suez and Sinai, Israel turned to their "Allies," the British and the French who withdrew from Suez and advised Israel to withdraw likewise. Only a decade after the Nazi German gas and torture chambers were shut down and the dead were buried, two million Israelis were threatened with annihilation. Once again an Israelite leader realized that his people could not depend upon princes, pharaohs, premiers or presidents; but if there was a chance for survival, it would depend upon Israel's human resources and ingenuity.

The issue of nuclear proliferation was a central issue in Kennedy's relationship with Israel. He did not wish to see Israel develop its own atomic bomb arsenal for fear that it would only further stimulate the race for the acquisition of such weapons throughout the world and by Israel's enemies. Israel sought an alliance with the United States, but since that goal seemed unattainable, it pursued various avenues of greater security including the development of sophisticated weapons systems. The essence of the relationship between Kennedy and Israel throughout his administration from January 1961 through November 1963 revolved around these seemingly incompatible issues.

In November 1959, Senator Kennedy observed,

> The ability of other nations to test, develop and stockpile atomic weapons will alter drastically the whole balance of power, and put us all at the mercy of inadvertent, irresponsible, or deliberate atomic attacks from many corners of the globe. For once China, or France, or Sweden, or half a dozen other nations successfully tested an atomic bomb, then the security of both the Russians and Americans is dangerously weakened.

In August of 1959, Kennedy observed that a less developed state might seek to develop or use a nuclear weapon in order to increase its prestige or achieve independence from "big power decisions." But regardless of their intentions, it was clear that this trend foreshadowed developments that would "alter every basic military and diplomatic premise of our time."

While Eisenhower was president and Dulles his secretary of state, he refused to help Israel with its defense needs, and in the last months of his administration, he agonized over the possibility of Israel's development of nuclear weapons. Secretary of State John Foster Dulles and Christian Herter, his successor, could only advise Israel to reduce its acquisition of weapons. As Herter explained it to Ben-Gurion on August 1, 1960, the task of acquiring weapons is "Herculean." In addition to the cost of such weapons they most often became "outdated" before normal production could be attained, and each new advance seemed to exceed its predecessor in "death-dealing capability." Herter hoped that Israel could be reassured by America's opposition to "aggression and its championing the cause of freedom."[4] The aim of U.S. policy was to reduce hostilities and avoid becoming a major supplier of arms to the Middle East. If the United States would depart from that policy it would contribute to the intensification of the arms race. Ben-Gurion's request for Hawk missiles would be a case in point.[5] Officials in the Eisenhower and Kennedy administrations maintained that if the United States would supply the Hawk system, some other outside power "anxious to exacerbate tensions in the Near East" might provide Israel's neighbors with surface-to-surface missiles. In the end, the Hawk missile was not an effective weapon against those missiles, and it did not secure Israel. Eisenhower observed that Israel could acquire tanks and aircraft elsewhere and could develop its own military production, and that the United States could provide Israel with aircraft detection devices.[6]

During the John F. Kennedy-Richard M. Nixon presidential debates of October 1960, Kennedy once again revealed his concern for the spread of atomic weapons. He thought that China might acquire such weaponry by

1963, and if they were disseminated around the world, mankind would move through "a period of hazard" in the next few years. He believed that "we ought to make one last effort" to prevent the spread of such weapons.

Nuclear proliferation was to remain a key issue in the relationship between Israel and the United States in the later part of the Eisenhower administration and throughout the Kennedy presidency.

In December 1960, Eisenhower's Secretary of State, Christian Herter, had confronted Israeli Ambassador Avraham Harman with photos of Dimona, taken by American agents. "Agents" was a polite euphemism for spies. Herter was able to describe the Dimona installation, its size, overall scope and its capacity lines. The United States estimated that costs for such an installation were more than $80 million. This had not been discussed during recent talks regarding Israel's economic plans and Israel's requests for U.S. financial assistance. If word spread of this potential nuclear weapons development, it would have a "very disturbing impact" on the Middle East as well as American interests. Herter asked for clarification so as to "remove the bases for concern," and it was America's desire to "explore the matter directly and frankly in order to avoid misunderstanding."[7] Ambassador Harman said that he was unaware of those facts and that he would report the American concerns to Jerusalem. He remained calm as Herter called for a "frank dialogue" and for Israel to make a "full accounting."[8]

According to a December 16, 1960, *London Daily Express* report, by October 1957, the French had agreed to sell Israel various equipment including a reactor that could produce plutonium and a reprocessing plant that could separate plutonium from irradiated reactor fuel. It was also reported that Norway was to provide the heavy water used as a coolant in the nuclear fission process, and that France had furnished Israel with eighty-five tons of natural uranium.[9] In 1955, the Eisenhower administration, in pursuit of its U.S. Atoms for Peace program, prepared to assist such states as Greece, Iran, Pakistan, Lebanon and Israel in their "atomic energy development program." Three years later Israel signed an Atoms for Peace contract with an American company, "American Machines and Foundry Atomics," to construct a one-megawatt reactor at Nahal Soreq, near the town of Rehovot. That same December of 1960, the British informed Eisenhower that Norway had provided Israel with twenty tons of heavy water, and the U.S. Joint Atomic Energy Interagency Committee observed that Dimona was an atomic facility.[10]

After Harman had met with Herter on December 20, he wrote to his superiors that he believed the United States would "draw serious conclusions" if Israel refused to allow a visit to the reactor. The issues of safeguards and plutonium were a key matter with the Americans, and they would continue to press Israel on these matters. It involved Middle Eastern and global considerations. The Russians had already accused the United States of being Israel's silent atomic development partner. When Kennedy became president he was concerned that the Arabs would pressure Russia to provide them with nuclear technology. Harman thought it was essential that Israel made it known that its installation was being constructed by Israeli experts. In this way Israel would be presented to the world as "an independent force to be reckoned with."[11] This was for the benefit of the Arabs as well as the major powers. Nuclear technology real or possible was to help Israel defend itself against possible Arab or even Soviet aggression. Even the possibility of nuclear technology might help persuade the United States to conclude an alliance with Israel. It was a gamble Israel was forced to take.[12]

Harman thought that the United States would continue to pressure Israel in the matter of plutonium and safeguards since the United States questioned Israel's real intentions. He advised that Israel should stress that the reactor would be completed in three to four years and that there would be plenty of time to solve the "pertinent issues."[13] After consulting with Jerusalem, Harman informed Herter that Israel was building an experimental reactor that had a capacity of twenty-four megawatts which was to serve the development of scientific knowledge for "industrial, agricultural, medical and other scientific purposes." It was part of a general overall program for the rebirth of the Negev, and it would enable Israel to build its own nuclear power station in the future. The reactor was begun in 1959 and might be operative within three to four years. Equipment and material had been obtained locally and abroad, but Israel had agreed not to reveal its sources because of the Arab boycott. Israeli scientists studied abroad in such places as France and the reactor was built by Israeli experts.[14]

Herter said, "This principle of peaceful utilization was very important," and that he wanted to know what would be done with the plutonium produced by the reactor. Again Harman claimed that he did not have that information, but he would seek to obtain it, and once the reactor would be completed, it would be open to qualified students from friendly states. Israel foresaw a need for a body of people trained in the industrial uses of atomic energy. Israel stressed that the facility was only for "peaceful purposes."[15] When Harman advised that Ben-Gurion would present a statement on this matter before the Knesset, Herter thought that Ben-Gurion's public remarks should emphasize "the peaceful and open character of the facility; the use to be made of the plutonium and the safeguards thereon."

Minister Gazit advised, "It would not be possible to guarantee precisely what the Prime Minister would say and that he might not go into as much detail."[16] Some American officials might even have liked to choreograph what the Israeli prime minister should say. Israel would not go along with such a scenario. Friendship and alliance, yes; rule by Pax Americana, no.

On December 21, Prime Minister Ben-Gurion advised the Knesset that Israel was constructing a twenty-four megawatt reactor for peaceful purposes, and the next day the State Department supported the Israeli position by stating that Israel's project was not a "cause for special concern."

It welcomed Israel's assurances that the reactor would be used only for "peaceful pursuits." Moreover, Israel advised that once the reactor would be completed it would welcome visits to the reactor by students and scientists of friendly states. Harman cautioned his superiors that for the United States this was a matter of global concern, and that it would not leave Israel alone on this matter.[17]

The *New York Times* reported on December 23, 1960, that according to U.S. estimates, the reactor would not be capable of producing enough plutonium for more than one bomb a year, within two and a half years. Reportedly while Ben-Gurion and his ambassador had reassured the United States that the reactor would be "dedicated entirely to peaceful purposes," the State Department had reiterated its opposition to the proliferation of nuclear capabilities and that it had "consistently advocated appropriate safeguards to insure that fissionable materials would be used for peaceful purposes."[18]

On December 24, Ogden Reid, U.S. ambassador to Israel, reiterated Kennedy's concerns. The United States wanted to know how the plutonium would be used, and what safeguards Israel might introduce if atomic weapons would be produced and when would there be visitations of Dimona. Moreover, did Ben-Gurion realize the potential international consequences of this project? How did Ben-Gurion think such concerns could be dispelled?[19]

The prime minister advised that Israel was three to four years from producing plutonium, and when it would get to that point, Israel would not be behind any power in the world with respect to safeguards. In any case, Israel would transfer the plutonium to the supplier of the uranium. Ben-Gurion agreed to secret visits to Dimona by a "friendly power."[20]

A detailed communication from the espionage services of the U.S. embassy in Israel on January 18, 1961, described Israel's development of nuclear weapons. The CIA noted:

With reference to the recent revelation of the existence of a nuclear reactor in Beersheba the fact that Israel is working in this field should have come as no surprise inasmuch as almost every nuclear scientist who has contributed to the development of nuclear weapons in the U.S. has been a Jew and a great number of prominent nuclear scientists have come to Israel. Furthermore, the Soviet-Egyptian project for the construction of a nuclear reactor in Egypt has been known for some time. It is also known that the Egyptians, not satisfied with the help they got from the Soviets, have approached the Germans with requests for the kind of men whose specialty is not the peaceful uses of atomic energy. Knowing this about what is going on in Egypt and being reasonably sure that the U.S. is not in a position to bring effective pressure upon the Egyptians, the Israeli government cannot

prudently wait until Egypt produces an atomic weapon before doing
something about one of its own.[21]

The CIA report regarding Israel's efforts at developing its nuclear capacity was not realistic. Since Egypt was receiving assistance from the Soviet Union and Germany in the development of its missile and nuclear bomb
projects, it was only natural that Israel would seek to develop its own nuclear capabilities. There was some anti-Jewish sentiment in the CIA report.
It assumed that "almost every nuclear scientist who has contributed to the
development of nuclear weapons in the U.S. has been a Jew," and that they
therefore helped Israel in its nuclear projects.[22]

In a January 26, 1961, memo, Kennedy learned that France had sold
arms to Israel from 1954 to 1958, and with France's assistance Israel had
survived.[23] During that time there had been "frequent and extended visits
by key Israeli military officers to France." Israeli submarine crews had received training in France and had participated in joint maneuvers with
French crews. During the Spring of 1960, Israel obtained thirty Super Mystere jets and sixty ultramodern Mirage-III jet fighters would be delivered
starting in September 1960 through 1962.[24]

Kennedy read that by 1952 the United States knew that France and Israel had concluded an agreement for nuclear cooperation. Reportedly from
1952 to 1959 France had assisted Israel militarily and in the development
of nuclear weapons. But that on April 15, 1958, Dr. Ernest Bergmann,
chairman of the Israeli Atomic Energy Commission had "stated categori-
cally" that the Israeli-French agreement was "limited to the exchange of
information on uranium chemistry and the production of heavy water."[25]
Bergmann claimed that the press reports of French-Israeli cooperation on
atomic bombs were fabrications designed to influence the United States,
not to aid the French nuclear weapons program.[26] On December 7, 1960,
the U.S. Joint Atomic Energy Intelligence Committee (JAEIC) observed that
the nuclear reactor complex under construction in the Negev near Beersheba could be interpreted as having a number of functions: research, plutonium production and nuclear electric power generation, but since Israel
chose to keep Dimona a secret the JAEIC suggested that the complex was
intended for the production of weapons-grade plutonium. There was "extensive" evidence that France was supplying "plans, materials, equipment
and technical assistance" and training Israeli personnel.[27]

French Premier Bourges-Maunury and the French army chief of staff had
decided that France would furnish Israel "complete information concerning atomic energy" in order to assist Israel in the construction of an atomic
bomb. The agreement may not have been discussed in the French Cabinet,
but it had been worked out by the staff of the premier and his defense
minister.[28]

Those who authored the report struck gold when they observed that Israel had long feared that, with the aid of the Soviet bloc, the Arab states might win the Middle East arms race. In early January 1961, one Israeli official observed, "Israel could not be expected to wait until Egypt produced an atomic weapon."[29] Even President Charles De Gaulle, who worked to improve France's relations with the Arabs, continued to assist Israel with its nuclear research as "concrete evidence" that France was a great power.[30] Since France had been excluded from the "nuclear club," it did not wish to accept the obligations of a club member, and it took a generally hostile attitude regarding safeguards in bilateral atomic energy agreements.[31]

In his January 30, 1961, memo to the president on Israel's atomic energy activities, Dean Rusk noted that in 1955, the United States had assisted Israel in its atomic energy development by providing it with a one-megawatt research reactor for Nahal Rubin, nearby Tel Aviv. In the summer of 1960 the U.S. embassy in Tel Aviv learned that the French were helping Israel to construct a "large" reactor in Dimona, and that by December 2, 1960, U.S. intelligence established that "a significant atomic installation had been constructed there." It was then that Secretary of State Herter had asked Israel's Ambassador Avraham Harman about this development.[32]

Ben-Gurion had publicly reassured the United States that Israel did not plan to develop nuclear weapons, and the French reassured the United States that they were only helping Israel develop atomic energy for peaceful purposes. Moreover, Ben-Gurion advised that Israel had kept this development a secret because of its concern for Arab retaliation against firms that had assisted Israel. Rusk found "considerable justification for this Israeli reasoning."[33] But American officials were greatly concerned, and they felt that Israel's acquisition of nuclear weapons would have grave repercussions in the Middle East, not the least of which was the probability that Russia would station nuclear weapons on the soil of Israel's "embittered Arab neighbors."[34] President Kennedy worked to persuade Israel to permit a qualified U.S. scientist, or a scientist from some other friendly state, to visit Dimona. Ben-Gurion thought that this could be done at an early date.[35]

This was confirmed by Ambassador Ogden R. Reid, in conversation with President Kennedy on January 31. Reid believed that very few Israeli officials had been aware of Israel's atomic research.[36] Perhaps even Foreign Minister Meir did not know about this research until she read the news headlines.[37]

Reid presented Israel's request for "more sophisticated weaponry to protect itself against surprise attacks by the UAR." Israel was "merely 4 minutes from Damascus by supersonic jet." Reid urged the president to consider providing Israel with "ballistic missiles" as well as specific assurances of U.S. "willingness to help in case of invasion." If this were done, there might be more "stability in the Middle East." The United

States should shorten the delay by providing Israel with "early warning" systems.[38] Reid praised Israel's aid to Africa program and urged the United States to keep Israel in mind as an "adjunct to Western efforts in Africa."[39]

Assistant Secretary of State G. Lewis Jones welcomed Ben-Gurion's offer that an American expert visit Dimona as soon as the publicity died down both in Israel and the United States. Jones now claimed that Israel's Arab neighbors had raised the question of Dimona as a source of nuclear weapons,[40] and that the State Department wanted to know when, in fact, Ben-Gurion would invite someone to see Dimona. Harman said that an internal political crisis was taking up much of Ben-Gurion's attention and the ambassador did not think that Ben-Gurion would be inclined to extend an invitation at this time.[41]

Harman protested that no Israeli, "let alone Ben-Gurion, could conceive why there was such a hurry" about a visit to Dimona. There was no plutonium, and it would take at least two years to build a reactor. "In good time, when there was something more to see, the visit might be arranged."[42]

But this response was not good enough for the State Department officials and Jones pressed on. He insisted that a visit by qualified persons would help allay suspicions, and it would be most helpful if Harman could "in the next ten days suggest a visit by an American or some other friendly expert."[43]

On February 26, Theodore Kollek, director general of Ben-Gurion's office, informed Jones that he thought a visit by a qualified American observer to Dimona could take place during the month of March.[44]

U.S. pressures on Israel served to further undermine Israel's confidence in U.S. security commitments which had ostensibly been made from 1950 to 1960. The Tripartite Declaration of May 25, 1950, provided that the United States, Britain and France declared "their deep interest in and their desire to promote the establishment and maintenance of peace and stability in the area and their unalterable opposition to the use of force or threat of force between any of the states in that area."[45]

On July 12, 1956, John Foster Dulles had written to Foreign Minister Abba Eban, "that the United States would, within constitutional lines, oppose any aggression in the Near East and render assistance to the victim of aggression; and that United States foreign policy embraces the preservation of the independence of the State of Israel."[46]

A year later on September 12, 1957, Dulles wrote to Golda Meir:

I want there to be no doubt in the mind of the Israel Government of the deep interest of the United States in preserving the independence and integrity of Israel. I do not believe that the world at large, and particularly the Soviet Union, can have any doubt as to the reaction of the United States should the Soviet Union launch an attack upon Israel.[47]

Despite such words of reassurance, Israel's defense position became more precarious as Arab states like Egypt acquired great quantities of sophisti- cated weapons from such sources as the Soviet Union. Ambassador Har- man reported that Egypt had acquired the MiG-19s with air-to-air missiles, and that some of those jets had been delivered to Iraq. Soviet training crews had gone to great and successful efforts to raise the quality of Egypt's train- ing and interservice coordination. All of which made Israel more vulner- able.[48]

Harman suggested that if the major powers could agree to stop selling this "deadly stuff"—these weapons, they could help establish a regional disarmament.[49] But since such an agreement could not be achieved, Israel had to seek arms with which to defend itself, including atomic arms. Some American officials still embraced their prosaic and oblique view that Israel did not need the Hawks since the Jewish state had a "splendid" air force, and that an early warning electronic system offered by the United States would increase the effectiveness of its air force. As for its air bases, more could be built in the Negev. In case of an "unprovoked attack" the Sixth Fleet and other U.S. forces could be put into action.[50] They continued to argue that if Israel were provided the Hawks, the Arabs would be driven into the arms of the Soviets.[51]

Nuclear proliferation was one of Kennedy's greatest concerns. He recalled that when Eisenhower had shown him how to operate the satchel that car- ried the codes to the U.S. nuclear arsenal, he had asked which countries might soon join the nuclear "club," and Secretary of State Christian Herter replied: "Israel and India." The Russians were helping India, and France helped Israel. At the pace Israel was going it would probably have weapons- grade plutonium before Kennedy would seek reelection by 1964. Kennedy was advised to insist on inspections of the Israeli reactor at Dimona.[52]

Some members of Congress were likewise uneasy with Israel's atomic re- search. Senator Albert Gore, chairman of the Near East-Sub-Committee of the Senate Foreign Relations Committee and Senator Bourke B. Hicken- looper seemed annoyed that Israel had not only concealed its activity, but had "deliberately" misled the United States. Hickenlooper claimed that he had "definite" knowledge that Israel had "lied" to an American official in the late summer or early fall.[53] Fulbright claimed that it was the secrecy factor that troubled him. If the Israelis had nothing to hide, then "why did they hide it?"[54]

Ambassador Harman suggested that Israel should exercise greater care in its relations with members of Congress like Senator Fulbright. The sen- ator had complained that he had been "branded" as "anti-Israel," and he insisted that this was not the case. He felt that the Israel lobby organized by I. L. Kenen had exercised "continuous Jewish pressure on all members of Congress." Fulbright told Harman that there was a good deal of censorship in Israel and that the United States was not getting enough information about what Israel was doing with respect to its Dimona reactor.[55]

Harman accepted Kennedy's and Fulbright's view that the United States should be a friend of Israel and the Arabs. Moreover, a "central" element of Israel's "national policy" was to achieve "friendship" with the Arab states. While Israel did not object to the Arabs receiving economic aid or that anyone would seek their friendship, Israel felt that it was wrong to equate Arab and Israeli attitudes. Harman tried to help Fulbright understand that there was a difference between censorship in Israel and censorship in Egypt. It was not right to equate Egypt's desire to "eliminate Israel" with Israel's desire to live in peace with the Arabs.[56] Fulbright agreed that "an attitude of impartiality did not involve an attitude of equation," but he claimed that he had been harshly "attacked" in Israel on the issue of censorship and felt certain that censorship existed in Israel. That was why he had made an issue of it in Congress.[57]

Harman did not find his conversation with Fulbright "particularly cordial," but he thought it was good that it had taken place for it might be possible to talk with him at a later date about "substantive issues." Harman felt that Fulbright was "deeply wounded," particularly by demonstrations against him at the Hebrew University. He was also upset by a feeling that Jews had a hand in his not being appointed secretary of state. A good friend of Fulbright told Harman that the senator felt that the real reason for his nonappointment as secretary of state was the possible reaction of some African states[58] since Fulbright was a segregationist. But Fulbright felt that he was not "temperamentally fitted" to be secretary of state. He thought Rusk was more suitable.[59]

Harman thought it was not good that the chairman of the Senate Foreign Relations Committee should be regarded as an enemy of Israel. Harman observed that there could be "no doubt of the very high intellectual caliber of this man and it must be possible for us to be able to reach him on some point and it will be most valuable if we were able to do so."[60] More than likely his concerns for Israel's secret defense programs had helped ignite Fulbright's attacks on American supporters of Israel.

The difficulties between Fulbright and Israel would continue for years to come, and in May of 1963, Fulbright once again tried to discredit Israel and its American supporters.

The senator from Arkansas encouraged an investigation into the activities of American Zionist organizations and tried to discredit them. Myer Feldman was advised in an unsigned memo dated May 2, 1963, that Fulbright had investigated the American Section of the Jewish Agency and that the Department of Justice had suggested that the American Zionist Council—a unit that represented various Zionist groups in America—should be registered as a foreign agent since it received funds from the Jewish Agency in Jerusalem. For the same reason the Department of Justice suggested that the Jewish Telegraphic Agency (JTA) should likewise be registered as a foreign agent. The JTA had been established after World War I to collect news of interest to the Jewish people throughout the world. According to the report Feldman received, Fulbright and the Department of Justice knew that any unfavorable publicity attending the investigation of such organizations would "inevitably cause irreparable harm" to all those organizations, to the American Jewish community and to Zionists as well as non-Zionists, who were "deeply concerned with the problems of Jews throughout the world."[61] Moreover, Fulbright's investigatory committee did not concern itself with "other American groups with overseas ties" or with the "activities in the United States of representatives or proponents of anti-Israel or Arab interests."[62] Fulbright's investigations and resultant publicity left "the false impression that any attempt by American Jewish groups to present their views with respect to Israel, to the Government or the Congress may be regarded as subversive or against the best interests of the United States."[63]

The unsigned memo defended the right of American citizens "to present to their Government their views on proposed policy, or action, by the U.S. on matters which, in their opinion, affect the well-being, or security, of the State of Israel and its inhabitants."[64]

Kennedy became concerned as Fulbright seemed to run amuck with his personal war on Zionism and American Jews. President Kennedy tried to balance things out by inviting "responsible" people of the national Jewish organizations—both Zionist and non-Zionist—to present their views. He thought that such discussions might be helpful.[65] The memo described the philanthropic assistance provided by Americans, regardless of their religious affiliation, and their "deep-rooted" concern for the well-being of the people of Israel. Contributions through the United Jewish Appeal since 1939 had reportedly amounted to one billion dollars. This financial support made it possible for more than one million Jewish survivors of Nazi persecutions and refugees from Arab lands to find refuge in Israel. American Jews were motivated by their concern for their fellow Jews overseas and their "deep conviction" that they were "acting in consonance with the policies and objectives of the U.S. to strengthen democracy in the free world." Kennedy felt that it was in the best interest of the United States that this generous philanthropic work should continue, for it was "in the best American tradition." But these endeavors would be "seriously impaired" if any doubt or stigma was attached to them. America was the first country to recognize Israel, and in addition to giving technical assistance to Israel, it gave grants and loans to Israel of more than $879.1 million by the end of 1962. This also enabled Israel to provide technical assistance to the newly emerging nations in Asia and Africa. Such assistance helped keep those countries in the Western orbit. The United States "is publicly committed to the territorial integrity of Israel and of its people." It was "difficult to reconcile the friendly and active concern for Israel" with Fulbright's investigations and the accusations made by the Department of Justice.[66]

Ultimately some senatorial critics of Israel, like Senator Hickenlooper, agreed that atomic energy was forthcoming and if applied peacefully, was like electricity: "Whether we like it or not countries are going to get it." While he felt that the United States should not try to keep states like Israel from developing its atomic resources, he wondered if there could be any guarantee that such energy would be used only for peaceful purposes.[67]

Lyman L. Lemnitzer, chairman of the Joint Chiefs of Staff, provided a response to that inquiry on January 17, 1961, as he revealed that the highest level of the Israeli government had assured the United States that it had no plans to produce atomic weapons. Furthermore, Israel had hoped to have a "power reactor in ten to fifteen years." The French assured the United States that their cooperation with Israel was limited to the twenty-four megawatt research reactor. While the French agreed to supply the uranium, whatever plutonium the reactor might produce would be returned to France. Allegedly, arrangements were made to assure that the reactor would be used only for peaceful purposes.[68]

On January 11, 1961, Harman, in conversation with Herter, observed that Ben-Gurion was the central figure in Israel with respect to the "Negev and atomic energy." Moreover, Harman tried to make Herter understand that "Israel had no plans to develop atomic weapons,"[69] and he made it perfectly clear that Ben-Gurion was greatly annoyed by the "leakages to the press and the number and detail of the leaks." This resulted in "excessive excitement and turmoil" and gave the appearance that the United States seemed concerned with Israel's atomic research, but not proliferation in general.[70]

Ben-Gurion felt that Nasser's stance was a consequence of America's airing of Israel's atomic research and that the publication of this very private matter also had an "adverse effect on Israel."[71]

Herter defended U.S. policy and claimed that the United States had tried to help dispel suspicions that had emanated from "many quarters."[72]

This explanation was not at all satisfactory to Harman.

Herter denied that it had been someone from the State Department that had leaked this controversial matter, but that it had been John McCone, chairman of the U.S. Atomic Energy Commission, who chose to make those remarks before TV cameras.[73]

Israel was likewise concerned with other aspects of U.S. "big brother" spying as American U-2 spy planes flew over Israel and photographed its land. The United States and Israel were friends, but was this what friends did to one another?[74]

Herter insisted that his information had come from photos taken on the ground, not far from the Dimona complex.[75]

Ben-Gurion was greatly disappointed with the Eisenhower administration's bias in favor of the Arabs and that a "friendly" United States did not find statements made by Israel's ambassador and its prime minister to be enough to put closure to this atomic energy matter. After all, "I am Prime Minister of a sovereign and friendly state and formal unequivocal assurances should be sufficient without the need for reiteration of inquiries." Moreover, all this came at a bad time because of "internal political difficulties."[76] Issues such as these should have been more easily resolved especially since the United States and Israel stood "together on broad world issues."[77]

It was agreed that both Israel and the United States should inform the press that the Israeli project was "exclusively" directed for "peaceful uses of atomic energy."[78]

Harman said that he was no expert about such things, but from his observations its construction was in the "very early stage" and that it would take at least three to four years for it to be completed. There was "definitely no plan to attempt even an experimental power station" at Dimona.[79]

When Ambassador Harman met with Assistant Secretary Lewis Jones on February 3, 1961, Jones said that the United States "fully accepted the statements of Prime Minister Ben-Gurion with respect to the peaceful uses of the Dimona reactor," but nevertheless Kennedy wanted an inspection of Dimona.[80]

Ambassador Harman advised that there was no need for such an inspection. As far as he was concerned, the story of Dimona was "very simple." They were "building a reactor" which would take some two years to complete. Ben-Gurion had given all the assurances that anyone could give and had proposed to hand back the plutonium to the country that supplied the uranium. "In good time, when there was something more to see, the visit might be arranged but no Israeli, let alone Ben-Gurion, could conceive why there was such a hurry about it."[81]

G. Lewis Jones held to his view that a quiet visit "without publicity at an arranged date" would be "invaluable in allaying suspicions."[82] As a "good friend" Jones advised Harman that the United States would continue to have an interest in this matter. Harman thought that "getting the visit over with" would be a good thing.[83]

On February 13, 1961, Harman assured Secretary Rusk that his government would give the "earliest attention" to the question of arranging a visit by the representatives of "one or more friendly powers to Dimona."[84] Rusk was encouraged and once again explained U.S. sensitivity to atomic developments particularly at a time when nuclear test talks were imminent. He said that Israel's complete "candor" in this field was of "great importance" in the relationship of the two governments.[85]

During Harman's talk with American officials on February 16, 1961, he reported that Egypt and Iraq had obtained the Soviet MiG-19 jet fighter and created a military imbalance since it was greatly superior to the French

"Super-Mystere." Not only could it carry missiles, but it had "tremendous speed and high flight ceiling." Israel was trying to obtain the French "Mirage," but it would take some eighteen months before that plane would be delivered.[86]

Harman pointed out that Israel could not withstand a sudden air attack since it was a small country with no defense in depth, a narrow ten-mile waist, and altogether it was no more than 50 miles by 350 miles. While the UAR had twenty-six airfields and it could shuttle back and forth over Israel, the Israelis only had three operational airfields and one civilian airfield. All this meant that Israel's jet fighter capacity could be knocked out immediately and its communication system destroyed. This would create great difficulties for manpower mobilization, which depended upon quick communications with its large reserve forces that had to augment its small standing army. Because of these difficulties, Israel asked the United States for the Hawk anti-aircraft missiles. If it were "possible to begin training now, Israel would be in a state of preparedness from a manpower" viewpoint. Israel anticipated that at the time of "maximum danger," the United States would consent to provide the Hawk.[87]

McGeorge Bundy asked Harman about Israel's construction of an atomic reactor.[88]

Harman still insisted that Israel had no intention to build "the bomb," and that the reactor was three to four years away from operation.[89]

Bundy observed that "the manner of its revelation to the world had created unnecessary tension," and that it had "spilled out in an unfortunate manner." Harman agreed that it had been "leaked out quite unnecessarily" and consequently Nasser had threatened to mobilize some four million men, all of which was most unpleasant for Israel.[90]

Harman insisted that all of this great noise was over a modest project "devoted exclusively to scientific experimentation and the training of a corps of scientists" who perhaps in fifteen years would be an important asset.[91]

While State Department officials felt that the French Mystere was on a par with the MiG-19, Israel again raised the issue of the Hawk ground-to-air missile.[92] The State Department still opposed providing Israel with the Hawk. Officials warned that it would produce a new element in the "never-ending pursuit of better arms." Harman continued to express his government's unhappiness with the manner in which Israel's nuclear development had come to the public's attention. The State Department insisted that it had tried to keep the matter secret as it waited for Israel's official explanation, but it had been forced to comment when the story broke in the British papers. While Israel may have been justified in keeping the matter secret, there were a "number" of congressmen who remained unhappy that Israel had kept this secret from the United States.[93] On March 3, Dean Rusk reported that Theodore Kollek had informed G. Lewis Jones on February

26, that a visit to Dimona by "a qualified American observer" might be possible in March.

On March 3, 1961, Rusk sent a circular to various U.S. embassies that the United States was seriously concerned with "Israeli nuclear activity" and was determined to "oppose the proliferation of nuclear weapons capabilities as firmly in Israel as elsewhere." The U.S. goal was to persuade Israel "to allow inspections and safeguards so that the fears of Israel's neighbors may be allayed." Prospects were good that "a qualified American observer" would be permitted to visit Dimona in the near future. This would enable the United States to better assess the Israeli statements concerning the peaceful purposes of Dimona and help alleviate fears of Israel's neighbors. Like electricity, atomic energy would be developed by "a number of states," but the United States would seek to promote its development for "peaceful purposes." It was known to the United States that a number of states including India were in the process of constructing reactors. India was building a reactor that was "considerably larger than that of Dimona." The United States planned to maintain "vigilance" with respect to such reactor programs in Israel as well as the rest of the Middle East, including Egypt. Rusk instructed American embassies and officials that "any such reports coming to the attention of our missions in those countries should be carefully checked, investigated and fully reported to the Department."[94]

Once again Jones had asked to talk with Ambassador Harman about Israel's atomic energy program. He complained that the United States had been waiting since January 4 for the invitation to send U.S. experts to Dimona. On February 26, 1961, Theodore Kollek had said that the invitation would be forthcoming in March, irrespective of the political squabbles in Israel. But March came and went, and there was still no invitation. Jones said that the United States was "keen" on visiting Dimona. On March 27, Kennedy inquired as to when the visit would take place, and he wanted a report by March 31.

Jones identified himself as a "friend" of Israel and observed that it would not do Israel much good if it appeared that Israel was stalling on that invitation.[95]

Harman did not have any news to give Jones. He had tried to "push" his government as much as he "dared." Ben-Gurion found it difficult to comprehend why "there was such a hurry." "The visit had been promised," and the promise would be kept.[96]

Jones continued to pressure Harman. He insisted that there could be no further delays and that Israel should give a favorable reply within the next few days,[97] but Ambassador Harman doubted that anything could take place until after the Passover holidays which started that year on April 3 and would continue until April 10.

On May 4, 1961, Israel informed the United States that the American observer scientists would be received in Israel on May 18. They would be guests of the Israeli government during their four-day stay in Israel. Their immediate hosts would be Israel's atomic energy officials.

The two American observers were Ulysses M. Staebler, senior assistant director of the Division of Reactor Development of the AEC, and Jesse William Croach Jr., Dupont scientist, stationed at AEC's Savanna River Laboratory. Rusk promised Kennedy that their reports would be available for the president before his meeting with Ben-Gurion.[98]

A week later Rusk responded to Kennedy's suggestion that American scientists should have a neutral scientist with them so as to improve the credibility of any report. The Department of State tried to persuade the Israelis to do that, but without success, and McGeorge Bundy suggested that the president introduce this idea when Ben-Gurion would visit with him,[99] but the Israeli prime minister was quite sensitive about having a "neutralist" visit Dimona. He pointed out that Israel's national pride would not permit it to be "singled out" from all other nations; and unless and until other states agreed to international inspection and control, Israel was not prepared to submit to such inspection.[100]

Before the JFK–Ben-Gurion meeting the National Security Council had provided Kennedy with its views on Israel's nuclear researches. The NSC clearly opposed the proliferation of nuclear weapons. The introduction of such weapons would have as deleterious impact on the "Middle East." Inevitably, the NSC reported, the Arabs would appeal to the Russians. Israeli nuclear capability would be "contrary to the interests of peace."[101]

That same day, Staebler and Croach presented their Dimona findings to the Department of State. They had been well received in Israel and they were permitted to visit the "several installations which are engaged in nuclear research, including the reactor at Dimona." They reported that "nothing" had been concealed from them and that the reactor was of "the scope and peaceful character previously described" to U.S. officials by Israel.[102]

The State Department advised that a further visit would not be necessary before another year, that Israel kept the project secret because of its concern of a possible boycott by Arabs against the manufacturers on whom Israel was dependent and because it was concerned that there might be sabotage. Furthermore Arab awareness of Israel's scientific ability would not be in Israel's interest. According to U.S. estimates, the reactor would produce small amounts of plutonium suitable for weapons, but there was no "present evidence" that Israel planned to produce atomic weapons. State officials seemed impressed that Israel had achieved "a most creditable accomplishment both in content and execution."[103] Attached to that memo was a censored hand scribbled note on White House stationery: "Tone leaves Scoville worried. We can't be completely satisfied Unanswered questions."[104]

Despite objections from Dean Rusk and other top State Department officials, President Kennedy agreed to meet and talk with Prime Minister Ben-

Gurion on May 30, 1961.[105] Just before this meeting, American embassies in the Middle East were informed that Ben-Gurion would meet with JFK on May 30, 1961. It was anticipated that President Kennedy would be in New York for a speech prior to his departure to meet Charles deGaulle in Paris. Ben-Gurion would arrive in New York on May 28 for a private visit, but would, at his request, be received by President Kennedy who hoped to emphasize U.S. views on "Israel's nuclear reactor" and the need to "move forward with respect to Arab refugees."[106]

The Department of State was "keenly interested in any measures" which would minimize adverse reactions in the Arab world to Ben-Gurion's visit. It was hoped that Kennedy's letters, cast in warm friendly tones, would be helpful. They thought that the letters should be delivered "well before" news of Ben-Gurion's visit would become public.[107]

CHAPTER 4

Ben-Gurion's Gallant Fight

When President Kennedy met with Prime Minister Ben-Gurion on May 30, 1961, Ben-Gurion expressed his great concern with the growing disparity of power between Israel and Egypt. The gap with respect to arms available to Egypt and those available to Israel was growing. Russia provided Egypt with at least three times the quantity of arms that Israel had, and those Russian arms were of a "superior quality." Perhaps Israel had "superior" manpower but the Egyptians were "improving the quality of their manpower."[1]

Israel's struggle with Egypt was not just a question of power, said Ben-Gurion, it was a matter of survival. "If Nasser were to defeat Israel he would do to the people of Israel what Hitler had done to the six million Jews of Europe."[2] Ben-Gurion spoke of Israel's need for air defenses. While the Egyptians had twenty-six airfields, Israel only had three and a civilian airport. In order to deal with this situation and to defend its airspace, Israel needed the Hawk missiles: "If we get the Hawk missile we are more or less safe." Within its arsenal Israel had "nothing against the MiG-19 or the MiG-21."[3] Egypt had twenty MiG-19s; 96 MiG-17s; thirty MiG-15s and fifty IL-28s. Overall, Egypt had at least three hundred planes.

Kennedy listened intently and expressed his concern. He promised to watch the "count very carefully" because "our interests are closely involved with yours. We want to make sure that you will not be open to attack. We would be involved by that. I want to make it clear that our interests are very in accordance with yours."[4]

Ben-Gurion then asked Kennedy to arrange for a U.S.-Soviet declaration supporting "the integrity and independence of all the countries in the Middle East." While such a declaration might not "guarantee peace," it might help, but Kennedy did not believe that the Russians would agree to such a declaration. He revealed his great concern over America's widespread international commitment. America was involved in Europe, Latin America, Asia and Africa. One such involvement was Berlin. "What use would a declaration on our part be to you if we were to get run out of Berlin? I am not sure that our problems are not as great as yours."[5]

Prior to Ben-Gurion's meeting with John F. Kennedy, the National Security Council had provided the president with its views regarding possible Israeli atomic developments and clearly stated its opposition to the proliferation of nuclear weapons. Such weapons, the report indicated, would have "Middle East repercussions" and Arab concerns were "widespread and deep." Inevitably the Arabs would appeal to the Russians. The NSC claimed that the development of Israeli nuclear capability was "contrary to the interests of peace."[6]

Winston Churchill had once described Israel as "invincibly established," but Ben-Gurion did not see it that way at all and wrote "some fifty-five letters to heads of state describing the dangers Israel had to face." He wanted to see Israel securely established. "Nuclear research" was one way he hoped to promote that security.[7]

In the course of its struggle for survival and its search for security, Israel developed expertise in the field of nuclear technology. The Eisenhower and Kennedy administrations were concerned lest this would encourage a greater and an even more dangerous arms race as well as the proliferation of nuclear weapons. The CIA had estimated that such an Israeli nuclear development would bring Egypt even closer to the Soviet orbit. American intelligence speculated that the Soviets would not provide Egypt and other states with nuclear know-how or weapons, but that they might base some missiles and atomic bombs in Egypt under Soviet control. By late 1962, early 1963, the CIA believed that Israel already had nuclear weapons or the ability to piece the weapons together. While Ben-Gurion informed Kennedy that Israel would not be the first to introduce nuclear weapons to the region, Levi Eshkol advised Johnson that Israel would not stand by if Egypt tried. Israel could not "let Nasser be the first to introduce new categories of weapons into the Middle East."[8]

As the United States was preoccupied with the balance of power in the Middle East and elsewhere, President Kennedy tried to find out from Ben-Gurion whether Israel was pursuing the development of nuclear weapons. Ben-Gurion reminded Kennedy of Israel's special circumstances: "We are the remnant of a people struggling for its last hold of its existence. Israel is our last stop."[9] As the questioning of Israel's harnessing atomic energy came up, Ben-Gurion reminded Kennedy that the United States had sent an investigating team to Israel and that the president had its report. The prime minister said that he was prepared to answer any further questions.

Kennedy said that he found the report "very helpful," but then, "A woman should not only be virtuous, she should appear to be virtuous. We must take away any excuse for the argument that what you are doing is connected with the proliferation of nuclear arms." He felt that if it even appeared that Israel was "preparing atomic weapons, [the UAR] would try to do the same. Perhaps in the next few years atomic weapons will proliferate, but we don't want it to happen." Kennedy appreciated the report and wanted it published, but he asked that some scientists from neutral states should be invited to investigate the Israel atomic energy project. Ben-Gurion agreed that the report might be published, but he was somewhat skeptical about having a "neutral" intervene in this matter and he wanted to know what Kennedy meant by "neutral."[10]

Perhaps someone from Switzerland, Sweden or Denmark? "Would you object to our sending such a neutral scientist?" asked Kennedy.

Ben-Gurion did not voice any objection.[11]

Ben-Gurion made no secret of the fact that Israel needed atomic power for its peacetime projects and that it considered atomic energy for defense purposes. Israel had begun an atomic energy project for desalination in order to obtain more water for the Negev, Israel's desert which was two-thirds of its total land area. Israel had no coal or oil of its own, this was why Israel turned to atomic energy. France had lent Israel some assistance in its efforts to build an atomic reactor. For the "time being the only purposes are for peace. But we will see what happens in the Middle East. It does not depend upon us. Perhaps Russia won't give bombs to China or Egypt, but maybe Egypt will develop them herself," said Ben-Gurion.[12]

In June 1961, the U.S. embassy in Israel had reported that Israel planned to build a nuclear reactor in the Negev. The plan had apparently been initiated by Moshe Dayan and Shimon Peres. No date was given. It was brought before the entire Israeli Cabinet for approval. Dayan and Peres believed that if they were to ask the United States for aid to build the reactor, they would be turned down, but if they asked France, they would receive a favorable reply. The Israelis believed that the only question Israel would have to decide would be whether the United States would consider this matter as vitally affecting its interests or whether it would merely respond angrily. The Cabinet, influenced by Dayan and Peres, concluded that the United States would do no more than display an angry attitude.[13]

As far as Ben-Gurion was concerned, his meeting with Kennedy had been fruitful. Finally an Israeli prime minister had personally made the president aware of Israel's special circumstances and its security difficulties, and he had outlined Israel's military situation so that the president might begin to understand Israel's predicament. Perhaps John F. Kennedy might begin to understand why it was necessary for Israel to pursue nuclear research. Ben-Gurion had tried to persuade Kennedy to join Khrushchev in a joint declaration advocating the end to war in the Middle East. Despite his years of experience and savvy, he seemed not to comprehend the chasm that separated the Soviet Union and the United States. For his part, Kennedy tried to help Ben-Gurion, Foreign Minister Golda Meir and later on Levi Eshkol understand his situation. But the primary focus of Israeli leaders was the survival of the State of Israel and the Jewish people. They knew that almost nothing had been done to help rescue the Jews during the Holocaust and that without the courage and determination of the Israeli people there would have been no rebirth of Israel. They knew that by the mid-1950s the Arab states led by Egypt were prepared to annihilate Israel. Had Israel not preempted, with the help of French and British arms, Israel might very well have been annihilated. Egypt would have completed Hitler's plan to wipe out the Jews. Ben-Gurion and his government tried to move heaven and earth to make Israel as strong as possible so that no one would even dream of harming it.

After his meeting with Kennedy, the Israeli prime minister traveled to Ottawa to meet with Canada's prime minister, John Diefenbaker, on June 7, 1961. Ben-Gurion spoke of Israel's satisfactory relations with Turkey and Iran and observed that Iran was in serious trouble. The Shah was well-meaning, but weak, and he spent most of the Western aid he received on military and urban development. Diefenbaker asked Ben-Gurion about Israel's atomic research. Ben-Gurion once again denied that Israel's atomic research program led to the production of nuclear weapons. He insisted that Israel's atomic program was designed to meet Israel's needs for electrical power and water. It was unfortunate that the countries of the Middle East devoted so much of their energies and resources on war, and he reiterated the need for a Soviet-American detente that would guarantee the independence and integrity of the Middle Eastern states. Diefenbaker, like the American president, thought that the idea was not very practical. Perhaps America would keep its word, but the Russians would not. Ben-Gurion insisted that it would be useful even if the Russians were insincere, as it would provide a face-saving device for Nasser and allow him to back away from a commitment to destroy Israel. Diefenbaker found Ben-Gurion's thesis interesting and promised to talk with Kennedy about it before the president would meet Khrushchev in Vienna.[14]

Ben-Gurion's next stop was Paris where he met President Charles De Gaulle who indicated that France needed to change its policy of assistance to Israel. French government assistance for Israel's reactor would have to be replaced by private French firms.[15] Israel was more alone than ever.

Rumor spread from Beirut that the Federal German Government had entered into a secret agreement with Israel to develop an atomic bomb. Reportedly the Germans hoped to make progress in the area of nuclear research by "utilizing" Israel's know-how and technology.[16]

The State Department doused that rumor. Officials from the Near East Division advised American embassy officials that there was "no substance" to the reports that Israel planned to develop atomic bombs with West German assistance. "Ben-Gurion gave President Kennedy clear assurances that Israel was not contemplating the development of nuclear weapons and we doubt Ben-Gurion would deliberately prevaricate to the U.S. President."[17] Furthermore, the recent visit of two U.S. scientists to Israel's atomic energy installations gave no indication that Israel was attempting to develop nuclear weapons. Nonetheless, "in accordance with the firm U.S. policy of opposing the proliferation of nuclear weapons the U.S. expected to continue its vigilance of nuclear weapons development possibilities in Israel and elsewhere."[18]

Ambassador Barbour reported that Ben-Gurion had been very pleased with Kennedy particularly because of the president's understanding of the underlying importance of Israeli security problems and his reaffirmation of America's determination to assist Israel in and outside of the UN if Israel became a victim of aggression. But it was apparent to some Israeli officials that Kennedy had done very little more than "reiterate" America's longstanding position on mutual defense.[19]

President Kennedy was likewise impressed by Ben-Gurion. Some of his officials hoped that the mutual confidence established by their Waldorf Astoria meeting would be useful for progress on matters of common interest in the future.[20]

Kennedy tried to understand the complexities of the Near East and somehow achieve harmonious relations with all the states therein. But as Komer observed, no matter which Arab faction the United States would support, it would "outrage all whom we did not support." Komer believed that in the end "a hands-off policy of trying to be friendly with everybody is the best course."[21]

When Ambassador Harman talked with Assistant Secretary of State Talbot on March 9, 1962, he heard him evaluate conditions in the Arabian Peninsula as unstable. There was "a cadre of intelligent and modern people in Saudi Arabia," but there were far fewer in "Yemen." Oil was one of the greatest problems. The Arabs were finding oil "in many of the small sheikdoms all the time." It was likely that there would be "a very uneven development" and this would lead to clashes. In Abu Dhabi with a total population of about 20,000, oil was discovered, and within five years it would become as wealthy as Kuwait. The annual income would be $10,000 per capita. The local sheikh kept his money in an iron box under his bed. When the sheikh asked how much money he would invest for Arab development, he said that he would invest as much as other Arab countries had invested in his country's development in the past.[22]

In Kuwait they had formed a development company, and there was some talk about investing in Arab countries. Jordan hoped to benefit therefrom, but Talbot observed that the Kuwaitis interpreted development to mean investing in Beirut apartment houses. He found bad relations growing amongst the Arab states. The Saudis were upset with Cairo's propaganda and this was the case with Yemen as well. Harman thought that Egypt's subversive propaganda reflected Egypt's lack of concern with its internal problems. Talbot observed that people in the Arab countries claimed that they would be reconciled with Israel's present population, but what they feared was the growth of Israel through immigration. Harman "had heard that line before." The Arabs had a number of arguments and they could be "depended upon to try them all at the same time." One of their favorite arguments against Israel was the Jewish immigrants, another was that Israel consumed everybody's waters, and still another was that Israel was an alien force in the Middle East since it affiliated with the European Common Market. They hoped their misinformation would be accepted by the international community and that Israel would thereby be weakened or blocked in its development. Israel would never accept Arab restriction of Jewish immigration to Israel. "If the Arabs were to face me across a peace table to offer me peace on a platter in return for an agreement on my part to restrict Jewish immigration I would turn it down. If I accepted that condition I would undermine the foundations of my existence and abandon my self-respect."[23]

Talbot reported that amongst the State Department Arabists there were different estimates as to what direction the Arab world would take. Some felt that a general consolidation of the Arab world was in process and had been in process since 1918 and would probably be brought about by someone like Nasser or whoever was leading Egypt. Others believed that there would be further fragmentation, and that one regime after another would fall. They all felt it to be unwise for the United States to support one particular leader like Nasser since others, like the rulers of Saudi Arabia, were very much against him. Saudi Arabia and Egypt were constantly at loggerheads with one another, which was best seen when Egypt invaded Yemen. They were likewise opposed to the United States identifying itself with Israel.[24] The region was very complex, and there was a great deal of instability within such countries as Syria, Iraq and Lebanon with its Christian-Muslim divisions.[25]

On May 21, 1962, McGeorge Bundy asked Shimon Peres, Israel's deputy minister of defense what he thought about the introduction of nuclear weapons into the Middle East. Peres said it would be better for Israel if they could be kept out, but if others might move in that direction, Israel would have to consider its own position.[26] That May, Peres had come to Washington to lay the groundwork for Israel's request for military aid for the purchase of such sophisticated weapons as the Hawks as well as conventional military equipment. Egypt had significantly increased its military strength. It acquired MiG-21s and Soviet naval vessels. In the end, U.S. economic aid had enabled Egypt to devote its resources for the purchase of military supplies.

For some time President Kennedy had tried to get Israel's nuclear facilities inspected, but whatever inspections did take place did not seem to satisfy some of America's experts. Kennedy, and later LBJ, tried to get Israel further interested in scientific nuclear research in such fields as desalination rather than nuclear weaponry. They would even provide Israel with "heavy water" materials for such research. Israel's university of technology and science—The Technion—would be one of the recipients of that "heavy water" material.

On June 22, 1962, Phillips Talbot proposed another "quiet visit by U.S. scientists to Dimona." Talbot said that the May 1961 visit had "served to remove Israel's atomic energy development as an irritant in the Near East situation" and he believed that a similar visit could further prolong a "relaxed attitude."[27]

The Kennedy administration did not always get good grades from Congress for its Middle East policy. Among Kennedy's critics there was Democratic Senator Stephen M. Young of Ohio who found Kennedy's policy to be "weak, vacillating and inconsistent." He observed that in most respects Kennedy's foreign policies were good, but in the Middle East they were disappointing. He recalled that in 1957 and again in 1960, Senator Kennedy had presented proposals for the Middle East which would "do much toward achieving a permanent settlement of the problems of the Middle East." Said Senator Young, "they were valid then and they are valid now." Young called upon Kennedy not to abandon his past ideals and to initiate "broad, vigorous and dynamic initiatives," for the United States merely reacted to Russian initiatives and took the defensive. He urged Kennedy to do all in his power to arrange a conference between Arab and Israeli leaders and to help establish a Middle East development fund under the auspices of the UN to help develop the resources of that region.[28]

On June 13, 1962, President Kennedy sent Ben-Gurion a letter that dealt with a variety of issues, some of which gave rise to "concern and anxiety" while others "provided a basis for hope" that peace in the Near East could be achieved. Shimon Peres's discussions with U.S. officials were being "carefully examined," and American officials hoped that Israel would make use of UN services to keep its borders quiet. The president was pleased that progress was made with respect to the development of water resources in the Middle East. Israel's plan to draw from the Jordan-Yarmuk River waters, to which Israel was entitled, should be carried out as scheduled by Israel and its neighbors. Each was to use their fair share of the water system to improve their economy and advance the general welfare of their people. It was Kennedy's hope that cooperation in this water project could lead to cooperation "toward the ultimate objective of peace."[29]

On June 24, 1962, Ben-Gurion wrote Kennedy that he was thankful for the way President Kennedy and his staff had received Shimon Peres on matters of "vital importance to Israel's security," and he reiterated the importance of peaceful settlement of disputes in order to establish a lasting and permanent peace with its neighbors. He thought JFK's support of Israel's water project reflected "a deep and sensitive understanding of one of Is-

rael's most vital needs and interests." While Israel hoped to use its fair share
of water for the benefit of its people, it had no intention of depriving its
neighbors of their rights to water. Israel welcomed 10,000 new immigrants
each month. Most of these immigrants came from backward and oppressed
states and they came with nothing. While America had achieved something
of the same thing over a period of several hundred years, Israel was expected to do the same in a short time, and it was constantly confronted
with a most difficult security problem. Once again Ben-Gurion expressed
his concern that what had been done to six million Jews, with the participation of such Arab leaders as Haj Amin el Husseini, could be done to the
two million Jews of Israel, "if, God Forbid, the Israel Defense Forces were
defeated." In order to secure its defense, Israel needed "sufficient deterrent
strength." For as long as the peace of the world was "not secure everywhere we have to secure our peace through our strength."[30]

Tensions mounted as Egypt successfully launched its test rockets on July
21, 1962. Initially Israel brushed off the rockets as having no "immediate
military significance." But that was more a matter of politics than strategy.
The Israeli chief of staff warned that the real danger of those rockets was
that they would attract attention away from the flow of conventional armaments the Egyptians were receiving from the Russians.[31] It was this development that helped persuade Kennedy that Israel should be supplied
with the Hawk defensive missile system.

On August 15, 1962, President Kennedy informed Prime Minister Ben-
Gurion that he was sending Myer Feldman to consider the matter of the
Hawk missiles and the Arab refugees. "As you know . . . the Department
of State and members of my staff have been reviewing intensively certain
matters that are of prime importance to Israel's security and well-being as
well as to the improvement in the atmosphere in the Near East and in
prospects for peace."[32]

Ben-Gurion thanked President Kennedy for his support, "his magna-
nimity and friendship," as reflected in his decision to sell Israel the Hawk
missiles. Ben-Gurion appreciated Feldman's "great skill" in presenting with
"clarity and eloquence" the American position and he appreciated "profoundly" Kennedy's decision to supply Israel the Hawk missile. Ben-Gurion
also appreciated Dr. Johnson's mission regarding the Arab refugees, but his
plan would only complicate matters "even more" for Israel without any
advantage "accruing to the refugees themselves."[33]

Although the Hawk missile was a welcome departure from previous U.S.
policy, that defense system did not restore the balance of power between
Israel and the Arab states. Soon thereafter Israeli leaders would request
ground-to-ground missiles, tanks and naval craft provided by the Soviet
Union.

Amidst this alteration in U.S. policy there were some Israeli diplomats
who were much more blunt than Ben-Gurion and Golda Meir in their crit-

icism of U.S. policy towards Israel. One such critic was Nachman Ran, third secretary of the Israeli Legation to Budapest, who wanted to know why the United States had embarked on an anti-Israeli policy when it gave aid and support to Egypt, a country that had voted to destroy Israel. Why did the United States oppose bilateral Israeli discussions with Egypt on common problems? Nachman Ran pointed out that there was "a dangerous imbalance of power" as the Arabs received arms from the USSR, and this gave the Arabs a preponderance of power against Israel. It was an absurd charge that a small country like Israel with a population of two million might embark upon an aggressive military policy when it was surrounded by forty million Arabs. In Ran's view, the economic aid to Egypt supported an aggressive Arab war policy against Israel. What Israel needed, and what it wanted more than arms, was bilateral talks with Egypt that would help settle outstanding differences and disputes, and bring peace.[34]

Shimon Peres observed on July 27 that because of the extensive supplies received by the Egyptians, Israel would need foreign help to prevent war and establish a balance of arms that might deter its enemies from launching a war of aggression. Ben-Gurion warned that any conflict with Nasser would be a life and death struggle for Israel and any weapons obtained by Egypt had to be regarded with the utmost seriousness.[35]

By September 14, 1962, Peres observed that Israel had to adopt a new military doctrine in view of the weapons in the hands of the Arabs. The time Israel had to meet the new challenges was short. Two weeks later he noted that the decision of the United States to sell Hawk missiles to Israel did not absolve Israel from its efforts to keep from falling behind.

Kennedy tried his best to maintain U.S. friendship with Egypt and the other Arab states while at the same time being supportive of Israel. Israeli diplomats like Ambassador Harman thought that the administration was somewhat naive in believing that Nasser could be tamed or converted into a peace loving neighbor and friend of the West. Individuals like Carl Kaysen, Deputy Special Assistant to the President, believed that Nasser should be persuaded to better his country and that the United States should continue supplying him with economic aid for this purpose.[36] But as Harman talked with Feldman, he discovered that Kennedy was greatly displeased with Nasser's actions in Yemen, Saudi Arabia and Jordan. Kennedy wanted to hear the Israeli viewpoint regarding Nasser.[37]

As Israel struggled to survive, the United States had major diplomatic and military confrontations with the Soviet Union over Cuba, Berlin and Southeast Asia.

Months before Kennedy took office, President Eisenhower had decided in favor of a CIA plan to overthrow the pro-Communist Castro regime. Some 2,000 anti-Castro Cubans were to be trained for an invasion of Cuba which was supposed to spark an insurrection in Cuba against Castro. JFK inherited that plan from Eisenhower and apparently accepted the word of

CIA, Defense and State Department experts that it was a worthwhile undertaking.

During JFK's April 12, 1961, news conference, he denied widely circulated reports that the United States was supplying the training facilities and armed support for an invasion of Cuba:

> First, I want to say that there will not be under any conditions, an intervention in Cuba by the U.S. armed forces. This Government will do everything . . . to make sure that there are no Americans involved in any actions inside Cuba.
>
> The basic issue in Cuba is not one between the U.S. and Cuba. It is between the Cubans themselves. I intend to see that we adhere to that principle . . . .[38]

One week before the invasion, after having received assurances from the joint chiefs of staff, Secretary of State Rusk and Secretary of Defense McNamara that the invasion plan would work, Kennedy approved the invasion with the understanding that there would be no overt American participation. But on April 15, 1961, U.S. B-26 bombers attacked three Cuban military airfields, one was on the outskirts of Havana.

At the UN the Cuban foreign minister accused the United States of being involved in the air attack. U.S. Ambassador Adlai E. Stevenson denied the charge. The Cubans produced photographic evidence that revealed some of the U.S. equipment captured by the Cuban authorities. U.S. reports indicated that the first strike had succeeded, and the second strike was canceled, but when the reports proved wrong, Kennedy ordered a second strike. Poor weather conditions made a second strike impossible.

On April 17, U.S. Naval craft escorted a fleet of ships to the Cuban territorial waterline, and the fleet proceeded to the Bay of Pigs. Some 1500 exiles disembarked and began their invasion. The Cuban Air Force fired at the ships and managed to sink two vessels. The Cuban planes chased away additional supply ships and a group of B-26s that had tried to assist the invaders. An hour after the B-26s had been driven off, unmarked U.S. Navy jets flew in and out of the area.

After seventy-two hours the invaders surrendered to Castro's forces. Contrary to CIA expectations, the Cuban people did not rise up in arms against Castro. Two hundred exiles were killed and 1200 were captured and given thirty-year prison terms.

The invasion to liberate Cuba had failed. Latin American states were apparently outraged by this unilateral American intervention, and the Russians sent ominous letters to Kennedy.

Kennedy accepted full blame for the fiasco. He learned not to depend upon CIA or other such governmental experts. From April 1961, he would rely more upon such close associates as his brother Robert Kennedy, the attorney general, and less upon the so-called "professionals."

Postscript: After extensive negotiations, Castro released 1133 prisoners and 900 of their relatives who were still living in Cuba in exchange for $53 million in pharmaceuticals and agricultural equipment.

As a consequence Castro moved closer to the Soviet bloc orbit. Soviet Russia's military buildup in Cuba became a matter of growing U.S. concern as more Russian "technicians" and more military equipment was shipped to Cuba. U.S. observation planes and ships photographed Russian ships heading for Cuba, but aerial reconnaissance flights over the island did not report sighting offensive weapons. Some congressmen and newsmen called for an invasion of Cuba since reportedly the Russians had placed their missiles on the island. Castro spoke of an imminent American invasion.

On October 14, American U-2 reconnaissance flights revealed that Soviet medium-range missile bases were being installed in Cuba. President Kennedy met with Soviet Foreign Minister Gromyko who warned that if the Berlin question would not be settled after the U.S. elections, Russia would conclude a separate peace with East Germany, and he complained about how badly the United States had treated Cuba. Kennedy sat in his rocking chair and listened, astonished, while Gromyko asserted that Russia trained Cubans only in the use of defensive weapons. Kennedy read his statement of September 4, warning the Russians against the introduction of offensive weapons into Cuba. Gromyko assured the president that this would never be done and that the United States need not be concerned. Robert Kennedy came by to see his brother soon after Gromyko had left and observed that the "President of the United States, it can be said was displeased with the spokesman of the Soviet Union."[39]

Kennedy tried to find possible alternatives to a missile confrontation, but he made sure that the Russians did not know that he was aware of their offensive weapons preparations in Cuba. Then on October 22, 1962, he addressed the nation on the Cuba situation. He informed the American people of "unmistakable evidence" that the Russians were preparing offensive missile sites "on that imprisoned island." It was clear that the "purpose of these bases can be none other than to provide a nuclear strike capability against the Western Hemisphere." The Soviet medium-range ballistic missiles were capable of carrying nuclear warheads for more than 1000 nautical miles. Each could strike Washington, D.C., the Panama Canal, Mexico City or any other city in the southeastern United States, Central America or the Caribbean. The president advised that he had taken some initial steps. First, he aimed to "halt this offensive buildup" and that there would be "a strict quarantine on all offensive military equipment" headed for Cuba. Second, there would be a continued surveillance of Cuba. Third, "It shall be the policy of this nation to regard any nuclear missile launched from Cuba against any nation in the Western Hemisphere as an attack by the Soviet Union on the United States requiring a full retaliatory response upon the Soviet Union."[40]

On October 24, as Russian ships neared the 500-mile barrier, the United States had to intercept them or announce a withdrawal. As RFK recalled it was "the moment we prepared for, which we hoped would never come."[41] Secretary McNamara announced that two Russian ships were within the quarantine barrier. Interception would probably be between 10:30 and 11:00 a.m. Then word arrived that a Russian sub was positioned between the two Russian ships. It was decided to send an aircraft carrier and helicopters with anti-sub equipment. RFK recalled that this had been a "time of gravest concern for the President."[42] How would all this end up? "His hand went up to his face and covered his mouth. He opened and closed his fist. His face seemed drawn, his eyes pained, almost gray. We stared at each other across the table. For a few fleeting seconds, it was almost as though no one else was there and he was no longer President."[43] Robert Kennedy thought of times of strain and hurt as when John had been ill and almost died; when he had lost his child; when they had learned that Joseph P. Kennedy their oldest brother had been killed over Germany. The president had made his decision and had initiated the course of history, but at this point the president was no longer in control over those events. "What could we say now—what could we do?" Within a few minutes the president learned that the Russian ships had been ordered to stop. They were stopped dead in the water. Then Kennedy gave another order. The Russian ships were not to be interfered with. If the ships were to turn around, there was to be no interference. They were to be given every chance to do so.[44] The tension had eased, the Russians had been stopped, but the danger was far from over.

For thirteen days in October the United States and Russia were on the brink of a nuclear holocaust. But they were able to negotiate and defuse the situation. While Cuba remained a Russian base, most, if not all Russian missiles were removed from Cuba as were American missiles from Turkey.

Ben-Gurion and much of Israel watched the challenge and response which Kennedy had faced with great interest. They were impressed by the courage and determination of the young American president. Ben-Gurion wrote President Kennedy on October 29, 1962:

I appreciate the fact that your Government kept us informed of your policies in relation to the grave question of Soviet missile bases in Cuba. Since your historic speech of 22nd October I have been following the situation closely. I would not burden you at this time with a lengthy communication. It is sufficient to say that I have the utmost understanding of the motivations of your action and the highest admiration for its courage. I want to congratulate you on the utmost success you have achieved. Your leadership and determination have strengthened the cause of world peace.[45]

That same day Kennedy sent Adlai Stevenson a personal letter of thanks for the work he had done at the United Nations:

I want to tell you how deeply and personally I appreciate the contribution you have made to the security of the United States and the peace of the world in the last week. Your vindication of American policy before the U.N. was superb. . . . [But] we are not yet out of the woods and I count on you in the days ahead.[46]

Understandably the Cuban missile crisis near head-on nuclear collision made Kennedy and his administration even more concerned and sensitive about nuclear proliferation. They expected greater reciprocity and concessions in return for Kennedy's willingness to meet with Foreign Minister Golda Meir. They expected concessions on the issue of repatriation, and cooperation with UN peacekeeping machinery, among other things.[47]

On December 27, 1962, during Foreign Minister Meir's meeting with the president she expressed her admiration for his leadership and reassured him that there would be no difficulties between the United States and Israel on such matters as nuclear proliferation.[48]

The State Department's view, as reported by Robert Komer, was that: "Our policy to date toward Israel has been one of all give and not get."[49] Komer felt that it was necessary "in our own interest to bring more balance into this relationship."[50]

The day before President Kennedy was to meet with Foreign Minister Golda Meir, he sent Feldman to talk with her and prepare the groundwork. Feldman advised Meir that there was some disagreement between Kennedy and his advisors on the refugee question, and if Israel could help resolve the matter, it would be most beneficial to Israel. Moreover, he told Meir that Kennedy viewed Israel as part of the free world and that it should be defended. He then brought up the issue of Dimona, since the president was greatly concerned with nuclear proliferation. He asked if she thought Israel had given U.S. inspectors enough time to see everything in Dimona. The president was most concerned that if Israel would use the reactor to produce atomic bombs, the Arabs might attack Israel. Feldman explained that the president had tried to prevent Soviet expansion in the Middle East and the formation of an Arab bloc against the United States. Furthermore, Kennedy had provided economic aid to the Arabs in order to promote greater friendship between the United States and the Arab states. President Kennedy expected some help from Israel to keep Dimona a civilian project, provide a resolution of the refugee problem and exercise restraint with respect to border incidents. While Kennedy felt that the Johnson refugee plan was dead, he asked Israel to help the United States resolve this issue.[51]

After this preliminary talk between Meir and Feldman, the Kennedy-Meir meeting was held in Florida at 10 a.m. on December 27, 1962. Mrs. Meir reviewed Israel's security needs and said that Israel was "perfectly prepared to live within its present borders," it did not seek Arab lands, it was not anti-Arab and it did not need "the sands of Jordan." Israel just wanted the Arabs to stop shooting, and it was prepared to help resolve the refugee issue. It had accepted some 40,000 refugees, but it had gained nothing from it—neither acknowledgment nor credit. The Arabs were inflexible. Israel's Arab population was some 230,000 to 240,000, that was already 11 percent of Israel's population, and not all of them were "peaceful citizens." As Ben-Gurion had said, Israel would not gamble its future on "deficient peace plans."[52]

Meir wanted to know for what purpose the Arab refugees wanted to enter Israel? Arab delegates at the UN repeatedly proclaimed that Israel had no right to exist and that it should be made to disappear. Israel knew quite well what the Arabs planned to do: They wanted to make Israel into another Algeria. Israel wanted to see all the Arab countries democratic and developing rapidly and that cooperation for the common good.[53]

Egypt had threatened Israel with its military buildup. Soviet made TUs had bombed Yemen and then flew back to Egypt. If the Egyptians could do that to Yemen, what could they then do to Israel? Egypt was arming itself with Soviet ballistic missiles and radiological warheads. It had a budget of between $220,000,000 and $250,000,000 for that endeavor. As Ben-Gurion had advised Kennedy in May of 1961, Meir once again tried to help Kennedy understand the special circumstances and history of the Jewish people. The government of Israel was not just responsible for the welfare of its people, it had another responsibility. Twice before in its long history Israel had lost its sovereignty. The country was occupied and its people dispersed. In 1948, Israel reestablished its independence as a state, and this might be its last chance. The entire world remembered what had happened to the Jews of Europe. At the time of the outbreak of World War II, Eastern Europe held the reservoir of Jewish people who wanted to come and make a fresh start in Israel. They were murdered by the German Nazis and their collaborators. Who knew what might happen to the three and a half million Jews in the USSR? They might never get out. If something happened again so that the Jews would be dispersed from Israel, this could be the last time. Would the Jewish people have to wait another 2000 years for the restoration of their Israel? That was not "a happy idea."[54]

Foreign Minister Meir confessed that she realized everybody seemed to bring their problems to the president and that Israel was no exception.[55]

President Kennedy smiled as he listened to Foreign Minister Meir and then confided that he had a great many difficulties to face. America, he said, was in a unique position. No other country carried the responsibilities of the United States. It was concerned with the developments in Korea, Vietnam, India, Pakistan, the Middle East, Africa and Latin America as well as Europe. The United States tried to maintain the "balance of power in the interest of the free world," and for that reason it found itself involved in "controversies between Somalis and Ethiopians, Indians and Pakistanis, Cambodians and Thais. . . ." Perhaps Israel has "enormous security problems, but we do too." In recent months the United States had come close to a direct confrontation with Russia and Cuba.[56]

After describing the variety of American commitments, Kennedy then tried to clarify America's commitment to Israel. The United States "has a special relationship with Israel in the Middle East really comparable only to that which it has with Britain over a wide range of world affairs." But the United States had to maintain its friendships with the Arab world. If it would lose those friendships, it would be detrimental to the interests of the United States and Israel.[57] He asked that Israel try to understand American interests and commitments. Because of its ties with the United States, the State of Israel did not have to depend "wholly on its own efforts for security but on the U.S. as well."[58] Kennedy did not demand concessions from Israel, but he did ask for Israel's friendship and understanding as an ally. He observed that obviously Israel could not accept a flood of refugees, and the Arabs had their own troubles. Perhaps no compromise might be possible on this issue, said Kennedy, but hope should not be given up. The Arab refugee situation cost the United States a good deal of money since the United States was the main country that supported UNWRA. And the refugees caused "great damage" to the prospects of peace. The "great majority" of refugees would have to be resettled outside of Israel. No progress had been made with the Johnson plan, and it was "gone," but that did not mean that we should not keep trying for it was not "impossible" to find a resolution of this issue. If the dispute would be allowed to fester it would most likely "blow up" some day.[59]

Those sentiments had never before been expressed so succinctly by an American president to an Israeli official. Seldom, if ever, had an American president exhibited such insight into the problems of the Middle East. Seldom had any leader of the twentieth century revealed such wisdom and understanding concerning that troubled part of the world. And yet Israeli leaders like Ben-Gurion and Meir did not grasp nor appreciate what Kennedy had tried to tell them. From their perspective, private assurances as to Israel's security were well and good, but they could not take the place of public declarations that might enhance Israel's chances for survival.[60] They could not appreciate the constraints that restricted President Kennedy's choices. Despite all their efforts, and to their dismay, Israeli leaders were unable to obtain a public declaration of alliance from President Kennedy.

A FRIEND IN THE WHITE HOUSE

While Kennedy spoke to Israeli leaders as a friend of Israel, American officials continued to pressure Israel to make concessions. Robert Komer advised Minister Gazit that he felt Israel's policies in the 1960s reflected "too many past wounds and not enough future prospects." He observed that Israeli policy was "too hard-nosed and inflexible to permit adequate movement toward the settlement of outstanding issues," such as the Arab refugees. He reminded Gazit of Kennedy's reassurances to Mrs. Meir of December, "Our special relationship with Israel was comparable only to that with the UK." Israel's "constant harping on security reassurances, intelligence exchanges, direct negotiations or contacts (with the Arabs) sounded suspiciously like a dodge in which the Israelis were using our presumed reticence as an excuse for their own unwillingness to move."[61]

Komer observed how Israeli diplomats had remarked that Kennedy's support of Israel's security was "going a step further than previous words," but they were greatly concerned with Egypt's development of unconventional warfare capabilities. Komer suggested that a "tacit agreement not to develop unconventional capabilities" might be arranged between Israel and the Arabs.[62] Gazit thought that was very unlikely.

On February 12, Komer advised the president that Israel had been working on its own rockets as far back as July 1961, but that Israel was behind Egypt. With "a major effort plus some outside help," in three to four years Israel would have a number of 200- to 300-hundred mile range missiles. Komer thought Israel was recruiting foreign scientists, and among them were some Americans to help develop its missiles. Komer thought it necessary to have another inspection of Dimona soon. Unless it were "deterred by outside pressure" Israel would seek to produce "a weapon sometime in the next several years and it could have a very limited production capability by 1967–1968."[63]

Two years after Ben-Gurion and Kennedy had met, President Kennedy was still trying to work out some kind of agreement for the inspection of Dimona. A March 6, 1963, CIA report on the consequences of Israel's nuclear capability indicated that there would be "substantial damage to the United States and the Western position in the Arab World" if Israel were to develop an atomic arsenal. There was Israel, and then there was the "Arab World."[64] It was the CIA's estimate that ultimately Israel's nuclear potential would result in a Middle Eastern confrontation between the Arabs and the Soviet bloc against Israel and its friends in the West.[65]

CIA officials were concerned that the Arabs would turn to the Soviet bloc for assistance. It was unlikely that the Russians would be willing to provide the Arab governments with nuclear weapons. They had not provided such nuclear weapons to their satellites and would not assist the Arabs to develop their own nuclear weapons. They preferred to increase

Arab dependence upon the Soviet Union rather than "create an independent Arab nuclear capability."[66] It was thought that the Russians might place "nuclear weapons on Arab lands and keep control over such weapons." This might involve no more than a few bombs which could be dropped by Egyptian planes, or they might establish missile bases under Russian control. But then the Arabs would not wish to have foreign bases in their lands under Russian control.[67]

The CIA believed that Israel's "acquisition of a nuclear capability" might result in either the detonation of nuclear weapons or Israel's announcement that it had such weapons. They believed that Israel could manufacture such weapons without testing them. Israel had a "clear military superiority over its Arab adversaries" and once it acquired nuclear weapons, it "would become more rather than less tough." While Israel would not seek to make war, it would seek to "exploit the psychological advantage" of its nuclear capability to intimidate the Arabs and to prevent them from making trouble along the frontier.[68] That same report noted that possession of such weapons might result in some Israelis being inclined to "adopt a moderate and conciliatory posture in order to allay as far as possible the world-wide concern arising from the further proliferation of nuclear weapons." Some Israelis might even hope to reach a settlement of the controversy with the Arabs, by "negotiating magnanimously from their new position of strength." But an Israeli bomb would have a negative impact on U.S.-Arab relations because ultimately the United States would be blamed. There would be Arab feelings of "resentment and betrayal," and America's influence with the Arabs, "limited at best, would be drastically reduced."[69]

According to CIA estimates, "Nasser might be tempted to strike at Dimona, but would probably be deterred by the fear that Israeli retaliation would destroy him before the international peace-keeping machinery could intervene to suppress the conflict." The Arabs might seek to persuade the major powers to force Israel to submit its nuclear capacity to international control, but such "an attempt would almost certainly be unsuccessful." Nasser "might embark upon a nuclear weapons program of his own, with whatever technical help he could beg or hire from abroad; but this would at best be a lengthy and expensive enterprise, highly provocative to Israel."[70] Perhaps the Arabs might turn to the Soviets for nuclear assistance, but the CIA still did not believe the "U.S.S.R. would be willing to provide Arab governments with nuclear weapons, if only because of the difficulty of extending to such regimes what it is unwilling to give to its own satellites. We doubt also that the U.S.S.R. would give the Arabs any substantial assistance in developing nuclear weapons of their own." It was "conceivable that the Soviets might place nuclear weapons on Arab territory, retaining them under Soviet control." Perhaps the Russians "would establish missile bases, with an extensive Soviet military presence." But in any case, the Soviets would use this situation to gain "political advantage."[71]

By March of 1963 Kennedy spoke of his frustrations with respect to pro-liferation of nuclear weapons: "I am haunted by the feeling that by 1970, unless we are successful, there may be ten nuclear powers instead of four, and by 1975, fifteen or twenty. . . . I regard this as the greatest possible danger and hazard."[72]

American officials became more and more suspicious of Israel's inten-tions. As Israel complained about German technicians and scientists, some suspected that Israel used the German scientists in Egypt as justification for its nuclear program. Komer admitted that the UAR was seeking to develop "surface-to-surface missiles, using hired German help," but he believed that the UAR missile program was "far less menacing than the Israelis suggest." There was no evidence that the Egyptians were working on "cobalt or strontium 90 isotopes" as warheads. Komer claimed that Israel used the so-called Arab nuclear activity as a cover for its own nuclear projects and he urged President Kennedy to promote arms control as a means to fore-stall a "missile and nuclear race."[73]

But as Ben-Gurion saw it, American diplomats and officials refused to appreciate that Israel was threatened with extinction by its Arab neighbors. Egypt was getting stronger economically, culturally and militarily. It had some 120,000 students in its universities, ten submarines, seven destroyers and quite a number of torpedo boats, sixty heavy bombers and twice as many planes as Israel had. Egypt's armed forces had become better trained since the war in Yemen. Ben-Gurion believed that within two years, when the Egyptians would have their missiles operational, they would attack Is-rael.[74] The Arabs are "virulently anti-Israel," they aim to launch a war of destruction against Israel, and if Nasser would be able to break Israel's air defenses, the war would be over in two days. It might take the United States ten days to come to Israel's rescue, but by then it would be all over. When Ben-Gurion had talked with Presidents Eisenhower and de Gaulle about this situation, they had both "agreed that it would be too late."[75]

On March 26, 1963, McGeorge Bundy noted that Kennedy wanted "as a matter of urgency that we undertake every feasible measure to improve our intelligence on the Israeli nuclear program as well as other Israeli and Egyptian advanced programs and to arrive at a firmer evaluation of their import." He wanted to see the forthcoming informal inspection of the Is-raeli nuclear complex to be undertaken promptly and to be as "thorough as possible."[76]

President Kennedy had a practical intellect and was capable of studying various viewpoints that his advisers might present. He wanted to hear more than just the opinions of such establishment State Department officials as Dean Rusk, Phil Talbot, Adlai Stevenson and W. A. Harriman. That was one of the reasons he kept Myer Feldman as a key advisor on such mat-ters as Israel and the Middle East.[77]

In March 1963, there were reports in the *Jewish Observer and Middle East Review* that Israel sought to acquire "an independent deterrent," possibly a nuclear deterrent, and that the CIA had submitted its reports regarding Israel's nuclear research program. In early April, Shimon Peres, Israeli deputy minister of defense, assured U.S. officials that Israel would not work in this field unless it discovered that "other countries in the region were involved in it."[78]

At the same time Middle East tensions grew more severe. Egypt, Syria and Iraq prepared to form one state. Cairo would be the capital of a new "United Arab Republic." The United Arab Republic flag would acquire a third star which represented Iraq. The other two stars were for Egypt and Syria. Even though Syria had quit the UAR in 1961, Syria's star had not been removed. Now Syria returned and joined in the declaration to liberate Palestine. For Israel this was a declaration of war. For that matter Jordan and Saudi Arabia were not any too happy with this turn of events.

On April 2, 1963, Peres expressed the belief that "American influence in the Middle East had grown, that the Soviets had been shown to be a bogeyman; not strong militarily nor successful economically," but one should "not exaggerate" for the Russians were not yet out of the picture. He observed that the Arab world had become more unstable as did its militarism. Nasserism might seem the most "popular" in the Middle East, but its influence was not "all-pervasive." Jordan was one of the countries that had the potential for instability. Perhaps some Israelis admired King Hussein, but his position seemed "hopeless."[79]

Africa was abandoning its neutralism and moving toward militarism. There was a dramatic collision between the Pan-African and Pan-Islamic movements which created "a troubled Africa looking for new directions." For Egypt it meant a challenge which Nasser would seek to exploit, and for Israel it meant that "it must constantly reassess its policies." The Egyptians had acquired air-to-air missiles, ship-to-shore missiles, as well as ground-to-air and ground-to-ground missiles. At the time apparently there were "no countermeasures to missiles." Administration officials like Deputy Under Secretary of State for Political Affairs U. Alexis Johnson discounted some of Peres's information regarding the Egyptian missiles. "It is one thing to put fuel in a rocket and shoot it; it is quite another to provide the missile with accurate guidance," and Egypt was some years away from being able to do that.[80]

Peres believed that Egypt would be able to achieve missile accuracy and reach Tel Aviv within one and a half to three years. Missiles would be a greater temptation in the Arab countries and cause "an increasingly greater apprehension in Israel." Even if the missiles were no more deadly than a rifle, it would have a psychological impact since there were no countermeasures to missiles. Israel felt that Egypt was trying to develop a terror weapon against Israeli cities. As far as Israel was concerned, "human lives in a kibbutz 15 to 20 kilometers from Tel Aviv were as important as human lives in the heart of the city." There was no way of knowing what "cynical forces" might do. Moreover, Israel had information that Egypt was "going into other" areas of weaponry. It had already used gas warfare in Yemen. The Soviet Union assisted Egypt and it was "impossible to prejudge with assurance what the Soviets might do to advance their interests." Later on there would be the Chinese, and they would be "even less responsible than the Soviets" since they were quite short of oil supplies.[81] Israel called upon Washington to make it clear that it would oppose any such aggressive move with military intervention and that it would "push all possible means of negotiations between the Arabs and Israel. Nasser is the key."[82]

Alexis Johnson concluded that all this missile business in the Near East was "very bad business," but the United States would be "even more deeply opposed were developments to move beyond that into a nuclear phase."[83]

As Feldman walked with Peres through the corridors of the White House they "casually" met the president who invited Peres to drop into his office.[84]

The president told Peres that the United States was "very concerned about proliferation of nuclear weapons," and he hoped that Israel "would not develop or obtain this kind of weaponry."[85] Peres confided in President Kennedy that Israel was greatly concerned with Nasser's armament program, including his missiles and his intervention in Jordan. He likewise emphasized that Ben-Gurion was especially concerned with the UAR union of Iraq, Syria and Egypt and their proclaimed vow to "liberate Palestine," which was a code phrase calling for the destruction of Israel. Ben-Gurion could not recollect a state charter that called for the annihilation of another state.[86]

Kennedy listened sympathetically to Peres, but was not much impressed with his line of thinking. Kennedy's main concern was Israel's development of nuclear weapons. He thought that Israel was "more than able to defend itself" and did not need nuclear weapons for that purpose. "I strongly hope Israel would not develop or obtain that kind of weaponry." Peres gave Kennedy "unequivocal assurances that Israel would not do anything in this field unless it finds that other countries in the area are involved in it."[87] Or as Mordechai Gazit recalled, Peres assured the president that "if no one else produces such weapons we shall not be the ones to introduce them."[88]

Israeli politicos, amateur and professional, commented and speculated on the Peres-Kennedy meeting and its ramifications. Some said that Peres had obtained more concessions and "definite assurances" than Foreign Minister Golda Meir and David Ben-Gurion. Some came to believe that the United States had agreed to provide armaments to Israel on a continuing basis. General Moshe Dayan observed that no army had supplied itself with ground-to-ground missiles in order to load them with conventional warheads. It could be assumed that the UAR was developing or would develop nuclear warheads. Nuclear weapons would serve Nasser's goal which was to eliminate Israel altogether and thereby gain dominion over the Arab world.[89] Therefore, said Dayan, "During the age of the missile and its conventional and nuclear warheads . . . the main deterrent will be the Israeli army's strength and arms." Israel must diligently develop these, so that it will not lag behind. American diplomats in Israel reported that Dayan left "little doubt that he would favor the development of nuclear weapons by Israel."[90]

In message after message Kennedy advised Ben-Gurion that he wanted to see semiannual American inspections of Dimona, but Ben-Gurion stood his ground and insisted that such semiannual inspections would make the U.S.-Israel relationship appear to be no more than a "satellite relationship."[91] Ambassador Harman elaborated on that when he advised that Israel felt that a regular schedule of visits to Dimona would further reduce Israel's sovereignty. He wanted to know why the United States did not ask to examine Arab nuclear facilities.[92]

Israel continued to be concerned that German scientists helped Egypt develop missile and nuclear technology. Congress was likewise concerned. On April 5, 1963, Senators Hugh Scott, Jacob Javits, Thomas J. Dodd, William L. Prouty, Kenneth Keating and Thomas Henry Kuchel called upon Kennedy to persuade West Germany and other European states not to encourage their scientists and technicians to help the Arabs construct missiles and nuclear weapons.[93] Kennedy advised that the United States was opposed to the spread of weapons of mass destruction and tried to reduce Middle East tensions. Moreover, the United States was aware that Egypt and Israel sought to develop their own missile and jet industries. Germany might listen to American requests, but then the Germans might well be replaced by Soviet advisors.[94]

In early April as Ben-Gurion evaluated the threat from Nasser, he thought of Israel's 1948 war of independence and concluded that Nasser would go to war against Israel once he was convinced that he would win. Egypt was getting stronger economically, culturally and militarily day by day. It had 120,000 university students, nearly a dozen submarines, seven destroyers, and a number of torpedo boats, while Israel had none. In the Yemen war the Egyptian army showed that it had become better trained, and Ben-Gurion estimated that in two years, when Nasser would have his missiles in place, he would "feel strong enough to attack."[95]

JFK sailing, his favorite pastime. *Courtesy The John F. Kennedy Library.*

The Kennedy family, September 4, 1931. *Courtesy The John F. Kennedy Library.*

The Kennedy family together. *Courtesy The John F. Kennedy Library.*

Robert Kennedy visited Israel in 1948 during the War for Independence. *Courtesy The John F. Kennedy Library.*

Senator John F. Kennedy, Franklin Delano Roosevelt, Jr. and Prime Minister David Ben-Gurion, Israel, October 7, 1951. *Courtesy The John F. Kennedy Library.*

Presidents Eisenhower and Kennedy at the time of JFK's inauguration. *Courtesy Dwight D. Eisenhower Library.*

President Kennedy and Foreign Minister Golda Meir, December 27, 1962. *Courtesy The John F. Kennedy Library.*

Robert Kennedy talks before the United Nations Assembly as Ambassador Stimson listens. *Courtesy United Nations.*

President Kennedy and Attorney General Robert Kennedy at the White House, March 28, 1963. *Courtesy The John F. Kennedy Library.*

President Kennedy consults with his father, Joseph P. Kennedy. *Courtesy The John F. Kennedy Library.*

President Kennedy listens to Foreign Minister Gromyko. Center is Ambassador Federenko. *Courtesy United Nations.*

John consults with his brother, October 5, 1962. *Courtesy The John F. Kennedy Library.*

Robert Kennedy at the United Nations, January 24, 1964. *Courtesy United Nations.*

John F. Kennedy at a press conference, May 9, 1962. *Courtesy The John F. Kennedy Library.*

White House advisor Myer Feldman. *Courtesy The John F. Kennedy Library.*

John F. Kennedy at a press conference, June 27, 1962. *Courtesy The John F. Kennedy Library.*

CHAPTER 5

"A Gravity without Parallel"

Ben-Gurion wrote President Kennedy on April 25, 1963, of his great concern about the future of Israel. He prefaced his letter by saying that ordinarily he would not seek to impose on JFK who carried "super-human burdens" regarding domestic as well as international issues the world over. But the threat that came from the UAR "increased the danger of a serious conflagration in the Middle East" and had "adversely affected Israel's security."[1]

The Kennedy–Ben-Gurion correspondence was heavily preoccupied with Ben-Gurion's search for an American alliance and weapons with which to defend Israel on the one hand, and with the Kennedy administration's effort to discover if Israel was developing atomic bombs in Dimona. The Kennedy administration wanted semiannual inspections of Dimona, but Ben-Gurion insisted that such semiannual inspections would convert the U.S.-Israel friendship into a "satellite relationship."[2] Ambassador Harman advised that Israel felt that a regular schedule of visits to Dimona would reduce Israel's sovereignty. He asked why the United States did not likewise examine Arab nuclear facilities.[3]

Ben-Gurion found that conditions in the Middle East had assumed "a gravity without parallel," and he shared that concern with President Kennedy on April 26, 1963. Ben-Gurion chose to make President Kennedy aware of this situation because he was "conscious of the interest the American people has always evinced in the preservation of peace as well as the welfare of Israel," and "more particularly," because of President Kennedy's "personal interest," of which he had been "given signal proof" in his conversations and through the "personal and confidential letters" Kennedy had addressed to him and in Kennedy's talk with Foreign Minister Golda Meir in December of 1962.[4]

For a good many years the rulers of such Arab states as Egypt, Syria and Iraq issued public declarations of their "firm determination to obliterate Israel." Ben-Gurion said that he could "fill quite a thick booklet with the pronouncements of rulers, army commanders, official newspapers and radio broadcasts from Cairo, Damascus, Baghdad and other Arab capitals," of their intention to seek the destruction of Israel. But in "recent days, something unique" in the history of states had transpired. On the 17th of April, a treaty of federation had been signed in Cairo between Egypt, Syria and Iraq. Nasser prayed to God before he signed that document and said that the federation of these three states had "as its sole objective the well-being of the Arab people." In that document the federation declared its determination to establish "a military union that will be in a position to liberate the Arab homeland from the Zionist danger and imperialism." The treaty made no mention of Israel or the people of Israel. "Palestine" and "her liberation" were referred to as "the essence of the revolution." It was the first time that an official Arab constitutional document declared that one of its objectives was the obliteration of Israel.[5] The so-called "liberation of Palestine," said Ben-Gurion, would be impossible without the total destruction of the people of Israel. But Israel would not permit itself to be obliterated. The people of Israel were not in the "hapless situation of the six million defenseless Jews who were wiped out by Nazi Germany." It may be that the Arabs are greater in number and greater in arms, but Israel can "defeat all three—not without very serious losses, of course."[6]

Ben-Gurion did not seek war, nor did he seek a victory, because that would not solve anything, for as he said it would be "followed by a second and a third round and it might have world-wide repercussions. The scope and significance of which I hesitate to spell out." He did not think America would "acquiesce in the liberation to which the three Arab states inscribed on their banner."[7]

It would be "unpardonable" and the height of "irresponsibility to make light of this Treaty." Hitler had openly declared to the world that "one of his objectives was the destruction of the entire Jewish people." At that time the "civilized world, in Europe and America, treated this declaration with indifference and equanimity." The result was "a holocaust unequaled in human history." Six million Jewish people—"men, women, old and young, infants and babies, were burned, strangled or buried alive." And now, said Ben-Gurion, even though the entire world knew of Nasser's declaration and intention to "wipe out Israel," he still received assistance from many parts of the world. The Russians provided Egypt with weapons and equipment, and Egypt received large-scale aid from such quarters as the United States and Western Germany.[8] If Egypt were not planning the annihilation of Israel, then western financial aid to Egypt could be considered as a very positive action, but in the present circumstances the aid served to set the Russian arms in motion against Israel. For this reason, the most effective method of preventing the disaster of the "liberation of Palestine," which was the essence of the treaty of federation of the three Arab states, was for the president and the prime minister of Russia to publish a declaration to "jointly guarantee the territorial integrity and security of every state in the Middle East." They should advise all the parties concerned that if any state might threaten its neighbor or refused to recognize its existence, that state would receive no assistance of any kind—financial, political or otherwise from the two powers and their allies.[9] A similar joint declaration had been published on April 26, 1956, by Chairman Nikolai Bulganin, Nikita Khrushchev, Prime Minister Anthony Eden and Foreign Minister Selwyn Lloyd. They declared their intention "to do everything in their power to facilitate the maintenance of peace and security in the Middle East" and called upon the states of that area to "take measures to prevent the increase of tension in the area. . . ." But since their declaration made no provision for "effective measures in case of aggression and they did not insist upon the immediate cessation of Arab hostility against Israel it did not lead to any practical result."[10]

Ben-Gurion did not think that Khrushchev was prepared to sign such a declaration, nor did he think that Kennedy was ready to make such a proposal to the Russians, but if his suggestion was not feasible, then the Middle East situation assumed "a gravity without parallel."[11] If the president could spare an hour or two, Ben-Gurion was prepared to fly to Washington for a conference.

The Israeli prime minister was thankful for the release of the Hawk missiles to Israel, but this defensive weapon alone could not serve as a deterrent to Israel's neighbors. The Arabs were accumulating weapons "whose offensive potential" could not be "reduced by the Hawk." The Arabs had come to believe that Israel's defense forces were no longer capable of defending Israel and that the "hour" had come for the "liberation of Palestine." Ben-Gurion warned that the disaster which this "liberation" would involve, "must be averted, for the sake of Israel, for the sake of the Arab people and for the sake of the world."[12]

By April 27, it was evident that the UAR and elements of the Jordanian army planned to overthrow King Hussein. George Ball, Undersecretary of State for Economic Affairs informed McNamara that there might be an attempt to overthrow King Hussein.[13]

By this time, Kennedy had his fill of Nasser's intrigues and threats and he wanted to know from his staff what, if anything, his administration's policy of pouring millions of dollars into Egypt had achieved. But it seemed that President Kennedy, George Ball, Robert Komer and Phil Talbot were more concerned with Israel's reaction to the crisis in Jordan rather than the crisis itself. Kennedy was likewise concerned by Israeli critics who claimed that America's economic assistance of Egypt had only served to encourage Egypt's expansionist ambitions. Kennedy was concerned about "the dangers of Israeli building a case that our aid to Nasser made him play his hand more boldly, . . ." and he called upon his staff to "find the ways and means of refuting this charge."[14]

In his memo of May 2, 1963, Robert Komer had summarized some of America's concerns and worries regarding the Middle East. He believed that America's "chief leverage" over Israel and the Arabs was a "flat guarantee" against aggression by each other so as to reduce the tendency to "escalate" the conflict. And even if the arms race were to be reduced, the United States would have to provide such a guarantee anyway. But there were great risks involved "if both sides were going lickety-split towards nuclear weapons and missiles."[15] Israel might intervene in the West Bank if Nasser indicated that he would intervene. If Egypt tried to bomb Israel, then Israel would retaliate against "UAR nuclear sites, missile plants and airfields. . . ."[16]

Journalist Roland Evans asked Komer if Israel's complaints were real or exaggerated. Komer thought it was a little of "both." He told Evans that Israel had real concerns that Jordan might become absorbed by the UAR and that the UAR was developing "advanced weapons"—missiles. Both Israel and the UAR were "developing capabilities in the nuclear reactor field which they could attempt to turn into military purposes." Soviet Russia had poured in arms into the UAR, Iraq and Syria, all of which contributed to greater instability and tensions.[17] For the time being Komer did not see any "immediate" threat to Israel.[18]

The State Department anticipated that some legislators like Senators Javits, Gruening and Humphrey would sponsor a resolution calling for collective defense and restriction of aid to the Arabs.[19] The State Department remained rather cool, if not antipathetic towards Israel. As Israel celebrated its independence it raised its flag at the Hebrew University's Mt. Scopus campus. The American embassy in Israel reported that for the fifth consecutive year Israel had "provoked Jordan's wrath by erecting a huge illuminated Star of David and Israeli flag on Mt. Scopus's disused buildings." Those officials had likewise complained that as part of Israel's mourning for the death of President Yitzhak Ben-Zvi, it had lowered the UN flag and raised the Israeli flag at half-mast.[20]

Members of Congress were greatly concerned by Egypt's aggressive approach toward Israel and were opposed to Kennedy's continued pro-Egyptian policies, including his foreign aid to the Egyptian dictatorship. Senator Jacob Javits, Republican from New York, called upon Kennedy to establish a defensive pact with Israel and to implement a sharp change in U.S. policy of dealing "evenhandedly with friend and foe alike in the Middle East." Javits felt that the United States should do everything possible, including phasing out foreign aid to Egypt, "in order to force Egypt to abandon the arms and missile race as a useless and senseless waste of resources."[21] Unless strong measures were undertaken, Javits warned, Nasser would seek to crush Israel.[22]

Senator Hubert H. Humphrey, Democrat from Minnesota, called for a UN arms embargo against all Middle Eastern states. Congressman Seymour Halpern introduced a bill that would cut all foreign aid to Egypt since such aid allowed Egypt to devote its resources to military expenditure.[23]

Senator Wayne Morse of Oregon thought that Kennedy was "dead wrong" since he was helping states that were "a threat to the peace of the world."[24] Most of the senators and congressmen likewise referred to Nasser's use of former German Nazi officers and technicians to develop Egypt's missile program.[25]

Senator Ernest Gruening, Democrat of Alaska, noted that Soviet arms, German Nazi scientists and U.S. money made "a wonderful combination" in the UAR. If the United States did not reverse the buildup of Nasser, it would result in a "bloody war" in the Middle East for which the United States would bear "a certain responsibility," and ultimately the United States might very well be drawn into that war.[26] Other critics of Kennedy's Middle East foreign policy included Senators Kenneth Keating of New York, Clifford P. Chase of New Jersey, Leverett Saltonstall of Massachusetts, Hugh Scott of Pennsylvania and John Sherman Cooper of Kentucky.[27]

President Kennedy responded to Ben-Gurion on May 4, 1963. He repeated his reassurances that America was deeply "concerned over the security and integrity of Israel," and promised to watch "closely the current developments in the Arab world." He would try to make sure that those developments did not "take a form dangerous to the security of any nation in the area." The United States had Israel's "defense problems very much in mind."[28]

As with U.S. policy since the Truman Doctrine of 1947, Kennedy supported those Arab states that preferred to remain independent and whose freedom of action might be jeopardized, but he agreed that Israel and the Unites States "must continue to be alert to all the developing implications of the current movement for Arab unity." He found the "future of this movement and the rapidity of its development not at all clear. . . ."[29]

Kennedy agreed that it would be "irresponsible" to make light of continued Arab threats to "liberate Palestine" and he "fully" understood the concern which Ben-Gurion and his government felt with respect to certain phrases of the April 17, 1963, document signed by Egypt, Syria and Iraq. But in the long run such proclamations were not "substantially different from many similar statements of the past." He was particularly concerned about the possible effects of the current developments on Jordan. He intended to do his best to "prevent a dangerous situation from arising." But it was not only a matter for the United States, it was also a matter for Israel. That was why Kennedy thought it was essential for Israel and the

United States to be in close touch and to avoid "precipitous actions or re-actions" which might "exacerbate rather than improve the situation" and provide the Soviet Union with a further chance to "extend its influence in the area."[30]

Once again Kennedy advised that a joint U.S.-USSR declaration did not seem possible in view of the differences between the United States and Russia and the role Russia played to instigate the Arabs and to supply them with armaments. Moreover, even if the Russians would be willing to join the United States in such a proclamation, it would help increase Soviet influence in the Middle East and thereby reinforce those elements that supported instability in the area. Kennedy could not appreciate Ben-Gurion's concern that if there would be no joint declaration, conditions in the Middle East would assume "a gravity without parallel." Kennedy believed that the risks in Jordan had been somewhat reduced and Jordan was "more than able to defend itself." Unless there was some "hasty and shortsighted action" that might upset the present situation, the president believed that it was time to work for "increased stability with a somewhat longer view of the problem."[31]

What concerned Kennedy more than an Arab attack was "a successful development of advanced offensive systems which . . . could not be dealt with by presently available means."[32] He believed that if the United States could continue to develop good relations with the Arab states, it would help bring peace to the region and it would be to the benefit of Israeli security. U.S. aid to such Arab states can help reduce the spread of Soviet influence.

Moreover, Kennedy would not permit Arab objections to warm relations between the United States and Israel to interfere with those relations—"as demonstrated most recently in our agreement to make Hawk missiles available and U.S. help in the matter of water from Lake Tiberias."[33]

President Kennedy concluded his observations with his reassurance of how important Israel's friendship and security was to him. He reaffirmed what he had told Foreign Minister Meir in December.[34] As to Ben-Gurion's suggestion to meet privately in D.C., the Kennedy administration felt that it was unlikely that such a meeting could be arranged without causing an uproar in the Arab world. As an afterthought Kennedy added that "when circumstances change, or if the urgencies should increase, I shall certainly bear in mind your generous suggestion."[35]

Ben-Gurion was not especially reconciled by President Kennedy's May 4 response. He thought that perhaps he might approach Premier Khrushchev directly about a U.S.-USSR declaration to the effect that neither would supply Nasser with aid and assistance unless Nasser recognized the existence of Israel. It might deter Nasser from his expressed warlike intentions. Ambassador Barbour tried to make Ben-Gurion realize that his idea was unrealistic since Israel represented "everything the Soviets disliked in the

Middle East." Israel was a "democratic, progressive, and stable state," and it was not Soviet policy to promote stability of this "type" in the area.[36]

Barbour also reiterated U.S. interest in semiannual visits to Dimona, but Ben-Gurion avoided a definite reply about those visits. He recalled that Kennedy had talked to him in terms of visits from a small neutral state. Even though Ben-Gurion considered Kennedy a friend he still opposed regular visits to Dimona.[37]

Kennedy insisted that Israel was "more than able to defend itself" and that he was concerned for the "long-term" high-tech arms race. While Kennedy said he believed that it was necessary for the United States to maintain good relations with the Arabs, Walworth Barbour, his ambassador to Israel, advised Ben-Gurion that Kennedy had a "deep interest" in arranging semiannual American inspections of Dimona.[38] Harman once again told the Americans that Israel opposed regular visits to Dimona, and that the United States should visit the nuclear facilities of the Arab countries.[39]

On May 5, 1963, Ben-Gurion's entire Cabinet approved his suggestion that the Soviet Union and the United States jointly guarantee Israel's borders against attack. The Cabinet likewise approved Ben-Gurion's proposal for a defense pact between Israel and the United States, something Israel had hoped for since Ben-Gurion abandoned Israeli neutrality in 1951 to side with the United States, at the time of the Korean War. Such a pact would help protect Israel from an attack. Ben-Gurion believed that a joint warning by the Soviet Union and the United States to Nasser that all financial aid would be cut off unless Cairo abandoned its belligerent policy towards Israel would reduce the threat coming from Nasser.[40]

Feldman met with Ambassador Harman to review Ben-Gurion's reaction to Kennedy's May 4, response. Feldman thought that Ben-Gurion's suggestion that the Russians might agree to reduce Middle East tensions would only serve to increase Russia's prestige. It was unreasonable to expect that the Russians would discontinue providing military supplies and assistance to the Arabs since this was Russia's "primary source of influence" in the Middle East.[41] But Harman recorded that Ben-Gurion felt that the attempt should be made since a similar effort by the British had been successful. The only reason it did not succeed as an "instrument of peace [was] because firm implementation had not been negotiated."[42] When Feldman asked why Ben-Gurion had denied the request for inspection of Dimona, Harman said that the prime minister had promised President Kennedy that a "neutral" could inspect the reactor, but he had not anticipated that there would be "regular" inspections of Dimona. While Ben-Gurion had been cooperative about inspections, Israel had not heard about U.S. inspections of Arab nuclear facilities. Just as the Americans claimed that inspections could help reassure the Arabs, Ben-Gurion felt that inspections of Arab facilities could be reassuring to Israel. Harman noted that the suggestion of a guarantee of Israel's borders was not particularly comforting. Israel had asked for and preferred "joint defense consultations" with the United States concerning Israel's security problems.[43] Secretary Rusk wrote a notation that the United States could not negotiate with Israel as long as Feldman would be America's "interlocutor."[44]

On May 8, 1963, Kennedy reassured Israel and all the other states of the Near East that the United States was against aggression and would not only support the UN's efforts to stop aggression, but it would "adopt other courses of action on our own to prevent or to put a stop to such aggression."[45]

> The United States supports social and economic and political progress in the Middle East. We support the security of both Israel and her neighbors. We seek to limit the Near East arms race, which obviously takes resources from an area already poor and puts them into an increasing race which does not really bring any great security. We strongly oppose the use of force or the threat of force in the Near East. And we also seek to limit the spread of Communism in the Middle East, which would of course, destroy the independence of the people.
>
> This Government has been, and remains, strongly opposed to the use of force, or the threat of force, in the Near East. In the event of aggression, or preparation for aggression, whether direct or indirect, we would support appropriate measures in the United Nations and adopt other courses of action on our own to prevent or to put a stop to such aggression, which, of course, has been the policy which the United States has followed for some time.[46]

Kennedy's words of reassurance received mixed review in Israel. While some Israelis welcomed Kennedy's statement as a step in the right direction, they believed it fell short of what the Israeli government had hoped for, but its timing and the authority behind it were seen as important from the psychological viewpoint.[47] Editors of the *Jerusalem Post* observed that President Kennedy's statement was in the nature of the external "moral and political" influence that Ben-Gurion had described in his recent Knesset speech. It was one of the two ways that Israel was seeking to prevent war in the Middle East. The other way mentioned by Ben-Gurion was for Israel constantly to strengthen its military deterrent.[48] *Maariv,* another major Israeli paper, asserted that Kennedy's words entailed a clearer delineation of U.S. policy than the "evasive and calming" pronouncements of previous administrations and that the moral and political support of the United States was important to Israel's security, but that "its full force would be demonstrated if it were accompanied by deeds." The most important deed would be for Israel's defense forces to have a deterrent capability of assuring the status quo in the Middle East. Words did not not suffice.[49]

Senator Javits introduced a resolution calling on President Kennedy to initiate a mutual defense agreement with Israel and provide military and other assistance to protect Israel and any other threatened nation. His resolution urged Kennedy to invite Great Britain and France to guarantee the existing boundaries of Israel and other Middle East states. Senator Kenneth B. Keating, a cosponsor of the Javits resolution, said that the increasingly aggressive moves by Arab states had raised concern in Israel about her "ability to maintain her integrity and sovereignty." "The Israelis have every right to expect that this country would exert strong pressures on the nations involved to withdraw their outside scientists who are building Egypt's offensive missile capacity."[50] Senators Humphrey, Gruening and Hart asked for a "sense of the Senate" that called upon Kennedy to influence the Middle East states to negotiate a reduction and control of nuclear weapons in that area and to institute an international policing system to enforce such agreements. They also called upon Kennedy to devise the means to end the incitement to violence in the Middle East.[51]

Secretary Rusk suspected that Ben-Gurion might have tried to use Israel's atomic research and the visits to Dimona as a bargaining chip for things that Israel wanted from the United States such as security guarantees. Rusk advised the American ambassador to Israel that President Kennedy had made it clear to Foreign Minister Meir in December that nuclear proliferation was a matter of U.S. global responsibility. There were various discussions and communications on this matter: (1) May 1961 President Kennedy in conversation with Ben-Gurion did not suggest substitution of neutrals for Americans to inspect Dimona. When President Kennedy had suggested that it might be helpful to let neutrals also observe the reactor, Ben-Gurion raised no objections and President Kennedy expressed his satisfaction at Ben-Gurion's response; (2) When President Kennedy spoke with Foreign Minister Meir on "our need to be fully informed of developments regarding Israel's reactor," Meir told Kennedy that there would not be any difficulties between us; (3) Speaking with Peres on April 2, he was given "unequivocal assurance regarding Israel's present actions in that field"; (4) When Barbour spoke with the prime minister on April 2, Ben-Gurion "did not demur" when Barbour brought up the proposal for semiannual visits. Barbour insisted that the United States was Israel's friend and that no nation could consider Israel as a U.S. satellite. The United States had been "most helpful in giving quiet international support to Israel's statements of peaceful intention and thus damping down dangers of precipitate, ill-conceived reactions by Israel's neighbors." And as for Israel's accusation that the United States did not insist on inspection of Arab states, Barbour was to advise that the United States had a "good line on any Arab nuclear efforts and that those efforts were not serious."[52]

On May 12, 1963, Ben-Gurion wrote to President Kennedy that he was "somewhat disappointed" with the president's response to his letter of April

25. Nasser had called for the "Liberation of Palestine" and believed that once he accomplished this task he would "secure his role as the uncontested leader of all the Arab peoples." This would fulfill Nasser's highest ambition to establish dominion over the Arabs.[53] During World War II some Arab leaders had admired Hitler. Nasser adopted that Nazi ideology. The "civilized world" did not take Hitler's word seriously that he would "exterminate the Jewish people," and Ben-Gurion warned that the same thing could happen if Nasser got his way. In pursuit of a belligerent policy the Arabs might very well seek to annihilate Israel. "As a Jew I know the history of my people and carry with me the memories of all it has endured over a period of 3,000 years." The great effort extended to establish the State of Israel had been made not only for the sake of those who "already arrived in Israel" but for the "survival of Jewry as such. . . . Mr. President, my people have the right to exist—both in Israel and wherever they live, and this existence is in danger."[54] Moreover, Ben-Gurion insisted on Israel's right to "threaten a potential perpetrator with annihilation."[55]

Ben-Gurion thought that the safest way would be if the USSR and the United States would issue a joint declaration that any Middle East state that refused to recognize the territorial integrity of Israel and the Arabs states and refused to live in peace with any other country in that region in conformity with its obligations as a member of the UN, would receive no financial, political, and military aid from the USSR or the United States.[56]

> It is not Arab unity that endangers Israel today or in the near future, but the dogma that Israel must be wiped out, which the Arab rulers have implanted in the minds of their peoples. The United States and the Soviet Union, if they were able to act jointly, could compel the Arab countries—and first of all Egypt—to abandon their belligerency practiced by economic boycott, the blockade of the Suez Canal, political warfare and hate propaganda, and to cease their military preparations to destroy Israel.[57]

Ben-Gurion held to his viewpoint that a two-power declaration, accompanied by effective measures could prevent war and catastrophe. Egypt could not develop its war machinery without arms and assistance from abroad.[58] If a joint USSR—U.S. would not be possible, Ben-Gurion suggested that other ways might be found to deter Egypt from pursing its belligerent policy against Israel:

1. If Jordan's regime might be challenged, the West Bank should be completely demilitarized under suitable international supervision.
2. Israel and the United States should conclude a bilateral security agreement to which America's allies might be invited to join.

3. As long as there was no arms limitation agreement in the Middle East and the Arabs would receive massive modern Soviet arms, it was imperative that the United States should provide Israel all the equivalent kinds of armaments.
4. Establish a general disarmament agreement between Israel and the Arabs under a system of mutual and international inspection and control.

Ben-Gurion again thanked Kennedy for the Hawk missiles, the reassurances he had given Meir during her December 1962 visit and the reassurances he had sent Ben-Gurion. And finally, he thanked Kennedy for his May 8 press conference statement.[59]

On May 10, 1963, Ambassador Harman had spoken with Ambassador W. Averell Harriman about the grim developments in the Near East. It was not a question of whether the new UAR federation worked or not. The "critical" question was Nasser's role in the Near East instability. Nasser's invasion of Yemen revealed his readiness to use "massive force to achieve his goals of domination and control" and that the April 17 federation declaration regarding the liberation of Palestine had to be taken seriously and as an "expression of Nasser's design."[60]

Harriman agreed that Israel had to take all this seriously. But he thought the Near East situation had improved somewhat. Russian influence had been reduced. Nasser knew of U.S. support for Israel, and it was doubtful that he would defy Kennedy's statement of May 8, that clearly expressed America's willingness and ability to protect Israel. Jordan was a problem, and there would be a "new dimension" if it were to fall to Nasser. Harman reiterated Israel's position that any change in Jordan would be dangerous. Jordan reflected the instability of the Near East. Israel asked for a "thorough discussion" with the United States of new and constructive steps which might be taken to "stabilize the area."[61]

Perhaps there was no momentary threat from Iraq and Syria, but that was "not really germane." Ben-Gurion had "always seen the issue of war and peace as one between Israel and the UAR," and the threat would be only the more serious if Nasser succeeded in establishing the union. Nasser's constant military threat was the issue. Stability in the Near East would depend upon his being advised that there was to be a firm line.[62]

On May 13, 1963, Ben-Gurion went public with his concerns regarding the dangers Israel faced. He openly declared that JFK's arms policy was "dangerously one-sided." He felt that not all of Israel's friends understood the need for deterrence. The U.S. attempt to limit the arms race in the Middle East was likely "to intensify the danger of war" in the Middle East. If such a limitation were attempted, it would only be applied against Israel and not against the Arabs, because the Arabs received arms from both the West and the Soviet bloc. "It is just such a one-sided withholding that is liable to intensify the danger of war in the Middle East."[63]

By a majority vote of 52 to 4, the Knesset voted to increase Israel's deterrent power and strengthen the security of the border settlements, but Ben-Gurion advised his fellow members of the Knesset that "not all our friends understand the vital need to increase the deterrent strength of Israel's Defense Forces as the most effective means of preserving peace in the region."[64]

Public criticism and especially Congressional criticism upset the Kennedy administration. Kennedy was concerned with its impact on the forthcoming election. Robert Komer advised Minister Gazit that this "hullabaloo" over U.S.-Israel relations had upset the Kennedy administration. Gazit noted that the "hullabaloo" would get worst unless the United States did "something to meet Israeli security requirements."[65]

Komer wanted to know if Israel meant to threaten the administration with an increase in the already substantial Israeli "pressure on us for new security guarantees unless we caved."[66] Gazit advised that the concerns expressed by members of Congress and the American people were a fact of life with which the administration would have to live. Israel had not tried to inspire the "current noises" from Congress, but Kennedy officials "must recognize the genuine concern of the top-political level in Israel over the growing Arab threats."[67] A formal U.S. defense pact with Israel and needed arms would serve as a warning to the Arabs that the United States meant business in its future security commitments to Israel.[68] Gazit could not understand why the United States failed "to go all the way instead of pursuing half measures" and restating existing policy. If President Truman had concluded a defense pact with Israel, and if he had provided Israel with arms in 1949, "the unfortunate developments of the intervening years would not have transpired." He did not believe that an open U.S.-Israel defense arrangement would have "settled once and for all the question of Israeli security" and it would not have undermined U.S. security.[69]

Komer thought it would be more useful if the United States and Israel engaged in private nonpublic talks and that propaganda should be avoided. He reminded Gazit of the Kennedy administration's "deep concern" with nuclear proliferation and that Israel's stalling tactics on the biannual inspection of Dimona, only helped raise "suspicions." Komer had the impression that the statements by Ben-Gurion, Dayan and other Israelis regarding Israel's defense needs were made in order to strengthen its requests for arms or they "could be part of a campaign to justify Israeli development of nuclear weapons, or to threaten this as an alternative if we didn't come through with a security pact."[70]

Gazit did not respond.[71]

Komer seemed convinced that Israel would go ahead with its nuclear weapons program unless it received security guarantees from the United States. The State Department proposed entering into quiet negotiations with Israel, conditioned upon their agreement to call off their pressure campaign, to preserve secrecy, for Israel not to move into the West Bank while talks were under way, and for Israel to cooperate on nuclear inspection. Komer thought this was "a tall order, but a good opening bid." The negotiations were envisioned as lasting several months, and ending up with a UAR-Israel arms limitation agreement plus security guarantees or in a nuclear limitation-security arrangement with Israel alone. The agreement would be in the form of an executive agreement or presidential letter rather than a treaty in order to avoid "Congressional problems."

Nasser was to receive a letter to calm him down. If the United States could get the Israelis to "lay off public agitation in return for opening a private dialogue," it should buy time to find out what Israel might accept and what the United States could get in return. Komer advised that before the United States could extend a guarantee of Israel's security, Israel would have to cooperate on Dimona. Robert Komer recalled that Israel got the Hawk missiles, but it did not deliver or agree to the Johnson refugee plan, and now the United States should go easy with respect to guarantees.[72]

All this was not what Ben-Gurion had asked for in his latest letter. The Kennedy administration did not buy his idea that an alliance was to include U.S. arms assistance. W. Averell Harriman did not believe that Israel was imperiled by Egyptian missile and atomic research aided by German technicians and scientists. He recited State Department views when he said that Egypt was not into nuclear weaponry. While a matter of concern, it was not as "serious as pictured." But representatives of the Jewish community in America like Label Katz of the Conference of Presidents and National Commander of the Jewish War Veterans disagreed with Harriman and some of the other State Department officials. He called upon the United States and Israel to work together with a view to guarantee the territorial integrity of Israel and establish an appropriate military collaboration. The military balance shifted in favor of the Arabs. When it had been a question of man-to-man combat, Israel could hold its own even if outgunned and outmanned. But Israel had no missiles, and the relationship had turned into one of missile-to-man. As Israel was at a disadvantage, such Arab countries as Egypt would be encouraged to attack Israel.[73]

Harriman claimed that there was "not the slightest doubt about our will and our ability to come to Israel's defense."[74] He did not know if it was right for the United States to provide Israel with a more "specific guarantee." But this was "a game" that two could play. If the United States would be "more specific" in its assurances to Israel, the Arabs might very well seek assurances from the Soviet Union and that sort of confrontation would "vastly increase the dangers of the Middle East situation."[75]

Katz outlined some of the developments in the Near East. Egypt had tried to occupy Yemen, there were coups in Iraq and Syria and there were attempts to overthrow King Hussein of Jordan. In all those instances the Nasserites had played a key role.[76] The deteriorating situation in the Middle

East was of deep concern to the American Jewish community and to the prime minister.[77]

Harriman agreed that a "Nasserite coup in Jordan would be of greatest danger and concern." He agreed that the April 17 statement regarding the liberation of Palestine was "utterly shocking" and that the propaganda which emanated from Egypt was the most "vicious in the world," but the United States was not as concerned as Israel that there was a likelihood of "implementation." "We must deal with realities, not propaganda." One reality was that the United States stood firmly besides Israel. "Israel knows this, the Arabs know it, and Nasser knows it." He tried to reassure supporters of Israel that President Kennedy "will do everything he feels is appropriate and useful in pursuance of these common objectives." Harriman concluded that the United States was "convinced that Israel is militarily so strong that it has a very effective deterrent against any Arab action, individual or collective."[78]

Foreign Minister Meir described Harriman as "one of the finest men she had ever met and as a friend of Israel," but his observations were "very unfortunate" as he equated Israel's "defensive arms program with Nasser's "avowedly offensive" military buildup. Israel had never threatened Egypt with "obliteration," on the contrary, Israel was prepared for "complete, and total disarmament." If the State Department thought it necessary to balance every observation regarding Egypt's armaments with something about Israel, then at least the letter should have made it clear that Israel's programs were in direct response to those of Egypt's.[79]

As Harriman summed it up on May 15, 1963: America's goals in the Near East were to protect U.S. oil interests and prevent Soviet penetration. Assistant Secretary Talbot viewed the Middle East situation as uncertain with Egypt trying to gain control of Yemen and its expanding into Saudi Arabia. Russian advisors and technicians were increasing in number and seeking to replace the Iraqi government with a pro-Russian regime. There was a conflict between the Kurds and Iraq; Nasser tried to regain his influence in Algeria and to control Syria. Conditions in Jordan were unbalanced and Egypt's intervention helped to keep the situation unstable. Israel was quite concerned over all those developments and tried to obtain U.S. security guarantees as Egypt was on the "verge of the rocket age." And finally Talbot observed that the United States had to keep a check on the arms race and Soviet expansion.[80]

Ben-Gurion, in conversation with Ambassador Barbour, spoke of how the Egyptians were working on their reactors, and that they had used poison gas in war against the Royal forces in Yemen. Ambassador Barbour insisted that the United States had a "good line" on any Arab nuclear efforts and that they did not amount to a "serious program."[81]

Ben-Gurion wanted to know if the United States also wanted to visit the Egyptian nuclear installations twice a year.[82]

Barbour insisted that there was "nothing to visit," since the Egyptians only had some kind of "medical reactor."[83]

Deputy Director General Gideon Rafael reported that the Egyptians were building a second nuclear reactor. Foreign Minister Meir claimed that she had some rather interesting information regarding the so-called "medical reactor." Israel was very concerned about what the Egyptians were doing.[84]

But Barbour insisted that there was no such Egyptian program and that the president regarded the request for the Dimona visit as an "extremely serious matter."[85]

Ben-Gurion "flatly" rejected Barbour's assertion, and said that Israel did not agree with the U.S. assessment of the Egyptian nuclear program.[86]

Barbour observed that the Israeli program was "a large program," but Ben-Gurion insisted that Israel knew fully well that the Egyptians were building "something bigger than what we now have." And did he know that the "Egyptians had used poison gases against the Royal Yemeni forces?"[87]

"Yes, we had so heard from Israel that some tear gas had been used."[88]

But it was much more than tear gas that worried Ben-Gurion. "We have certain information that worries us very much about Egypt's nuclear development."[89]

Barbour reverted to the Israeli situation. "Our present problem is the matter of visits to Dimona." He dismissed Ben-Gurion's claim that the Egyptians were a threat to Israel.

"You do not realize the depth of our worry," said Ben-Gurion. "Israel is the only state in the world that is being threatened with extinction every day. We know that the Egyptians have unconventional weapons and that they are making more such weapons. Moreover, the disparity in arms between Israel and the Arabs is growing. American officials do not appreciate the danger to Israel." Nasser is "making unconventional weapons and the disparity between Israel and the Arabs was growing. He has foreign experts and he sent some of his people abroad."[90]

Ben-Gurion asked of Barbour: "When he has missiles with nuclear warheads what will you do to him then?"[91]

Kennedy's ambassador then repeated Kennedy's May 8, press conference words. The U.S. would "take all necessary measures in and out of the U.N. to assist Israel if attacked."[92]

"Yes, but that help could be too late. If it comes to war, we must rely on ourselves." The U.S. government simply did not comprehend the unique threat to Israel.[93]

Ben-Gurion asked again. "Twice a year?"

"I will have to ask my government, but unless I can tell them that the same thing would occur in Egypt . . ."

"But the two situations are not the same."[94]

"Why Not!" exclaimed Ben-Gurion.[95]

"The Egyptian program is not as advanced. We need to see Dimona."[96]

Barbour insisted that Peres had assured the president that Israel was not developing its nuclear research towards nuclear weapons in Dimona, and there were "suspicious people in the world. "We must be able to say that we have seen Dimona for ourselves."[97]

Ben-Gurion wanted to know by what right Nasser asked that Dimona be inspected. The prime minister did not think that telling Nasser about Israel's project would reduce Egypt's efforts to develop nuclear weaponry.

It was then that Barbour abandoned all diplomatic tact and aggressively asserted: "I simply cannot comprehend why Israel would want to risk a nuclear race and war."

"No, No, No!" Ben-Gurion responded.

Barbour insisted that if Israel worked on the atom, the Egyptians would increase their efforts. "Nasser has already stepped up his efforts."[98]

"We simply do not agree with this assessment," said Ben-Gurion.

Ben-Gurion was prepared to share his intelligence information with the Americans.

"O.K.," said Barbour, "but we want a reply to our specific request and we prefer that there be no strings attached to future visits to Dimona."[99]

Toward the end of the meeting, Barbour conceded, "It would be better to have regular visits even if the results would be withheld from others than to have no visits." But he reminded the prime minister that he had agreed to visits without any conditions as to what use the United States made of the results.

"But a number of things had happened in the interval. Nasser had some disappointments. Why reassure him? Why should the visits be twice a year?"

"Israelis have a well deserved reputation as very fast builders," Barbour interjected, and once again asked for an urgent response.

"O.K., I will consult my Cabinet, but the U.S. should very carefully consider the points I made on Israel's security in my May 12th letter to President Kennedy."

Barbour quoted Kennedy that sometimes it was not enough for a woman to be virtuous. "She must also appear virtuous."

Director General of the Israel Foreign Office Hayim Yahil suggested that "in certain circumstances a virtuous woman might not want to appear virtuous."[100]

In his report to Washington, Barbour conceded that Israel did not wish to commit itself to an "open-ended procedure of regular visits, so as to maintain full freedom of decision if and when it determined that it must embark upon a weapons program." But he warned that Israel might use this inspection business to get concessions before agreeing to biannual inspections.[101]

Ben-Gurion felt that in view of expressed Arab intentions to wipe out Israel, the nuclear deterrent was essential for Israel's survival, but the Kennedy administration could not understand that.

On May 18, 1963, President Kennedy once again stepped into the negotiations with Ben-Gurion. Ben Gurion had not agreed to Kennedy's demands regarding biannual inspections of Dimona, and he continued to ask for a bilateral U.S.-Israel defense agreement and "all the equivalent kinds of armament" which Egypt and the other Arab states had obtained. Kennedy wrote Ben-Gurion that he had read Barbour's report regarding Ben-Gurion's view on the nuclear issue, and he wanted to add a personal comment on the subject of the "dangers of nuclear proliferation." Kennedy reminded Ben-Gurion that he had repeatedly said that there was "no more urgent business for the whole world than the control of nuclear weapons. We both recognized this when we talked together two years ago. . . ."[102]

It is because of our preoccupation with this problem that my Government has sought to arrange with you for periodic visits to Dimona. When we spoke together in May 1961 you said that we might make whatever use we wished of the information resulting from the first visit of American scientists to Dimona and that you would agree to further visits by a neutral as well. I had assumed from Mrs. Meir's comment that there would be no problem between us on this.[103]

Kennedy was concerned with the "disturbing effects on world stability which would accompany the development of a nuclear weapons capability by Israel. I cannot imagine that the Arabs would refrain from turning to the Soviet Union for assistance if Israel were to develop a nuclear weapons capability—with all the consequences this would hold."[104]

As far as Kennedy was concerned, the problem was much more extensive than its impact on the Middle East. The Arabs would most certainly turn to the Russians for help in developing their own nuclear weapons. If Israel were to develop those weapons, it would lead almost certainly to "other larger countries" that had "refrained from such development to feel that they must follow suit." The United States has a commitment to Israel, but that commitment "would be seriously jeopardized in the public opinion in this country and in the West as a whole if it should be thought that this Government was unable to obtain reliable information on a subject as vital to peace as the question of the character of Israel's efforts in the nuclear field."[105]

Kennedy said that he appreciated Ben-Gurion's concern for developments in the UAR, but like his advisors, he apparently saw no "present or imminent nuclear threat to Israel from there." The Egyptians did not have any installations comparable to Dimona, "nor any facilities potentially capable of nuclear weapons production." If Israel had any information to the contrary, he would appreciate it if Israel would transmit that information through Ambassador Barbour. The United States had the capacity to "check it."[106]

"I trust this message will convey the sense of urgency and the perspective in which I view your Government's early assent to the proposal first put to you by Ambassador Barbour on April 2."[107]

Ben-Gurion was not intimidated by Kennedy's letter. He met with selected aides and ministers on May 26 and then wrote his response to President Kennedy. On May 27, he presented Ambassador Barbour with his response and thereby advised that Israel's nuclear research policy had not changed since May 31, 1961, when he had met with President Kennedy. While he sympathized with JFK's global concerns regarding nonproliferation, that was not Israel's problem. "I fear that in the absence of an agreement between the great powers on general disarmament" there was "little doubt" that such weapons would get into the hands of China, India and various European states. Israel would follow the developments of the Middle East and that would determine its defensive policies. Ben-Gurion agreed to annual visits to Dimona which would be similar to those that had already taken place. The most suitable time for the next visit would be late in 1963 or early 1964 when Dimona would reach its "start-up" time. Visits from neutral scientists would likewise be welcomed.[108]

Ben-Gurion expressed his appreciation for Kennedy's commitment to Israel's security and his concern regarding the proliferation, but "we in Israel cannot be blind to the more actual danger . . . of destructive conventional weapons" in the hands of Israel's enemies who plan to annihilate Israel.[109] Again he advised that the Dimona project was established for nonmilitary purposes, but its future would depend upon regional circumstances. Israel reserved the right to change the reactor's purposes.[110] Ben-Gurion would agree to only one inspection a year instead of the two per year as suggested by the Kennedy administration.

State Department officials insisted that there had to be two inspections yearly and that a visit should take place before the Israeli reactor was critical. Then a detailed examination of the structure would be possible. Once it was critical, certain portions of the reactor would not be accessible. They likewise felt that scientists needed sufficient time to conduct a thorough examination.[111]

The State Department proposed an Egyptian-Israeli arms limitation agreement according to which Egypt would give up its ballistic program and Israel was to forgo its production of nuclear weapons. Because the Egyptians would not sign an agreement with Israel, this might be accomplished through parallel, bilateral agreements with the United States. It would be monitored by means of photographic and unobtrusive inspections. The inspections were to be secret.[112]

Israel's concerns and worries relative to attacks from the Arabs increased. Ambassador Harman advised Arthur Schlesinger Jr., special assistant to the president, that Israel felt the Middle East situation was as dangerous for Israel as it had been in 1948. He realized that Washington's estimation was different, but then Washington had "badly underestimated the size, speed and efficiency" of Egypt's arms buildup. Israel estimated that Egypt would launch a war against Israel within two years. Nasser believed that the "physical destruction of Israel's industry would be worthwhile" for in this way they would be able to set back Israel's development and soften up Israel for future attacks.[113] Israel felt "increasingly lonely and isolated under the Egyptian gun" and needed "greater reassurance."[114]

Schlesinger reviewed President Kennedy's commitment that the United States would "not tolerate unprovoked aggression against Israel." Harman said that Israel "deeply appreciated and fully accepted these assurances," but they would not have sufficient deterrent effect in Cairo because "they were not in a context of concrete cooperation and commitment." Guarantees such as NATO were "accompanied by a great apparatus of joint planning, contingency planning, . . ." which made NATO guarantees "carry conviction." What was necessary was "a security arrangement with Israel involving joint planning, and joint intelligence estimates. . . ."[115]

As Arthur Schlesinger reiterated America's concern for nuclear proliferation, Harman declared "flatly that Israel had no intention of producing nuclear weapons" and that Israel welcomed "occasional visits" to its nuclear facilities, but the proposed systematic inspection would "raise questions of principle." There was no proposal to inspect Egypt's installations.[116]

But on June 15, Kennedy once again insisted on the biannual visits and he warned: "As I wrote you on 18 May, the Government's commitment to and support of Israel could be seriously jeopardized if it should be thought that we were unable to obtain reliable information on a subject as vital to peace as the character of Israel's efforts in the nuclear field."[117]

Once again Kennedy said that he knew full well that Ben-Gurion appreciated the "truly vital significance of this matter to the future well-being of Israel, to the United States and internationally" and he was sure that his request would receive Ben-Gurion's "most sympathetic attention."[118]

Before Barbour had a chance to deliver Kennedy's note, Ben-Gurion resigned.

Why did he resign?

Ben-Gurion realized that he had lost popular political support at home. Without such support he did not wish to continue to govern Israel. Barbour observed that the resignation had been triggered by "sticky domestic problems, including the issue of German scientists in the UAR," and by bickering among members of his Cabinet. He had been particularly upset by the "hypocrisy of leaders of other parties," who during closed Foreign

Affairs Committee meetings "had agreed with his German policy, but then attacked that policy in public."[119] His inability to persuade Kennedy to establish closer relations with Israel and his inability to persuade Kennedy that Israel needed his support with respect to the development of a nuclear preemptive striking force may have likewise influenced Ben-Gurion to resign as prime minister and defense minister.

Levi Eshkol would succeed David Ben-Gurion, and Israel would continue its struggle for survival and its search for friendship and alliance with the United States as well as its goal for self-reliant security.

CHAPTER 6

Levi Eshkol and the Dual Alliance

Israel's Finance Minister Levi Eshkol of Ben-Gurion's Labor Party replaced Ben-Gurion on June 24, 1963. At times he had served as acting premier when Ben-Gurion traveled overseas. Upon presenting the new government to the Knesset, Eshkol promised to continue the policies of Ben-Gurion. He described Ben-Gurion as the "maker of the state" and "one of our people's greatest visionaries and men of action in all generations."[1] President Kennedy advised Prime Minister Levi Eshkol that the U.S. "commitment to and support of Israel could be seriously jeopardized if it should be thought that we were unable to obtain reliable information on a subject as vital to peace as the question of Israel's effort in the nuclear field." This was the message Kennedy had sent Ben-Gurion on June 15, 1963, and it helped persuade Ben-Gurion to resign for he had failed to persuade Kennedy and his administration to establish a NATO type alliance between Israel and the United States. It seemed that would not happen and in place of such an arrangement Ben-Gurion continued to pursue the development of Israel's independent scientific, technological and presumably nuclear path for survival. He had tried to persuade the American president, but he had failed. It was time to step out of the picture.

Again Kennedy reiterated the visitation schedule that he had asked Ben-Gurion to fulfill: "Early this summer, another visit in June 1964 and thereafter at intervals of six months." He insisted that inspectors or "scientists" as Kennedy called them, should have access to "all areas of the Dimona site and to any related part of the complex. . . ."[2]

On June 24, 1963, President Kennedy called for an international curb on nuclear weapons. As the United States, Russia and Great Britain were about to sign a treaty to prohibit nuclear testing in the atmosphere, in space and under water, Kennedy urged that the parties signing the atomic test-ban agreement persuade other countries to avert the "disaster" of a spread of nuclear weapons. Alluding to Communist China and France, and perhaps Israel Kennedy said that he would regard it as a disaster if other countries chose to rely upon "the false security which goes with nuclear diffusion."

> I do not regard the atomic weapons and the prospect of its spreading and the realization that war has been the constant companion of mankind throughout our history and the conflict between the Communist system and the free system—when you mix all these tactics together, you have a highly explosive and a highly dangerous situation. When Pandora open[ed] her box and the troubles flew out, all that was left in was hope. Now in this case if we have a nuclear diffusion throughout the world, we may even lose hope.[3]

Kennedy continued to face great challenges in such places as Berlin, Germany, Indochina, Cuba and South America. He did not run from those challenges and met them with every power and ingenuity he possessed.

Two days later in Berlin, JFK spoke before an audience of over one million inhabitants of that divided city declaring that West Berlin was central to the survival of the West. He seemed persuaded that without a free Berlin the free world would go under.

"I want to say on behalf of my countrymen who live many miles away on the other side of the Atlantic. I know of no town, no city that has been besieged for 18 years that still lives with the vitality and the force and the hope and the determination of the City of West Berlin." The wall demonstrated the failures of the Communist system and it was "an offense not only against history, but an offense against humanity. . . ." Kennedy observed that peace could not be assured in Europe as long as Germany remained divided.

> Freedom is indivisible and when one man is enslaved who are free? When all are free, then we can look forward to that day when this city will be joined as one and this country and this great continent of Europe in a peaceful and hopeful globe.
>
> All free men, wherever they may live, are citizens of Berlin. And therefore as a free man, I take pride in the words: 'Ich bin ein Berliner.'[4]

The German masses were wildly enthusiastic as they responded to Kennedy's words. Some people were reminded of the enthusiasm with which a previous generation of Germans had greeted Hitler. Others believed that if Kennedy had asked them to tear down the wall dividing Berlin, they would have done so right there and then.

The event might have bewildered those who had been persecuted by a previous generation of Germans. They could recall the days of the Nazi rallies and wondered how an American president could speak with such fervor of a Berlin that had been the former capital of Nazism. The future of West Berlin was again challenged by Soviet Russia. The U.S. government wanted the world to believe that if it failed to support West Berlin and West Germany, it would mean the demise of the West and freedom.

Shortly thereafter Kennedy visited Ireland where President de Valera expressed "a hundred thousand welcomes" to President Kennedy. Ireland was proud of Kennedy, said de Valera, "We admire the leadership you are giving. We hope that your return here to the ancient motherland will give you, not merely pleasure but renewed bodily strength and an ever more determined will in the pursuit of the safety and happiness of mankind."

Kennedy recalled that eight of his grandparents had left Ireland and that they had come to America. He was proud and happy to visit Ireland because of de Valera who had been "an old and valued friend of (his) father" and had served Ireland for over fifty years with "so much distinction" and "stood for, the very best of Western thought, and equally important, Western actions."[5]

Kennedy visited his ancestral home in County Wexford on the Irish Sea where his family dated back to at least 1654 and from which Patrick J. Kennedy had sailed for America in the late 1840s. Patrick Kennedy had founded the American branch of the family of which John F. Kennedy was its most famous member. As he greeted his kin, JFK said that he was "glad to see a few cousins who did not catch the boat" for America. He spoke to a crowd of 10,000 at New Ross and then visited Dunganstown where Patrick Kennedy was born and where a cousin, Mrs. Mary Ryan and her two daughters, lived. From there he flew by helicopter to the Ancient Burrough of Wexford to address a crowd of 6,000 with a talk about freedom. The "Irish experience," said Kennedy, had shown the world that it was possible for a people despite "a hundred years of foreign domination and religious persecution . . . to maintain their identity and their strong faith." And again as he had said elsewhere, he observed that those "who may believe that freedom may be on the run, or that one nation may be permanently subjected and eventually wiped out, would do well to remember Ireland."[6] Many a Jewish person could well identify with Kennedy's words. One could only wonder what David Ben-Gurion and Levi Eshkol might have thought when they heard of Kennedy's remarks in Germany and Ireland.

The three-day visit to Ireland may have been the happiest part of his visit to Europe. It may even have been the happiest days of his presidency. Kennedy said that his stay in Ireland had been the "high point" of his

eleven-day trip to Europe, and he promised to come back some day and
"see old Shannon's face again." But that was not to be. Less than five
months later, Kennedy would be assassinated. As he left Galway he issued
an invitation to his brethren: "If you ever come to America come to Washington and tell them, if they wonder who you are at the gate, that you
come from Galway. The word will out and when you do, one hundred
thousand welcomes!"[7]

When he got back to Hyannis Port, Massachusetts, he responded to
Khrushchev's July Fourth Independence Day "congratulations and wishes
of peace and prosperity" to the American people. Kennedy appealed to
Khrushchev to help lead the world to peace. The world had

> long passed that time when armed conflict can be the solution to in-
> ternational problems. That is why I share your desire expressed in
> your message of today that we move forward with understanding
> toward the solution of those key problems which divide us. I am hope-
> ful that world peace, just and lasting, can be achieved.

On July 15, 1963, Egypt launched its first anti-aircraft ground-to-ground
missile. It was believed that the Egyptians had more than one type of missile and that some of the others might be displayed during their July 23
Cairo parade.[8] That same day Edward Heath, Lord Privy Seal, told the
House of Commons that "there are indications that some nuclear weapons
may already be in the Middle East." The Foreign Office retracted that statement some two hours later. It reported that Mr. Heath had "intended to
refer to missiles capable of carrying nuclear warheads" and that Heath had
not intended "to imply that nuclear weapons were in the possession of any
Middle Eastern country."[9]

Had Heath let the cat out of the bag? Whose bag was it? Whose cat?
Did Egypt have nuclear weapons by July 1963? Did Israel? Was it likely
that both Egypt and Israel had such weapons by that time?

Prime Minister Levi Eshkol wrote President Kennedy on July 17, 1963,
to thank him for his "friendly congratulations" on his becoming prime minister. He hoped to contribute to the development of Israel's ties with the
United States. But for an Israeli prime minister the "central issue" was the
security of Israel. "We are the only state in the international community
whose existence is challenged [and] openly threatened by all of its neighbors. This gives Israel's security problem a unique intensity and urgency."[10]
He was "puzzled" by Kennedy's indication that America's "commitment to
and support of Israel could be seriously jeopardized" over Israel's development of its "scientific capacity." But that was the nature of an alliance
with a "great" power such as the United States. If something displeased
Uncle Sam, he had the power to cool the "friendship" or "alliance." As

with most international understandings and treaties, they would last for as long as the parties found them supportive of their needs and sovereignty.

Eshkol told Kennedy's ambassador to Israel that he had been disturbed by Kennedy's reference that the U.S. commitment and support for Israel might become jeopardized. Eshkol advised the ambassador, "Israel would do what it had to do for its national security and to safeguard its sovereign rights." He hoped that in "pursuit of this course Israeli-American friendship would grow," and he hoped that Barbour would help clarify the meaning of Kennedy's sentence. Ambassador Barbour said that he had "no additional clarification," but he admitted that there were "a number of suspicious people and people less than favorably disposed to close U.S.-Israel relations, both in the U.S. and elsewhere, who would capitalize on our failure to obtain reliable information on this vital subject," meaning Dimona.[11]

Eshkol then asked how the United States might view the possibility of consultation in advance if future Middle East "developments" made it necessary for Israel to embark on a nuclear weapons program." Eshkol prayed that the day would never come.[12]

Barbour reiterated the importance the Kennedy administration attached to the problem of nuclear proliferation and that "in the explosive atmosphere of the Middle East the introduction of nuclear weapons would be especially grave."[13]

Eshkol "nodded in apparent acquiescence."[14]

Robert Komer thought that Eshkol would agree to the biannual inspection if the United States would provide a security guarantee, "a full-fledged alliance with all the trimmings."[15] The State Department as usual was opposed to such a deal.

With the evident introduction of Soviet missiles in Egypt, the situation for Israel had become more uncertain. The IDF (Israel Defense Forces) was kept on the alert. Israeli jet fighters forced down four U.S. "Weather Bureau" planes with thirty-two individuals on board. They were forced to land at Israel's Lydda airport. Israeli defense officials said that the planes were intercepted as they penetrated Israeli airspace without notification. "Weather Bureau airplanes with thirty-two individuals on board"?[16] Were they of the type of "weather planes" Russia had shot down in 1960?[17] The State Department claimed that the planes had filed a flight plan that involved crossing Israel, but through an error or a misunderstanding they had not actually obtained clearance.[18] Were they weather planes? President Eisenhower had also claimed that the U-2 shot down by the Russians in 1960 was a weather plane, but when the Russians produced Francis Gary Powers, the pilot of America's "weather plane," Ike openly admitted that the United States had sent its planes to spy over Russian territory.

A few days later two Israeli Air Force jets clashed with two Egyptian MiG-17 planes in the area of El Auja, along the Israeli-Egyptian border. For the rest of the day, large numbers of Israeli and Egyptian jets patrolled their borders. The incident occurred just as the Egyptians publicized their ground-to-air Soviet missiles, and it coincided with the eleventh anniversary of the overthrow of King Farouk.[19]

While Kennedy hoped for peace in the Middle East and pressed Israel to reveal its scientific works, he found it difficult to have peace with Cuba that July 17. He could not negotiate with Cuba until its government was prepared to cut political ties with Russia and to remove Soviet troops still stationed there. "I think the United States has indicated very clearly that we do not accept the existence and cannot coexist in the peaceful sense with a Soviet satellite in the Caribbean."[20]

On July 27, Fidel Castro called for a Cuban-style revolution in Latin America and claimed that Argentina, Peru, Columbia and Guatemala were ripe for revolution.[21]

Kennedy could not see a relaxation of relations with Cuba "as long as Cuba was a Soviet satellite. . . . The fact of the matter is that the Soviet troops are there. The fact of the matter is that Cuba does follow a satellite role, and that's what we consider unacceptable to us. I would hope that the situation would some day change."[22]

On July 25, the United States, the Soviet Union and Great Britain signed a treaty to prohibit nuclear testing in the atmosphere, in space and under water. The document was signed in Moscow on July 25 at 7:15 p.m. Undersecretary of State for Political Affairs Harriman signed for the United States, Soviet Foreign Minister Andrei A. Gromyko signed for Soviet Russia and Viscount Hailsham, British minister for science signed for Great Britain. Harriman opined that the test-ban treaty would relieve the fears of people all over the world about nuclear contamination of the atmosphere.[23]

President Kennedy called the treaty "a shaft of light" that "cut into the darkness" and provided "a concrete opportunity to extend its coverage to other nations and later to other forms of nuclear tests." It was a "victory for mankind [and] an important first step towards reason," and could be "a step towards freeing the world from the fear and dangers of radioactive fallout." He declared that it was essential to end this arms race and prevent the proliferation of nuclear weapons:

> If only one thermonuclear bomb were to be dropped on any American city—whether it was launched by accident or design by a madman or by an enemy, by a large nation or small, from any corner of the world—that one bomb could release more destructive force on the inhabitants of that one helpless city than all of the bombs dropped in the Second World War.
>
> We have a great obligation—all four nuclear powers have a great obligation—to use whatever time remains to prevent the spread of nuclear weapons, to persuade other countries not to test, transfer, acquire, possess or produce such weapons.[24]

Kennedy hoped that this treaty could be the "opening wedge in that campaign to end the proliferation of nuclear weaponry."[25] Perhaps it might persuade countries like Israel and Egypt not to seek nuclear weapons.

Ambassador Gazit, in conversation with Robert Komer, said that Israel needed U.S. military reassurances. He observed that American statements concerning its intention to protect Israel against attack, "even when given in the form of a Presidential declaration," did not have a useful political effect in Israel. Ben-Gurion, Golda Meir and others had been told by Kennedy that the United States would not "condone aggression against Israel," but there was "so little physical evidence in support of this stated intention" that the reassurance had not fulfilled the Israeli leadership's estimate of what was needed for its defense and the "creation in Israel of a psychological climate of confidence."[26]

While some nations might expect a few years of instability and insecurity after achieving independence, Israel, after fifteen years of independence, faced "severe political-military threats" and its "right to existence" had constantly been challenged by the Arabs. Israel had an "extraordinary" need for reassurances that either she could defend herself or that "others would help defend her." While the United States had treaties with some forty-two countries which committed the United States to "render assistance against attack," that same United States "found it impossible to give that degree of assurance to Israel."[27]

Gazit wanted to know how the United States might come to Israel's assistance. Komer said that the "standard U.S. doctrine called for immediate attack on an enemy's offensive base structure and capability."[28]

Gazit wondered if the United States could consider giving Israel "private but formal assurances" and that this might accomplish the desired political affect within Israel's leadership. Short of that, perhaps senior U.S. armed forces officers could agree to meet regularly—at least once a year—with senior Israeli officers. The United States might give a general indication as to how a typical strike might be executed by the Sixth Fleet against "any hostile offensive." Israeli officers could present an analysis of the military threat that they saw in connection with their "principal potential adversaries." U.S. officers could then listen and say "Thank you very much. We are glad to have your views." Israeli planners could "at least assume the general characteristic of a U.S. action and the U.S. would then know the relative priorities of Israel and their order of battle." Nowhere was the term "defense treaty" assigned to such an understanding.[29]

Eshkol informed Kennedy on August 19, 1963, that Israel agreed to Dimona visits by the U.S. representatives, and that the next visit should be toward the end of 1963. By that time, the "French group will have handed the reactor over to us and it will be undergoing general tests and a measurement of its physical parameters at zero power." The start-up stage would not yet have been reached. Thus, the "visit of your people will take place at the pre-start-up stage."[30] In his letter of July 5, Kennedy's proposed that from June 1964, U.S. representatives should be invited to visit Dimona biannually. Eshkol believed that Israel would be able to "reach agreement on the future schedule of visits."[31] Moreover, Israel would continue to return to France all the irradiated uranium fuel. Eshkol congratulated Kennedy on the test-ban treaty: "It may be the first step leading to a general improvement in the relations between the Great Powers." Israel followed "with sympathy" Kennedy's efforts to make this agreement the starting point of a more general relaxation of tensions. It was Eshkol's "earnest hope that the relations between states in our region will also improve in conformity with the present international climate."[32]

Eshkol's response may not have been what the Kennedy administration wanted, but it was the best they could get from Israel. Kennedy had asked for inspection every six months, Eshkol made no firm commitments, but spoke of reaching an agreement. Kennedy called for complete access to the Dimona facilities, but Eshkol was vague. Kennedy wanted to pass information along to Egypt, but Eshkol did not want the "information obtained from the visits" to be passed on to the Arabs. Nasser should not be assured that Israel was not working toward nuclear weapons production. In view of Nasser's "superiority in conventional weapons, his undenied production of missiles and his large preponderance of manpower, an element of doubt as to Israel's capabilities could have a useful deterrent effect against any Egyptian adventures."[33] In other words, if you don't have certain weapons, it is just as well not to publicize that fact.[34] But despite it all, Kennedy seemed satisfied, and in his August 26, 1963, letter to Eshkol, he was much more conciliatory. He thanked Eshkol and expressed his appreciation for inviting U.S. scientists to visit Dimona on a regular basis. Kennedy recognized that Eshkol had "acted from a deep wisdom regarding Israel's security in the longer term and the awesome realities which the atomic age imposes on the community of man." And finally Kennedy observed that Eshkol had been part of "the historic spirit of the test ban."[35]

Kennedy wrote Eshkol:

Your letter of August 19, was most welcome here. I appreciate that this was a difficult decision, yet I am convinced that in generously agreeing to invite our scientists to visit the Dimona complex on the regular basis that was proposed you have acted from a deep wisdom regarding Israel's security in the longer term and the awesome realities which the atomic age imposes on the community of men.

You have suggested that an initial visit take place toward the end of this year. . . . I am asking Ambassador Barbour to keep in touch with you so that the visit can be arranged for a time when the reactor's core is being loaded and before internal radiation hazards have developed.

The recent overwhelming endorsement of the partial test ban treaty has moved us all a small step in the direction of a more peaceful world. Our purpose must be to continue striving towards the effective control of the power of the atom so that it may be used only for the welfare of man. The spirit you have shown in your letter to me is a clear indication that you share that same high purpose.[36]

The test-ban treaty that banned atomic testing in space, the atmosphere and the oceans was initialed on July 25, 1963. Israel announced that it would join the limited test ban.[37]

There was trouble along Israel's northern and southern frontiers again. On August 11, 1963, Egypt claimed that Israel posed a threat. As Nasser greeted some of his troops that came back from Yemen battlefields, he warned that there could be no disarmament in the Middle East until the rights of the "Palestinian people would be restored in Israel." Egypt's armed forces, said Nasser, had to stand against Israel.[38]

On August 20, Syrian and Israel forces exchanged fire at Ashmura, an Israeli border farm settlement north of Tiberias. There were air battles between Israeli Mirage and Syrian MiG-17s. Haim Yahil, director general of Israel's Foreign Ministry warned that there was "a real danger to the peace if the Syrian actions" did not stop. Israel instructed their ambassador to the UN to request a Security Council session to deal with the "grave act of aggression committed by Syrian forces."[39] In response to the Syrian-Israeli battles, the Egyptians placed their forces on an emergency alert.[40] Iraq placed its forces under Syrian command in support of Syria's fight against Israel.[41]

Perhaps President Kennedy achieved a better understanding with Israel in respect to inspection of some of its scientific and nuclear programs. Eshkol did not agree to biannual inspections of Dimona, but he accepted annual inspections even though the Americans had not asked for similar inspections of Egyptian facilities. But there was no peace or security for Israel in the Middle East. While the Arabs continued their massive war preparations and attempted intimidations against Israel, the Israelis had not persuaded Kennedy to move closer to an American-Israeli understanding. Kennedy believed that America could uphold its friendship and commitments to Israel and the Arabs, but he would not agree to an Israel-American dual alliance.

CHAPTER 7

The Last Days of JFK and Israel's Continued Struggle for Survival

During the last months of JFK's life, he and Israel continued to negotiate over inspections of Israeli nuclear facilities, Israel's requests for an American alliance, coordination between Israeli and American military commanders and Israel's requests for sophisticated military equipment.

On September 9, 1963, Minister Mordechai Gazit met with Robert Komer to talk about Israel's continual struggle for survival.[1] Gazit wanted to discuss a number of items including better intelligence exchanges and military visits. Israel needed to secure itself against being "engulfed by the Arabs." If such security matters might be laid to rest, then Israel might be able to pursue a more flexible policy towards the Arabs.[2]

Kennedy had tried to persuade Egypt's President Nasser not to pursue the nuclear path and to give his assurances that he would not attack Israel. In his September 12, 1967, letter to Nasser, Kennedy welcomed Egypt's endorsement of the test-ban treaty and noted that Egypt seemed committed to "acquire nuclear weapons." Kennedy said he hoped that Nasser would pledge not to attack his neighbors.[3] But Nasser would not make such commitments, and Israel was alarmed by his tactics in the Yemen, including his use of poisonous gases, and the fact that German scientists were assisting him to develop his missiles and his nuclear program.

Gazit tried to encourage the Americans to provide for the long-term "survival" of Israel, to discuss the "demilitarization" of the West Bank should a regime change occur in Jordan and to provide aid to Israel in case of an Arab threat. Israeli diplomats anticipated that the United States would once again refuse to offer Israel security guarantees and they thought that it was "essential" that the United States "express a willingness to discuss other means of enhancing Israel's security," perhaps joint military and diplomatic planning. Gazit suggested that there should be discussions of these issues and that a senior Israeli military person should regularly visit the United States for such discussions. Perhaps Prime Minister Eshkol or Foreign Minister Meir might be invited to talk with the president.[4]

On September 26, 1963, Kennedy reiterated and did not alter his prior commitments: ". . . we believe that there is no Near Eastern leader today, whatever his attitude toward your nation, who does not fully understand the import of our public, national commitment as I reaffirmed it on May 8." Kennedy insisted that the United States could uphold its commitment to Israel and its neighbors. But, he still doubted that an explicit security guarantee to Israel would be advantageous to the United States or Israel. It was best for all concerned if the United States were free to talk openly and freely to all the concerned parties, and a bilateral security arrangement as Ben-Gurion had suggested would have a distinct contrary effect. "I know you need no reassurance as to the constant and special U.S. concern for the security and independence of Israel. We have the will and ability to carry out our stated determination to preserve it." In case of a security concern, the United States would most carefully consider with Israel the best ways and means of coping with it as in the case of the Hawk missiles.[5] JFK's response followed the State Department's policy towards Israel.

Foreign Minister Golda Meir expressed Israel's strong concern regarding Egypt's ground-to-ground missiles, but the State Department claimed that Egypt's guidance system of the missiles was "very primitive." That might have been true in 1962, insisted Mrs. Meir, but by early October 1963, the Egyptians had developed a 50-50 capability of hitting any large inhabited area. Moreover, she observed, that Israel's tank corps was not as up-to-date as that of Egypt's. While the Egyptians had the Soviet T-54 tanks, Israel was still using old World War II Sherman tanks. Gazit thought that there should be a thorough discussion and examination regarding Egyptian missiles, tanks, and warheads, which might contain possible chemical, bacteriological, or radiological elements.[6]

Prime Minister Eshkol continued to work for an alliance with the United States, but to no avail. Kennedy advised Eshkol that the existing series of informal arrangements were sufficient, and he believed that the Israel Defense Forces were more than able to defend Israel's interests. During his May 8, 1963, press conference, Kennedy had made his position clear that a bilateral security arrangement would only serve to encourage the Russians to sell arms to Israel's enemies. He concluded, "I know you need no reassurance as to the constant and special U.S. concern for the security and independence of Israel," but if there would occur an imbalance, the United States would rectify the situation.[7]

On September 30, 1963, Mrs. Meir had again advised Rusk of Israel's worries that German scientists were assisting Egypt to develop poison gases, missiles and other sophisticated weaponry. As of November 1963,

50 percent of the missiles dispatched by Egypt could hit target areas such as Tel Aviv, and by 1965, the UAR would have a quantity of accurate missiles. There was evidence that the UAR was building its nuclear capability and that it was seeking to buy cobalt for this purpose. The UAR was also doing advanced work in chemical and radiological warfare.[8]

In his letter of October 3, 1963, Kennedy expressed his concern for Israel's security, but he would not extend U.S. assurances beyond what had already been provided. Furthermore, "there is no Near Eastern leader today . . . who does not fully understand the import of our public, national commitment" as it had been reaffirmed on May 8, 1963. He was "fully satisfied" that the United States could "back up" its assurances to "halt swiftly any aggression against Israel or its neighbors." Moreover, he believed that Israel had a "substantial deterrent advantage." The existing "informal arrangements meet Israel's needs and give clear warning to the Arabs; to go further at this juncture would entail certain positive disadvantages" to Israel and to the United States. It would be to the advantage of both the United States and Israel if the United States maintained good relations with the Arabs. A "bilateral security relationship" as had been suggested by Ben-Gurion would work against the best interests of all concerned. It would encourage the Arabs to seek such a relationship with the USSR. It is Arab hostility plus Soviet arms and threats that destabilizes Israeli security.[9]

Eshkol apparently appreciated Kennedy's October 3, 1963, commitment to deter or halt swiftly any aggression against Israel. He was especially appreciative since Israel was the only state in the international community whose neighbors openly threatened to destroy its independence and territorial integrity. Israel took these threats seriously, particularly because they were being supported by "belligerent policies and intensive military preparations, especially by Egypt." Nevertheless, Eshkol wondered whether the U.S.-Israel agreements were sufficiently effective to ensure that security. He was concerned with the view that Israel's military capability could provide it with "a substantial deterrent advantage," and with Kennedy's conviction that the "U.S. commitment is understood in its full import by the Arab leaders and constitutes a clear warning to them." While the Prime Minister agreed that the preservation of peace could best be served by the maintenance of Israel's own deterrent capacity together with a clear American commitment to prevent aggression, he felt that each of these elements had to be strengthened.[10] Egypt moved rapidly toward developing a strong missile force and greater accuracy in the guidance and range of its missiles. Israel's few airfields and centers of dense population were prime targets of Egypt's missiles. "Missiles, unlike aircraft, cannot be intercepted" and Israel has no missile forces of its own. Conditions of "perilous temptation" for Nasser were coming within view. There was a similar disparity between Arab armored forces and Israel's. Unless Israel received help in ground-to-ground missiles and tanks, it would not be able to develop its deterrent advantage. It also needed financial assistance to develop that deterrent. Israel had never "received free defense assistance to meet a military danger which is predominantly of Soviet origin." Israel was the "only country of which this can be said." Eshkol accepted America's reassurances that it could back up its word and commitments, but the Arabs might come to some other conclusions if they came to realize that there was a "firm treaty engagement." In modern times there was a need for "speedy and automatic reaction" to any threat. Israel needed to prevent an attack, "not to remedy its effects after the event." There still was no "formal public commitment and no joint planning"—all of which opened the possibility of miscalculation.[11]

On October 17, 1963, Israeli Ambassador Harman called for a discussion of the Near East situation since the Israeli-Arab military balance of some eighteen months ago had changed. Missiles and sophisticated weapons would be on the agenda. General Yitzhak Rabin would be there. Rusk wanted the meeting to focus on missiles, while Golda Meir wanted to include tanks in the discussions.[12] U. Alexis Johnson, deputy undersecretary for Near Eastern affairs, had warned that if the Egyptians were to develop "a serious missile capability and Israel should match it, escalation would be in full operation, and this would not be to the advantage of either the U.S. or Israel. Answering missiles with missiles was not comforting to either side."[13] Again it seemed that some State Department officials assumed that the Middle East arms race, was in part, Israel's fault.

Israelis were not comforted by Kennedy's words of reassurance. They continued to feel vulnerable to a possible Arab attack. But they wanted more in addition to Kennedy's May 8 and October 3 reassurances. They wanted to know "how and in what manner the U.S. would fulfill these assurances." There also was a need to coordinate plans of action of American and Israeli forces.[14]

Late in October Jacob Blaustein of the American Jewish Committee met with State Department officials regarding Israel's need for tanks and ground-to-ground missiles as well as security assurances from the United States. He said that Israel was "profoundly grateful" for the assurances that it had received from Kennedy, but Israeli leaders felt that they had to know more precisely about how the United States planned to come to Israel's aid. There had to be some secret arrangement for joint planning between Israel and the United States. Egypt's acquisition of modern weaponry and its development of ground-to-ground missiles had reduced Israel's military superiority. It became a matter of life or death for Israel to acquire comparable weapons.[15]

Ambassador Harriman had stressed that America possessed the determination and the capacity to help Israel in case it were attacked. James P. Grant thought that Israel had little to worry about since the Arabs were in disarray. Iraqi forces were locked in a stalemate with the Kurds; Nasser was bogged down in Yemen, and even though the Arabs had acquired sophisticated modern weapons, their military was still "unimpressive." Moreover, the United States Sixth Fleet and American forces in Europe could respond within 24 to 72 hours in case of an attack against Israel, and this would serve as a deterrent. But "in the unlikely event this failed," Harriman thought, Israel had a "clear military superiority and could withstand an attack until assistance was rendered."[16] Even though they seemed to admit that the United States might not be able to do the job, individuals like Harriman and Grant would still insist that Israel should depend upon American military power. Ultimately Israel would have to depend upon its own "military superiority." But then how could Israel be militarily superior to the Arabs if it could not even get weapons equivalent to those obtained by the Arabs? Repeatedly American officials insisted that if Israel acquired modern missiles with sophisticated guidance systems from Western sources, the Egyptians would acquire similar weaponry from the Soviet Union and the threat to Israel would be increased.

Rodger P. Davies, deputy assistant secretary of state, thought that joint planning was out of the question. It would only encourage the Egyptians to ally themselves more closely to the Russians. Moreover, he reported, that the Egyptians were afraid of a possible Israeli attack. The "memories of 1956 were strong." Davies did not mention the fact that in the 1950s the Egyptians had been preparing for an onslaught against Israel.[17]

Harriman reiterated the State Department theme song that America's "intense" support for Israel was Israel's best defense, but he held "no illusions as to the dependability of President Nasser." His activities in Algeria and the introduction of Soviet equipment as well as aggression in Yemen were "examples of his irresponsibility." Nevertheless, Harriman believed that it was better to talk and influence Nasser rather than to be "at complete logger-heads" with him. He believed that the United States could best serve Israel if it remained on top of developments in the area.[18]

During the U.S.-Israeli talks, the Americans observed that the UAR military threat concentrated heavily upon tanks and conventional weapons and that Egypt's missile threat was useless for military targets, but capable of disrupting Israeli mobilization efforts by strikes upon heavily populated areas. General Rabin observed that Egypt's possession of missiles might stimulate an over-confidence in Egypt's offensive capability and thereby encourage them to launch a general conventional and nonconventional attack. To the American query as to the status of the Israeli missile program, Rabin said that there were preparatory studies, but there was a need for a good deal of "money, knowledge and know-how before Israel could get into business."[19]

Talbot believed that both Israeli and American experts agreed that UAR missile capability was limited, and that the acquisition of missiles by Israel would stimulate the Arabs to acquire more Soviet missiles and thereby enhance rather than reduce the threat of war in the Near East. The resulting cold war polarization in the area would cause more difficulties for Israeli security than did Egypt's missile capability. Nasser knew that an attack against Israel by Egypt would damage its international stature. Israel had both public and private American assurances of support, but if the United States would openly align itself on the side of Israel through security guarantees, joint planning or arms buildup, the Arabs would seek similar arrangements with the USSR. This cold war polarization would be harmful to the U.S. and Israeli security interests.[20]

State Department officials sought accommodations with the Arabs in addition to working on military preparedness. Ambassador Harman appreciated this discussion and U.S. concern for the security of Israel. He noted that there was a minimum margin of safety below which Israeli defenses should not be permitted to decline. The "safe" tank ratio was one Israeli tank for two or three Arab tanks. It was therefore necessary to replace 300 outmoded Sherman tanks with modern tanks and acquire 200 additional tanks in anticipation of a further Egyptian tank buildup. A similar margin of safety had to be established for Israel's naval requirements.[21]

As for missiles, the UAR had missiles, as well as a corps of experts, and it was working to improve its inventory. Cost did not seem to matter to the Egyptians. Israel was concerned that missiles plus a military buildup of other military supplies could inspire the UAR to launch an offensive.[22]

While Israel supported the concept of total disarmament and mutual inspection, there was no readiness on the part of the Arabs to pursue any form of disarmament.[23]

Eshkol responded on November 4, 1963, that he appreciated Kennedy's reassurances that the United States had "a national commitment to deter or halt swiftly any aggression against Israel," and he attached "great value" to the fact that under Kennedy's "personal leadership" it was "so emphatically underlined," but it was distressing that up to this point Kennedy had not given it a "more formal expression." The American commitment had to be "strengthened" in view of such developing conditions as Egypt's acquisition of missiles and tanks from the Soviet Union. Matters were approaching a dangerous point, which could "only be avoided by due preparation now." The Egyptians were preparing "an effective missile force" and they were receiving assistance from the West Germans to develop an accurate guidance system for their missiles.[24]

Once again an Israeli prime minister portrayed Israel's vulnerability to an American president. Israel had only a few airfields and its centers of dense population were within enemy missile striking distance. An enemy might destroy those few airfields in a swift first strike. Half of Israel's population was within a small densely populated area of the Tel Aviv vicinity. Israel could be "damaged to a demoralizing degree." Those results could even be achieved by missiles that did not possess a high degree of accuracy, and due to the time factor, such a strike could not be prevented by the prospect of aid from a friendly power. Such a situation could be counteracted only if Israel acquired a deterrent capacity "in the same military dimension."[25] Eshkol and Abba Eban pointed out that Nasser wanted to eliminate Israel and that he would try to do so when he believed his forces were ready to do so. Nasser believed that by eliminating Israel he would then have direct territorial contact with Syria and Lebanon and thereby isolate Hussein. Israel was especially vulnerable to attack. As Ben-Gurion, Foreign Minister Golda Meir and others had explained it to Kennedy and his advisors over and over again, Israel had no interest in expansion. Eshkol likewise reminded the American ambassador and his president that Israel constituted the last refuge for European Jewry. This created an added dimension to its defense responsibilities.[26]

Eshkol explained further that thanks to Soviet deliveries of weapons to the Arabs, there were other "factors of vulnerability in the grave disparity between Arab armored forces and those of Israel." There was also a "total lack of balance between the naval forces of Egypt and those of Israel."[27] Eshkol would send Deputy Chief of Staff General Yitzhak Rabin to Washington to present a "full picture of our appraisal." Israel did not have "the necessary deterrent capacity in the near future" unless it would obtain "considerable help." It needed ground-to-ground missiles, tanks and increased naval power. Eshkol hoped that these matters would "receive earnest and positive consideration"[28] from the Kennedy administration.

In the following week Eshkol advised that without a U.S. promise to come to Israel's rescue, Israel would have to find other ways with which to defend itself from Nasser's arsenal.[29]

Talbot said that he welcomed the opportunity to examine Israel's evidence regarding the UAR military buildup. The United States had a commitment to deter or halt any aggression against Israel or its neighbors. It was vital to establish facts concerning military capabilities of the Near East countries.[30] He noted that the United States was aware of Israel's longstanding concerns. He recalled that on December 27, 1962, Foreign Minister Meir had advised President Kennedy that Egypt, with German help, had been developing ground-to-ground missiles since 1960, that Egypt was preparing for radiological warfare and that they had a secret budget of some $250 million for their weapons project. Israel was likewise concerned about Egypt's submarine menace. Since March 1962, and particularly since the Yemen conflict, the Soviet arms flow to the UAR had increased. Among the supplies provided was the TU-16 bomber. By April 20, 1963, Shimon Peres had advised the Americans that the Egyptians would certainly get air-to-air missiles, ship-to-shore missiles and ground-to-ground missiles. Moreover, within one to three years Egypt would have missiles with the capacity to reach Tel Aviv.[31] The Kennedy administration knew of the UAR's missile buildup as early as August 27, 1962, and it was this knowledge that had helped persuade Kennedy to sell Israel the Hawk missiles. Kennedy had asked his Ambassador to Israel, Walworth Barbour, if Egypt was acquiring Soviet missiles: "Are they acquiring them?"[32]

"So far as our intelligence shows they are," said Barbour.[33]

"What kind of missiles?"[34]

Barbour reported that the Egyptians had acquired ground-to-air Nike Zeus type missiles and surface-to-surface missiles for their naval forces.[35]

On November 14, 1963, General Yitzhak Rabin, Aharon Yaariv, military attache of the Israeli embassy, and Minister Gazit met with Robert Komer. They talked about strategic and military matters. Rabin observed that the Egyptians followed Soviet tactical doctrine, partly because it minimized the need for individual initiative. The initial attack consisted of heavy artillery barrages followed by mechanized and infantry units that would seek to breach Israeli defenses.[36] While Komer chided the Israelis for overstating the dangers which they faced, Rabin stressed the psychological factors involved as Nasser might become overly confident once he obtained a missile force. Komer felt that Israeli intelligence gave the impression that they had much harder evidence of Egypt's nuclear development. While the United States did see the possibility of trouble, it questioned Israel's estimate. Nasser had ordered the production of his missiles even though his research personnel had not developed them to achieve "military desirable accuracy." The Israelis estimated that Nasser believed the "simple fact" of possessing them was "a major asset."[37]

Robert Komer tried to play down the threat from the Egyptians, but General Rabin would not do so. Rabin pointed out that the Egyptian cruise missiles were a threat to Israeli power plants—all of which were near the coastal cities.[38] But Komer also tried to persuade Rabin that the Egyptians were not getting all they wanted from the Soviet Union, and that was one of the main reasons they were seeking to develop their own "home-grown" missiles and jet fighters.[39] He also tried to persuade the Israelis that the United States would assist Israel in case of danger. The United States had its tactical air forces and the Sixth Fleet nearby at Dana, while the U.K. Bomber Command was on Cyprus. The United States was confident that it could meet any need and challenge. Komer asked why Israel always seemed to question America's "will or ability to act, which we had underlined again and again both publicly and privately?"[40] He could not understand that "after our consistent support of Israel over the years, our extensive aid, and our repeated declarations since 1950," Israel might still question America's "reliability."[41]

General Rabin was not persuaded that the United States was a reliable friend or ally. During Israel's war of independence, the United States and its Western allies had abandoned Israel. When the Arabs invaded Israel in 1948, no major Western power had helped Israel. Harry S Truman had embargoed the shipment of arms and men to the Middle East. Israel did manage to defeat the Arabs thanks to its soldiers and was able to purchase arms from Czechoslovakia, a member of the Soviet bloc.[42] Because of that American and West European policy, Israel had to give up its efforts to wrest the Old City of Jerusalem from Arab control. Rabin also recalled that the Eisenhower administration had been instrumental in stopping Israel from totally smashing the Egyptian forces during the 1956 Sinai war so that it could make sure that there would be no recurrence of Arab blockades of Eilat and the Suez Canal.[43]

Furthermore, Israel was not considered by the United States to be on the same level as the states within NATO. The United States confronted the Communists, but in the case of Israel vs. the Arabs, there was no Communist enemy involved even though Nasser was a customer of Soviet Russia and was influenced by the Soviet bloc. The United States had "open formal treaty commitments to other allies, but not to Israel." The United States had joint military planning with various states, but not with Israel, and without such joint military planning, the consequences could be chaotic. Rabin asked Komer to think of a situation whereby American and Israeli planes might be flying over a target area. What would happen if they had not provided for prearranged signals? He recalled that in the desert there often were dust storms and it was hard to distinguish between friendly and unfriendly elements without prearranged signals. Rabin confided that in 1956 Israel had "shot up a lot of its own tanks" because it had not made provision for such signals.[44]

Komer's response was to repeat the stated American position with respect to an alliance with Israel. Such an alliance would "drive the Arabs to seek compensatory arrangements with the Soviets" and this would bring the USSR back into the Middle East.[45] The United States aimed to keep the Russians from penetrating the Middle East, to protect Israeli independence, to keep Middle East oil flowing to the United States and to prevent the polarization of forces where the United States would back Israel while Russia would support the Arabs. As a consequence of such polarization, Israel would then become a "garrison state." Komer insisted that the United States was a truly reliable ally and that he could not understand how Israel could question its "reliability."[46]

Ambassador Gazit interjected diplomatically that Israel felt it could depend on the United States, but that it could not let its own margin of safety become too thin. As conditions became more threatening to Israel, it "needed either stronger security guarantees or a stronger deterrent posture."[47] Rabin insisted that Israel could not depend solely on assurances of outside support. It had to be able to defend itself "come what may."[48] He appreciated words of reassurance, but Israel could not rely solely on such words without joint planning.[49] Rabin said,

Israel greatly appreciated U.S. private assurances of help, but it could not rely solely on them, or expect them to be effective without the sort of joint planning allies must do. Furthermore, the deterrent value of vague public statements and private assurances was significantly less than that of a formal alliance. The only long run hope for Israel was to kill the last cell of Arab hope for the destruction of Israel.[50]

Until that Arab hope of destruction would disappear, Rabin saw no hope for the normalization of Arab-Israeli relations.[51]

Komer thought that Nasser understood America's determination to defend Israel "every bit as clearly as if we had a formal alliance."[52]

Rabin did not agree with Komer.[53]

While Israel sought to be independent weapons-wise, U.S. officials like Komer advised Israel to take it easy with respect to the purchase of such costly weapons as tanks and ships. (Israel asked to purchase some 500 new tanks.) Rabin said those weapons were necessary to end Arab aspirations to destroy Israel. Even if Egypt's acquisitions of armaments only represented a psychological challenge, Israel had to demonstrate that it was taking "adequate measures to deter an Arab second round."[54] Unless that were accomplished Rabin saw no chance for the normalization of Israeli-Arab relations.[55]

Komer observed that the United States wanted more information about Israel's own plans. The United States had heard that Israel was interested in a French solid fuel missile that was being developed by Marcel Dassault of France. Did the Israelis plan to buy those missiles or did they intend to build their own? Rabin said Israel was interested in the missile, but that it had made no decisions on what to purchase or how many. The matter was being studied.[56]

Komer reiterated the State Department's assertion that if Israel would deploy superior missiles with good accuracy, then the Egyptians would "almost certainly" seek Soviet SAM missiles. Thus Israel would have driven the Egyptians to acquire weapons which would be most dangerous. The Egyptians would be further encouraged to acquire even more sophisticated weapons from Russia if they realized that Israel "had a breeder reactor which could be turned into producing weapons material and provide Israel with warheads for its missiles." Komer warned that if Israel could manufacture nuclear weapons it would open a pandora's box of a "new and unpredictable" arms race.[57]

Gazit complained that the American intelligence exchange with Israel had been "abstruse and academic," and the question remained: "where do we go from here?"

Komer did not respond to Gazit's inquiry, but asked his own questions insisting that the United States had to know more about Israel's plans and programs.[58]

One of the great fallacies of State Department thinking was that it was simply an arms race between Israel and the Arabs. But it was much more than that. The Arab leaders used Israel as their scapegoat and a means to gather popular support from their people. They claimed that all their troubles came from the fact that Israel existed. Instead of improving the life of their people in such countries as Egypt, Syria, Jordan, Lebanon, Arabia, Iraq, the Sudan and Libya they bought weapons with which to dominate and control other countries and to control their own people.

For Israel it was a basic question of survival and not a desire to dominate or rule the world. It was not a question of an arms race. Israel needed weapons in order to protect itself from such countries as Egypt, Syria and Iraq that sought its annihilation.

On November 21, 1963, Komer advised Gazit that the Gruening amendment introduced by Senator Gruening which called for the cessation of aid to states that tried to make war against Israel had "so limited our freedom of action with the Arabs as to make it very difficult for us to be as forthcoming with Israel on the refugee or other issues as we would otherwise like."[59] But Gazit insisted that Israel had nothing to do with the "standard pro-Zionist reactions of Leonard Farbstein, Ernest Gruening, Kenneth Keating and Jacob Javits." He recalled that when Javits had come to the area and wanted to write a report on the Arab refugees, Israeli officials had tried to persuade him not to publish that report but Javits published it anyway.[60]

Gazit did not appreciate the "arms length" relationship between the United States and Israel that made it so difficult to achieve "our joint purposes." He cited the recent meeting between Rabin and American officials. Israel had "laid out" all of its intelligence information, but the United States had kept "mum." In response, Komer said that the United States had given Israel more of its intelligence information on the UAR than at any previous time, and he claimed that it was incredible that Israel was "so consistently coy about describing its own defense plans and programs to its guarantor, banker, and strongest friend in the world. If trouble developed in the Near East it was not the French nor the Germans, but the United States that had to come to Israel's defense."[61] Komer observed that while the United States was expected to subsidize Israel, privately and publicly, "to support her to the hilt on every issue, to meet all of her security requirements, and to defend her if attacked," but in return the United States did not know what Israel intended to do in such "critical fields as missiles and nuclear weapons." He referred to the way Israel handled Dimona and how it created "real suspicion" that it was seeking to hide its plans to acquire nuclear capability. When Rabin was asked if Israel was acquiring missiles from France, he had on two occasions refused to answer. Komer seemed perturbed as he asked, "What kind of a relationship was this?"[62]

Gazit regretted the way Israel had handled the Dimona situation, but he felt that American-Israeli relationships were entering a state of crisis as when the United States raised objections to Israel's relationships with third parties. Komer asked if the United States was not entitled to have a better idea of what Israel was doing since the United States was Israel's chief financial backer and guarantor. "If Israel undertook a reprisal raid against Jordan that could lead to war, should not the U.S. be informed?"[63]

William H. Brubeck, the State Department's executive secretary reviewed some of the U.S. policies since August 1962 that had been favorable to Israel: (1) The United States had tried to achieve a solution of the Palestine issue without endangering Israel. (2) When Syria fired upon Israeli farmers, the United States urged the UN Truce Supervision Organization to intervene and made forceful diplomatic demarches. This prevented the situation from escalating, and Israel resumed the cultivation of the area in dispute. (3) When Egypt invaded Yemen, the United States supported Jordan and Saudi Arabia, whose stability was important to Israel, and worked to bring about the withdrawal of Egyptian forces from the Yemen. In talks with Arab leaders, the United States made clear that it would not "brook aggression against Israel." From such conversations and United States intelligence analysis the United States remained convinced that "no Arab state regarded it as feasible to take aggressive military action against Israel." (4) The United States stood ready to use its best efforts to support Israel's withdrawal of water from Lake Tiberias. (5) The United States agreed to sell Hawk ground-to-air missiles to Israel. Combined with Israel's "first class air force" and the early-warning radar that the United States had made available to Israel, its major cities and airfields would receive full protection against a surprise air attack. The United States agreed to provide Israel with a loan of $25 million to cover the cost of the Hawk system. (6) President Kennedy, in conversation with Mrs. Meir, once again declared U.S. friendship for Israel and readiness to come to Israel's assistance in case Israel were attacked.[64]

At one point in time in June of 1963, President Kennedy thought of doing a tradeoff with Israel. The United States would give Israel "reasonable assurances" in return for Israel's agreement not to move into Jordan or develop nuclear weapons.[65] But that plan never came to fruition. To the very last day of Kennedy's life in November 1963, State Department officials stood adamantly opposed to providing Israel an alliance with security guarantees. They insisted that it would spoil America's relations with the Arabs and thereby promote Soviet interests in the Middle East and Africa. JFK went along with that State Department policy.

After three long years Israel had failed to achieve its goal of a security understanding or dual alliance with the United States, nor did Kennedy agree to help Israel match the weapons Soviet Russia provided its Arab clients. Perhaps Kennedy might have wanted to provide Israel with a security understanding and to assist Israel with weapons, but he had to consider America's relations with the Arab states, and he did listen to the advice of his State Department and White House experts.

AND THE TORCH WAS PASSED ON

President Kennedy was assassinated on November 22, 1963. To date we do not know the full history of that gruesome deed. More than forty years since that terrible time we still do not know what happened and who the guilty parties were. Was it a lone assassin or a conspiracy? Perhaps some day a thorough and complete history of that day of infamy will be written. The Warren Commission Report, as Lyndon B. Johnson wrote in his memoir, *Vantage Point*, had been used primarily to calm the American people.

In 1968 Robert F. Kennedy was assassinated by Sirhan Sirhan, a Jordanian Arab. As of 2005 that individual sits in jail. He admitted killing Robert Kennedy because Robert Kennedy had been pro-Israel when John Kennedy was president, and he was pro-Israel as he ran for president in 1968. If the truth lies buried in the archives, whatever the truth concerning the untimely deaths of John F. Kennedy and Robert Kennedy may be, it is time that the story be told.

Lyndon B. Johnson inherited Kennedy's presidency including the issues of the United States and Israel.

On December 23, 1963, Ambassador Barbour asked Prime Minister Eshkol to keep three things constantly in mind when considering U.S.-Israel relationships: the totality of U.S.-Israel relationship, the "great importance of Israel's making the best possible impression on the international scene," and "the absolute requirement that the U.S. retain considerable working influence with the Arabs."[66] On the first matter Israel should recall that the United States provided Israel with "an extremely sophisticated and classified weapon" to help Israel defend itself, President Kennedy's most important statement of May 8 and his personal letters to Eshkol. "These clearly attest to the nature of our special commitment,"[67] and President Johnson was apparently determined to maintain that special commitment to Israel "in every respect."[68]

America's influence with the Arabs had been built up "painfully and over a long period of time," but it could not be "considered secure." "The most careful conservation of this influence is vital if we are, with Israel, successfully to meet the forthcoming problems." Dimona will soon go critical and that would not remain a secret for long, Israel will undertake large scale withdrawal of Jordan basin waters, the United States was trying to find a solution to the Yemen conflict and for "fundamental progress of the refugee issue. All of which would require considerable U.S. influence with the Arabs."[69]

The discussions between Israel and the United States continued. Levi Eshkol wrote President Johnson on December 25, 1963, that he wanted to work for closer relations with the United States:

> As a matter of fact I am sure you really mean well. We have our differences of evaluation of situations and dangers, of action to be taken and of its effects. We are here directly involved. You are a world power and the Middle East is sometimes only a dot on a big map. We know . . . that in your Egyptian policy you hope to attain influence for the benefit of the whole region but what are the results? The Soviet Union supplies arms while you and other Western countries give Egypt economic assistance, loans and food which in effect makes it easier for Nasser to engage in his intensive arms build-up and foreign intervention.[70]

While Israel never publicly criticized U.S. policy towards Nasser, it was difficult to "comprehend" that policy. Nasser recognized and dealt with Communist China. Nasser continued his war in Yemen and he sent forces to Algeria. Israel's main battle was to maintain its security. As Egypt acquired all the arms that it might want from the Soviet Union, it imposed "a tremendous burden" on Israel. The way Eshkol saw it, Israel in its relations with the United States faced a situation wherein there was no formal treaty, no staff arrangements, and no real military assistance. The prospect for the next year was of very little economic assistance. Eshkol asked Johnson to make "a special effort" to help Israel overcome this "impossible burden of security."[71]

Observations and Conclusions on Kennedy and Israel

Some observers like National Security aide on the Middle East Robert W. Komer claimed that JFK was his own man; he broke from the Washington foreign policy establishment, and he was his own secretary of state when dealing with such matters as the Middle East. Even Phillips Talbot, Assistant Secretary of State for Middle East Affairs, noted that "one of the great things about the New Frontier was the President's own personal handling of the affairs of the Middle East. He really was the Secretary of State."[1] Komer felt that Kennedy "cleared personally almost every major policy move in the entire Middle East area. They were all given the personal Presidential chop, and when they weren't we heard about it. So we didn't try to conduct policy without keeping him fully clued."[2] Komer claimed that "Kennedy knew more about the Middle East than most everybody in his administration including the Secretary of State and McGeorge Bundy."[3]

Kennedy may have watched Middle East developments closely, but he could not separate himself entirely from the foreign policy establishment attitudes toward the Middle East and Israel that had been in the making since the time of President Woodrow Wilson. The Middle East was important for its oil, its geographic location and its vast number of Muslims. It was one of the areas of contention between the Soviet Bloc and the West. Since 1943 the Soviets worked to separate the Middle East from western influence. It was part of Russia's Cold War strategy. To achieve that goal the Russians provided the Arabs with all manner of weaponry and they undertook such major projects as the multi-billion dollar Aswan Dam project in Egypt. Kennedy may have been sympathetic toward Israel, but his State Department was pro-Arab. American business and especially oil companies were pro-Arab. As Komer observed, the State Department took on the "role as a deliberate, understandable counter to the great domestic pressures from the Israeli constituency on the White House." The Secretary of State was "the spokesman for the evenhanded policy against all that political advice that was going to the White House on how to be pro-Israeli." Komer thought that "In terms of strategic geography, Israel [was] a millstone around our necks and known as such to all and sundry."[4] If Israel were not inhabited by Israelis "our policy would be totally different." It was natural that the State and Defense department professionals were Arabists, because as individuals like Komer saw it, America's "strategic and economic interests were emphatically with the Arabs. Only our political interest was with the Israelis." Besides there were thirteen Arab countries and only one "little old Israel." Oil was a key element. "It comes out and hits you in the face. Oil and strategic real estate."[5]

Kennedy decided that the Hawk anti-aircraft missiles should be sold to Israel. It was a first, but it was not nearly enough. In view of the Soviet bombers, jet-fighters, ships, submarines, artillery and tanks provided by the USSR to such Arab states as Egypt, Syria and Iraq the balance of power tilted in favor of the Arabs. Kennedy supported Israel's water development project and he rejected the State Department notion that Israel should accept hundreds of thousands of Arabs into its minuscule frontiers. But perhaps most importantly Kennedy clearly indicated that he would not tolerate any harm coming to Israel. Again and again he would advise Israeli leaders that the Jewish State was as important to the United States as was Great Britain. But he would go no further. Israel would not be included in any NATO-type alliance. Regardless of the many requests made by Israeli leaders he would support the State Department stance: no dual alliance with Israel. While he backed Israel in its struggle for survival he could not agree to a dual alliance. For it was believed that if the United States agreed to such an alliance it might lose the Arabs to the Russians and the balance of power would tilt in favor of the Russians. When Ben-Gurion came to realize that an alliance with the United States was not attainable he suggested that the United States and Russia agree to guarantee the independence and territorial integrity of the Middle Eastern States. But the Kennedy administration rejected both propositions. As Arthur Schlesinger Jr. wrote in *A Thousand Days*, while Kennedy "believed strongly in America's moral commitment to Israeli security and took steps to strengthen Israel's ability to resist aggression," he followed the American tradition of placating Arab ambitions even those of President Nasser's empire goals.[6] As Kennedy gave Egypt economic aid for food, he in effect enabled the Egyptians to use their resources to purchase weapons for their expansionist wars against Yemen, Saudi Arabia and Algeria. The Russians continued to stoke the fires of discontent and to encourage the Arabs to plan their next "round" against Israel.

Fully convinced in the righteousness of the cause and realizing that his best efforts to persuade Kennedy to establish an alliance with Israel would not succeed, Ben-Gurion concluded that Israel had little choice but to develop such might that both Israel's friends and enemies would realize that Israel would pursue every possible path in order to survive.

Despite Kennedy's appropriate words and good deeds Israel remained at an immense disadvantage in relation to the vast lands, arms, wealth, and resources held by the Arabs. It was because of those great disadvantages that Prime Minister Ben-Gurion chose to develop Israel's scientific explorations, including its nuclear research. Israel was forced to pursue this path in view of the multitude of its enemies: Somehow Ben-Gurion did not consider that at least two could play at that game. Nor did he contemplate the possible opposition that might come from President Kennedy. The Cuban missile crisis and the resulting U.S.-USSR nuclear confrontation only served to further stimulate Kennedy's effort to prevent the proliferation of nuclear weapons.

Ben-Gurion learned that Israel could not rely upon the goodwill of the United States, France, Britain, Russia or any other earthly powers. Friendship among states was temporary and uncertain. It would last for as long as it was convenient for the states involved.

Although Kennedy sympathized with Israel's need for self-defense he would not condone its possible researches into nuclear weaponry. Kennedy stood fast against the proliferation of nuclear weapons. Since the United States provided Israel with some aid such as Hawk missiles, the Kennedy administration insisted upon inspections of Israel's research facilities. While Israel agreed to some inspections, Ben-Gurion was opposed to biannual visits as the Kennedy administration requested. Ben-Gurion felt that his country's capacity for self-defense was its own sovereign business. Whether his country had the nuclear means with which to defend itself was likewise its own business. It certainly was not the business of those like Egypt and Iraq who were prepared to massacre the people of Israel. The very idea that Israel might have such weapons could persuade its enemies from attacking. Israel felt that its sovereignty and independence came into question. Moreover, its diplomats and leadership repeatedly asked why such inspections were not demanded from such Arab states as Egypt. They could likewise have asked why such inspections were not demanded from France, Britain, India, Russia or the United States? The Israeli prime ministers did not want Israel to be dealt with as if it were a dependency or a satellite. They believed that a friend should be treated with respect. But the Israeli leaders seemed not to realize that the greater the friendship and alliance, the greater the dependence on the goodwill of that friend. With all the dynamism and wisdom that Ben-Gurion and his fellow Israeli leaders may have displayed, they were at times somewhat naive.

JFK and the State Department were likewise somewhat naive as they believed that they could persuade the Arabs to be true reliable towers of friendship. Kennedy provided Nasser with hundreds of millions of dollars so that Egypt could purchase American grains and foods. But President Nasser could not be diverted from his goals of establishing a greater Egyptian empire. Kennedy recognized a regime that Nasser helped establish through military intervention in Yemen, but that did not dissuade Nasser from his pursuit of empire and further ambitions in oil rich Saudi Arabia.

Ben-Gurion and his successor, Levi Eshkol, gallantly defended Israel's independence, and they pursued greater friendship with the United States, but they thereby exposed their country to the animosity of the Soviet Union.

Israel's struggle for survival never got easier. With the passage of time the challenges it faced grew more awesome and difficult, but then the same could be said for the challenges that the United States faced. While the friendship of the United States and Israel was useful to both countries it likewise brought greater responsibilities to both.

NOTES

PREFACE

1. Public Papers of the Presidents of the United States: John F. Kennedy, 1963 (Washington, D.C., 1964) p. 280.

CHAPTER 1

1. Joseph P. Kennedy to Secretary of State Rusk, Telegram, November 14, 1938, State Department File No. 840.48 Refugees/896, National Archives, Washington, D.C.

2. Nahum Goldmann and Louis Lipsky to Louis D. Brandeis, November 17, 1938, Robert Szold Papers.

3. Joseph P. Kennedy to Secretary of State, Telegram, November 14, 1938, State Department File No. 840.48 Refugees/896, National Archives, Washington, D.C.

4. Memo of Conversation between Sir Ronald Lindsay and Undersecretary of State Sumner Welles, November 17, 1938, State Department File No. 840.48 Refugees/9111/2, National Archives, Washington, D.C.

5. Joseph P. Kennedy to Secretary of State Hull, Telegram, November 18, 1938, State Department File No. 840.48 Refugees/916, National Archives, Washington, D.C.

6. Nahum Goldmann and Louis Lipsky to Louis D. Brandeis, November 17, 1938, Robert Szold Papers, Zionist Archives, New York.

7. Justice Louis D. Brandeis to Robert Szold, November 17, 1938, Robert Szold Papers, Zionist Archives, New York.

8. FDR to Harold Ickes, President's Office File 3186, December 18, 1940, FDR Papers, FDR Library, Hyde Park, New York.

9. Joseph P. Kennedy Diary entry for November 15, 1938, Diary Box 91, File 1938, October–December, Joseph P. Kennedy Papers, The John F. Kennedy Library, Boston, Mass. After having examined the JPK Papers at the Kennedy library they were rearranged by the archivist in charge.

10. A. Smith, ed., *Hostage to Fortune: The Letters of Joseph P. Kennedy* (New York, 2001) p. 110.

11. Ibid.

12. Ibid.

13. Joseph P. Kennedy Jr. (18 years of age), to Joseph P. Kennedy, April; 23, 1934, A. Smith, *JPK Letters,* pp. 130–132.

14. Joseph P. Kennedy Jr. to Mother and Dad, August 25, 1942, Family Correspondence, Box 1, File 7/1942–12/7/1942, Joseph P. Kennedy Papers, John F. Kennedy Library (JFKL), Boston.

15. Joseph P. Kennedy to Joseph P. Kennedy Jr., May 4, 1934, A. Smith, *JPK Letters*, p. 133.

16. Joseph P. Kennedy Jr. (23 years old), Notes, June 10, 1939, A. Smith, *JPK Letters,* pp. 338–340.

17. Ibid., pp. 340–341. William E. Dodd criticized the Nazi German government for its anti-Jewish policies.

18. A. Smith, *JPK Letters*, pp. 340–341.

19. Joseph P. Kennedy to George St. John, November 21, 1933, A. Smith, *JPK Letters*, p. 120.

20. A. Smith, *JPK Letters*, p. 298.

21. Joseph P. Kennedy to John F. Kennedy, December 5, 1934, Family Correspondence Box 1, File 1, 1929–1932, Joseph P. Kennedy Papers, JFKL.

22. Joseph P. Kennedy to Felix Frankfurter, December 5, 1933, A. Smith, *JPK Letters*, pp. 121–122.

23. Joseph P. Kennedy to Father Charles Coughlin, August 18, 1936, A. Smith, *JPK Letters*, p. 187.

24. Ibid.

25. Ibid., 231. Conversations with Roosevelt and Hull, February 22, 1938, JPK Diary, Box 91, File 1938, Joseph P. Kennedy Papers, JFKL.

26. A. Smith, *JPK Letters*, p. 236.

27. Ibid., 239.

28. Ibid.

29. Joseph P. Kennedy to Arthur Krock, March 21, 1938, A. Smith, *JPK Letters*, p. 246.

30. Conversations with Roosevelt and Hull, February 22, 1938, JPK Diary Box 91, File 1938, Joseph P. Kennedy Papers, JFKL.

31. Ibid.

32. Joseph P. Kennedy to Arthur Krock, March 21, 1938, A. Smith, *JPK Letters*, pp. 247–248.

33. Ibid.

34. Joseph P. Kennedy Diary entry September 27, 1938, JPK Diary Box 91, File 1938, JPK Papers, JFKL.

35. Ibid.

36. JPK Diary entry September 28, 1938, JPK Diary Box 91, File June–September, 1938, JPK Papers, JFKL.

37. Ibid.

38. Joseph P. Kennedy to T. J. White, November 12, 1938, A. Smith, *JPK Letters*, p. 299.

39. Kristallnacht, November 9–10, 1938.

40. Joseph P. Kennedy to Charles Lindbergh, November 12, 1938, A. Smith, *JPK Letters*, pp. 300–301.

41. JPK Diary entry, February 9, 1939, JPK Diary Box 91, File February–March 1939, JFKL.

42. Ibid., Smith, *JPK Letters*, pp. 231–233.

43. Joseph P. Kennedy to Kick, August 2, 1940, Family Correspondence, Box 1, 1940–1942, JPK Papers, JFKL.

44. Ibid.

45. Ibid.

46. Joseph P. Kennedy to Rose Kennedy, March 20, 1940, A. Smith, *JPK Letters*, pp. 410–411.

47. A. Smith, *JPK Letters*, p. 233.

48. Ibid. That sort of claim appears in such books as Ronald Kessler, *The Sins of the Father: Joseph P. Kennedy and the Dynasty He Founded* (New York, 1996) pp. 45–47; A. Smith, *JPK Letters*, pp. 233–299.

49. Ibid.

50. Ibid.

51. Ibid., pp. 233–234.

52. Ibid.

53. Joseph P. Kennedy to Robert Kennedy, September 11, 1940, *JPK Letters*, pp. 469–470.

54. JPK Diary Notation of conference with Winston S. Churchill, June 11, 1940, JPK Diary Box 92, File June–July, 1940, Joseph P. Kennedy Papers, JFKL.

55. JPK Diary, June 12, 1940, A. Smith, *JPK Letters*, pp. 438–439.

56. Joseph P. Kennedy, September 10, 1940, A. Smith, *JPK Letters*, p. 466.

57. Joseph P. Kennedy to Edward Kennedy, September 11, 1940, A. Smith, *JPK Letters*, pp. 470–471.

58. Joseph P. Kennedy, Press Release, December 1, 1940, A. Smith, *JPK Letters*, p. 497.

59. John F. Kennedy Memorandum for Joseph P. Kennedy dated December 6, 1940, A. Smith, *JPK Letters*, p. 498.

60. Ibid., p. 500.

61. Ibid., p. 504.

62. Ibid., p. 504.

63. JPK Diary notation, Box 92, File 1943, Newspaper Release August 20, 1943, Joseph P. Kennedy Papers, JFKL.

64. Ibid.

65. John F. Kennedy to Family, August 13, 1943, A. Smith, *JPK Letters*, p. 569.

66. Joseph P. Kennedy Jr. to Rose Kennedy and Joseph P. Kennedy, August 4, 1944, A. Smith, *JPK Letters*, pp. 590–598.

67. A. Smith, *JPK Letters*, p. 519.

68. Ibid., p. 599.

69. Ibid., p. 612.

70. Joseph P. Kennedy to Kathleen Kennedy Hartington, May 1, 1945, A. Smith, *JPK Letters*, p. 617.

71. H. Druks, *The U.S. and Israel, 1945–1973* (New York, 1979) p. 19.

72. Truman may have referred to the 982 people, most of whom were Jewish, who were brought to Ft. Ontario, Oswego, New York, at FDR's invitation in August 1944. FDR and the War Refugee Board's plan was to have these people re-

turned to Europe once the war would be over. It was Harry S Truman who decided in January 1946 to permit them to choose whether to remain in America, return to Europe or sail for the Land of Israel. Truman, or whoever wrote this "journal" entry had forgotten that Truman had given the "Displaced Persons" the right to remain in America. That journal entry was dated 1947. Had he so quickly forgotten his own decision and executive order of January 1946.

73. Harry S Truman Journal entry, July 21, 1947, Harry S Truman Library, Independence, Mo.

74. A. Smith, *JPK Letters*, pp. 512–513.

75. JPK Diary notation, Conversations with FDR 1944, JPK Diary Box 92, File 1944–1945, Joseph P. Kennedy Papers, JFKL.

76. Ibid.
77. Ibid.
78. Ibid.
79. Ibid.
80. Ibid.
81. Ibid.
82. Ibid.
83. Ibid.
84. Ibid.
85. Ibid.

86. Joseph P. Kennedy to J. Edgar Hoover, October 11, 1955, A. Smith, *JPK Letters,* p. 671.

87. John F. Kennedy to Eleanor Roosevelt, December 11, 1958, A. Smith, *JFK Letters*, p. 681.

88. Rose Kennedy: Recollections of the Bay of Pigs Crisis, April 19, 1961, A. Smith, *JPK Letters*, p. 697.

89. Ibid., p. 698.

90. Rose Kennedy to Robert Kennedy, No date, A. Smith, *JPK Letters*, p. 698.

CHAPTER 2

1. Arthur Hertzberg, *A Jew in America: My Life and a People's Struggle for Identity* (San Francisco, 2003) pp. 92–93.

2. Ibid.

3. Ibid.

4. H. Druks interview with M. Gazit, August 3, 1997.

5. Robert F. Kennedy interview volume 8, p. 636, John F. Kennedy Library, Boston. Hereafter cited as JFKL.

6. Ibid.

7. Jack Kennedy to Joseph P. Kennedy, 1939 (no other date is given to the letter), President's Office Files, 135, JFKL.

8. Ibid.

9. Ibid.

10. N. Hamilton, *JFK, Reckless Youth* (New York, 1992) pp. 290–293; Michael O'Brien, *John F. Kennedy, A Biography* (New York, 2005) 98–99; Andrea B. Goldstein, Reference Archivist, Harvard University Archives, to H. Druks, July 28, 2005; Michelle Gachette, Reference Assistant, Harvard University Archives, to H. Druks, September 16, 2005; JFK to JPK (n.d.) JFK Personal Papers, Box 4B, JFKL.

11. JFK to editor of *The Harvard Crimson*, June 9, 1940, JFKL.

12. Hirsh Freed Interview, Oral History Collection, JFKL.

13. Ibid.

14. Phil Fine Interview, JFKL.

15. Hirsh Fred Interview.

16. Myer Feldman Interview, Oral History Collection, JFKL, p. 643.

17. Ibid.

18. Ibid.

19. Ibid.

20. ZOA, *John F. Kennedy on Israel, Zionism and Jewish Issues* (New York, 1965) pp. 11–14. Hereafter cited as *JFK on Israel*.

21. Ibid., p. 14.

22. Ibid., p. 15.

23. Ibid.

24. Ibid.

25. Robert Kennedy's papers, JFKL.

26. *JFK on Israel*, p. 21.

27. Ibid., pp. 22, 24, 26.

28. John F. Kennedy, *The Strategy of Peace* (New York, 1960) p. 118.

29. *The New York Times*, July 16, 1960.

30. *The New York Times*, April 20, 1963, H. Druks, *From Truman through Johnson, A Documentary History* (New York, 1970) pp. 5–6.

31. *The New York Times* (August 26, 1960).

32. Ibid.

33. Ibid.

34. Ibid.

35. Ibid.

36. Myer Feldman Interview, p. 399.

37. Ibid., p. 461.

38. Ibid.

39. Ibid., p. 462.

40. Ibid., p. 463.

41. Ibid., p. 482.

42. Ibid.

43. Hirsh Freed Interview.

44. Ibid.

45. Ibid.

46. Ibid.

47. N. Hamilton, *JFK Reckless Youth*, 85–86; James MacGregor Burns, *John Kennedy A Political Profile* (New York, 1959, 1960), pp. 24–28; Michael O'Brien, *John F. Kennedy A Biography*, pp. 65–68.

48. Hirsh Freed Interview.

49. *JFK on Israel*, p. 11.

50. Hirsh Freed Interview.

51. John F. Kennedy speech November 14, 1951, JFKL.

52. W. Bass, *Support Any Friend, Kennedy's Middle East and the Making of the U.S.-Israel Alliance* (New York, 2003) p. 52.

53. *Congressional Record*, 1957, pp. 3178–3180.

54. Remarks of Senator John F. Kennedy before Temple B'rith Kodesh, Rochester, New York, October 1, 1959, JFKL.

55. Ibid.

56. Ibid.

57. Kennedy, *Strategy of Peace*, p. 107.

58. Ibid., p. 108.

59. Ibid., p. 109.

60. W. Bass, *Support Any Friend*, p. 54.

61. ZOA, *JFK on Israel*, p. 61.

62. Dean Rusk statement of July 12, 1962, President's Office Files, 118, JFKL.

63. Interview with Mordechai Gazit, August 3, 1997, Jerusalem.

64. Dean Rush Interview, JFKL.

65. Meyer Feldman Interview, p. 476.

66. Ibid., pp. 474–475.

67. U.S. Security Guarantees to Israel, Israel Foreign Ministry 3294/8, Israel State Archives, Jerusalem.

68. John F. Kennedy–Ben-Gurion meeting, May 30, 1961, Foreign Office 3295/32, Israel State Archives, Jerusalem. Hereafter cited as JFK–BG meeting. In 1951 BG had referred to Egypt as having about 20 million people. See page 22.

69. Ibid.

70. Ibid.

71. Ibid.

72. Ibid.

73. Ibid.

74. Ibid.

75. Sherman Kent, CIA Memo for the Director, March 6, 1963, President's Office Files, 119A, JFKL.

76. Ibid.

77. Memo from Dean Rusk to President John F. Kennedy, May 25, 1961, President's Office Files, 119A, JFKL.

78. JFK–BG meeting.

79. Ibid.

80. Ibid.

81. Ibid. For a more detailed discussion regarding Israel and the atom, see chapters 3, 4, 5 and 6.

82. Myer Feldman Interview, p. 469.

83. Ibid., p. 470.

84. Ibid.

85. JFK–BG meeting.

86. Ibid.

87. Department of State, *Foreign Relations of the United States 1961–1963*, vol. XVIII (Washington, D.C., 1995) pp. 56–58.

88. Ibid.

89. Ibid., p. 58.

90. Letter from President Kennedy to Prime Minister Ben-Gurion, August 14, 1962, *Foreign Relations of the United States 1961–1963*, XVIII, pp. 60–61.

91. Ambassador Barbour to Dean Rusk, June 9, 1962, JFK Presidential Papers, NSF 118, JFKL.

92. Ibid.

93. Dean Rusk to U.S. Middle East Embassies, May 24, 1962, JFK Presidential Papers, NSF 118, JFKL.

94. McGeorge Bundy memo to Phillips Talbot, May 28, 1962, regarding conversations with Peres, May 21, 1962, JFK Presidential Papers, NSF 118, JFKL.

95. Ibid.

96. Ibid.

97. President John F. Kennedy to Prime Minister Ben-Gurion, June 13, 1962, JFK Presidential Papers, NSF 118, JFKL.

98. Ben-Gurion to President Kennedy, June 24, 1962, JFK Presidential Papers, NSF 118, JFKL.

99. Ibid.

100. Ibid.

101. Ibid.

102. Myer Feldman Interview, p. 537.

103. Ibid., pp. 535–536.

104. Myer Feldman Interview, p. 537; Ambassador Barbour to State Department, August 19, 1962, NSF, 118A, JFKL.

105. Minutes of meeting at the prime minister's home, August 19, 1962, Foreign Ministry 4312/6, Israel State Archives, Jerusalem.

106. Myer Feldman Interview, p. 538.

107. Ibid.

108. Ibid., pp. 66–67.

109. Ibid.

110. Ibid., from Rusk to the U.S. Embassy in UAR, August 22, 1962, p. 71.

111. Myer Feldman Interview, p. 540.

112. Ibid., p. 540; From Feldman to President Kennedy, August 24, 1962, *Foreign Relations of the United States 1961–1963*, XVIII, p. 62.

113. Myer Feldman Interview, pp. 539–541.

114. Ibid., p. 549.

115. Ibid., p. 541.

116. Ibid., p. 543.

117. Ibid., p. 546.

118. Ibid.

119. Ibid.

120. Ibid.

121. Ibid.

122. Myer Feldman Interview, p. 546; Memo from Komer to President's Special Assistant for National Security Affairs (Bundy), September 14, 1962, *Foreign Relations of the United States 1961–1963*, XVIII, pp. 96–97.

123. McGeorge Bundy to Robert W. Komer, September 20, 1962, *Foreign Relations of the United States 1961–1963*, p. 111.

124. Meeting of Mrs. Meir with Secretary of State Rusk, September 26, 1962, signed by Avraham Harman, Israel Foreign Office Papers 3377/5, Israel State Archives, Jerusalem.

125. Ibid.

126. Ibid.

127. Ibid.

128. Interview with Mordechai Gazit, August 3, 1997, Jerusalem.

129. Meeting Minutes of Minister Gazit, Ambassador Harmon and Acting Secretary of State, Myer Feldman Interview, p. 489.

130. *The New York Times*, September 27, 1962.

131. David Ben-Gurion Interview, Oral History Collection, JFKL.

132. State Department Memo of Conversation with Foreign Minister Golda Meir, December 27, 1962, President's Office Files, 119A, JFKL.

133. Ibid.

134. Ibid.

135. Ibid.

136. Ibid.

137. *Foreign Relations of the United States 1961–1963*, XVIII, pp. 282–283.

138. Ibid.

139. Ibid.

140. Ibid.

141. Ibid.

142. *U.S. Foreign Relations of the United States 1961–1963*, pp. 485–486.

143. George Ball to U.S. Embassy in Israel, April 27, 1963, *U.S. Foreign Relations of the United States 1961–1963*, XVIII pp. 487–488.

144. Myer Feldman Interview, pp. 479–481.

145. Ibid.

146. Minutes of Meeting with Minister Gazit, Ambassador Harmon and Acting Secretary of State, *Foreign Relations of the United States 1961–1963*, XVIII, p. 489.

147. Myer Feldman Interview, pp. 578–580.

148. Ibid., p. 580.

149. President Kennedy to Prime Minister Eskol, October 2, 1963, JFK Presidential Papers, NSF, Komer 427, JFKL.

150. Ibid., p. 540.

151. Ibid., pp. 524–525.

152. Ibid.

153. Ibid., p. 526.

154. Ibid.

155. U.S. Department of State circular, April 11, 1963, President's Office Files, 119A, JFKL.

156. Ambassador Barbour to Secretary of State, April 19, 1963, President's Office Files, JFKL.

157. Myer Feldman Interview, p. 508.

158. Ibid., p. 509.

159. George Ball Memo which was the basis of Kennedy's letter to Ben-Gurion, May 4, 1963, President's Office Files, 119A, JFKL.

160. Ibid.

161. Myer Feldman Interview, p. 522.

162. Ibid., pp. 523–524.

163. Ibid.

164. Ambassador Barbour to Secretary of State, May 5, 1963, President's Office Files, 119A, JFKL.

165. Robert W. Komer's Memo for the Record, May 15, 1963, President's Office Files, 119A, JFKL.

166. Memo of Conversation, May 15, 1963, President's Office Files, 119A, JFKL.

167. Memo for the record by Robert W. Komer, November 18, 1963, President's Political Files, 199A, JFKL.

168. Ibid.

169. Ibid.

170. Ibid.

171. Interview with Mordechai Gazit, August 3, 1997, Jerusalem.

172. Ibid.

173. Ibid.

174. Ibid.

175. Ibid.

176. Mordechai Gazit, *President Kennedy's Policy Toward the Arab States and Israel. Analysis and Documents* (Tel Aviv, 1983) p. 48.

177. Myer Feldman Interview, pp. 519–520.

178. Ibid.

CHAPTER 3

1. Avner Cohen, *Israel and the Bomb* (New York, 1998) pp. 42–43.

2. Ibid., p. 43.

3. Ibid., p. 55.

4. Secretary Christian Herter to Prime Minister Ben-Gurion, August 4, 1960, Israel Foreign Office Papers, 3293/44, Israel State Archives, Jerusalem.

5. Ibid.

6. Ibid.

7. U.S. Department of State, *Foreign Relations of the United States 1958–1960*, XIII, *Arab-Israeli Dispute; United Arab Republic; North Africa* (Washington, D.C., 1992) pp. 393–394.

8. Ibid.

9. "Summary of Additional Recent Information on Israeli Atomic Energy Program," January 17, 1961, *Foreign Relations of the United States 1961–1963*, XVIII (Washington, D.C., 1995) pp. 5–6; A. Cohen, *Israel and the Bomb*, pp. 88–89; CIA Bulletin, April 27, 1961, NSF Box 119A, Israel, Ben-Gurion Visit, JFKL.

10. A. Cohen, *Israel and the Bomb*, p. 87.

11. Ambassador Harman to Israel's Foreign Office, December 21, 1960, State of Israel, *Documents on the Foreign Policy of Israel*, 14 (1960); Companion Volume (Jerusalem, 1997) pp. 178–179. Hereafter cited as DFPI 14.

12. Ibid.

13. Ibid.

14. Memo of a Conversation, December 20, 1960, *Foreign Relations of the United States*, XVIII, pp. 396–399.

15. Ibid.

16. Ibid.; Yahil to Harman, December 20, 1960, DFPI 14, pp. 175–176.

17. Ibid.

18. *The New York Times*, December 23, 1960; Department of State, *Foreign Relations of the United States 1961–1963*, XVII, pp. 1–3.

19. Ibid., pp. 10–12.

20. Ibid.
21. Ibid.
22. Ibid.
23. Memo on Israel's relations with France and its assistance in nuclear research programs, January 26, 1961, President's Office Files, Countries, Box 119A, JFKL.
24. Ibid.
25. Ibid.
26. Ibid.
27. Ibid.
28. Ibid.
29. Ibid.
30. Ibid.
31. Ibid.
32. Dean Rusk to JFK, Memo for the President, January 30, 1961, President's Office Files, 119A, JFKL.
33. Ibid.
34. Ibid.
35. Ibid.
36. Memo of Conversation between Reid and Kennedy, January 31, 1961, *Foreign Relations of the United States 1961–1963*, XVII, pp. 10–11.
37. Ibid.
38. Ibid.
39. Ibid.
40. Memo of Conversation between G. Lewis Jones, Assistant Secretary for NEA, and Avraham Harman, February 3, 1961, President's Office Files, 119A, JFKL.
41. Ibid.
42. Ibid.
43. Ibid.
44. Dean Rusk Memo for the President, March 3, 1961, President's Office Files, 119A, JFKL.
45. Undated notation, Israel Foreign Office Papers, 3294/7I, Israel State Archives, Jerusalem.
46. Ibid.
47. Ibid.
48. Memo of Conversation, February 16, 1961, President's Personal Papers, 118, JFKL.
49. Ibid.
50. Ibid.
51. Ibid.
52. Warren Bass, *Support Any Friend* (New York, 2003) p. 186; Richard Reeves, *President Kennedy: Profile of Power* (New York, 1994) pp. 29–33.
53. *Foreign Relations of the United States 1961–1963*, XVII, Near East, pp. 1–3.
54. Ibid.
55. Ambassador Harman to Israel Foreign Office, February 21, 1961, Israel Foreign Office Papers, 3294/19, Israel State Archives.
56. Ibid.

57. Ibid.

58. Ibid.

59. J. W. Fulbright Interview, JFKL.

60. Ambassador Harman to Israel Foreign Office, February 21, 1961, Israel Foreign Office Papers, 3294/19, Israel State Archives.

61. Unsigned Memorandum for Myer Feldman, May 2, 1963, JFKL.

62. Ibid.

63. Ibid.

64. Ibid.

65. Ibid.

66. Ibid.

67. Ibid.

68. Ibid., pp. 9–10.

69. Memo of Conversation between Harman, Gazit, Herter, G. Lewis Jones, January 11, 1961, *Foreign Relations of the United States 1961–1963*, XVII, Supplementary ISR1/1–2.

70. Ibid.

71. Ibid.

72. Ibid.

73. Ibid., ISR1/3.

74. Ibid.

75. Ibid.

76. Ibid.

77. Ibid.

78. Ibid.

79. Ibid. When Herter wanted to know where Israel obtained its funds for this project, Harman said, "a number of its friends felt that over the longer term nuclear power would be important to the Israeli economy and that Israel should have the means at this time to put itself in a position to take advantage of nuclear power."

80. Memo of Conversation, February 3, 1961, JFK Presidential Papers, NSF 118, JFKL.

81. Ibid.

82. Ibid.

83. Ibid.

84. Memo of Harman's conversation with Rusk, February 13, 1961, JFK Presidential Papers, NSF 118, JFKL.

85. Ibid.

86. Memorandum of Conversation, February 16, 1961, JFK Presidential Papers, NSF 118, JFKL.

87. Ibid.

88. Ibid.

89. Ibid.

90. Ibid.

91. Ibid.

92. Memo for McGeorge Bundy from Walter Stoesel Jr., Director Executive Secretariat, State Department, February 24, 1961, JFK Presidential Papers, NSF 118, JFKL.

93. Ibid.

94. Dean Rusk circular, March 3, 1961, *Foreign Relations of the United States 1961–1963*, XVII, ISR 2A/12, Supplementary.

95. G. Lewis Jones Memo of Conversation, March 28, 1961, JFK Presidential Papers, NSF 118, JFKL.

96. Ibid.

97. Ibid.

98. Rusk Memo for the President, May 5, 1961, JFK Presidential Papers, NSF 118, JFKL.

99. McGeorge Bundy Memo for the President, May 11, 1961, JFK Presidential Papers, NSF 118, JFKL.

100. L. D. Battle Memorandum for McGeorge Bundy, May 18, 1961, JFK Presidential Papers, NSF 118, JFKL.

101. Memo from Dean Rusk to President Kennedy, May 25, 1961, President's Office Files, 119A, JFKL.

102. L. D. Battle Memo for McGeorge Bundy, May 26, 1961, JFK Presidential Papers, NSF 118, JFKL.

103. Ibid.

104. Ibid.

105. John F. Kennedy to Ben-Gurion, May 30, 1961, Israel Foreign Office 3295/32, Israel State Archives, Jerusalem.

106. State Department of U.S. Middle East embassies, May 10, 1961, JFK Presidential Papers, NSF 118, JFKL.

107. Ibid.

CHAPTER 4

1. John F. Kennedy–Ben-Gurion meeting, May 30, 1961, Israel Foreign Office 3295/32, Israel State Archives, Jerusalem.

2. Ibid.

3. Ibid.

4. Ibid.

5. Ibid.

6. Memo from Dean Rusk to President John F. Kennedy, May 25, 1961, President's Office Files, 119A, John F. Kennedy Library (JFKL), Boston.

7. Myer Feldman Interview, Oral History Collection, JFKL, Boston, p. 520.

8. Aide Memoire for talks with President Johnson and Secretary Dean Rusk, undated, 3501/17/3, Israel Foreign Office Papers, Jerusalem.

9. John F. Kennedy–Ben-Gurion meeting, May 30, 1961, Foreign Office 3295/32, Israel State Archives, Jerusalem.

10. Ibid.

11. Ibid.; Ambassador Barnes, Tel Aviv to State Department, June 2, 1961, JFK Presidential Papers, NSF 118, JFKL.

12. Ibid.

13. Ibid.

14. U.S. Embassy Ottawa to Rusk, June 7, 1961, JFK Presidential Papers, NSF 118, JFKL.

15. Avner Cohen, *Israel and the Bomb* (Columbia University Press, New York, 1988) pp. 74–75.

16. Ambassador McClintock in Beirut to Secretary Rusk, June 23, 1961, JFK Presidential Papers, NSF 118, JFKL.

17. NEA State Department to Beirut, Bonn and Tel Aviv embassies, June 24, 1961, JFK Presidential Papers, NSF 118, JFKL.

18. Ibid.

19. Barbour to Rusk, June 21, 1961, JFK Presidential Papers, NSF 118, JFKL.

20. Rusk to Barbour, June 22,1961, JFK Presidential Papers, NSF 118, JFKL.

21. Robert W. Komer Memo, October 10, 1961, President's Office Files, NSF 3223, JFKL.

22. A. Harman to Israel Foreign Office, March 9, 1962, Israel Foreign Office Papers, 3378/13, Israel State Archives, Jerusalem.

23. Ibid.

24. Phillips Talbot Interview, Oral History Collection, JFKL.

25. Ibid.

26. McGeorge Bundy to Phillips Talbot, May 28, 1962, regarding conference with Peres, May 21, 1962, JFK Presidential Papers, JFKL.

27. P. Talbot notation, June 22, 1962, JFK Presidential Papers, NSF 118, JFKL.

28. *The Congressional Record*, June 22, 1962.

29. President Kennedy to Ben-Gurion, June 13, 1962, President's Office Files, NSF, Komer 427, JFKL.

30. Ben-Gurion to John F. Kennedy, June 24, 1962, President's Office Files, 119A, JFKL.

31. Barbour to Rusk, October 5, 1962, JFK Presidential Papers, 119, JFKL.

32. President Kennedy to Prime Minister Ben-Gurion, August 15, 1962, JFK Presidential Papers, NSF 118, JFKL.

33. Prime Minister Ben-Gurion to President Kennedy, August 20, 1962, JFK Presidential Papers, NSF 119, JFKL.

34. Joseph O. Sherman, Second Secretary of the Legation to Department of State, September 14, 1962, JFK Presidential Papers, NSF 119, JFKL.

35. Ibid.

36. Ambassador Harman to Dr. Levavi, June 20, 1962, Israel Foreign Office Papers, 111.1/21, Israel State Archives, Jerusalem.

37. Ibid.

38. *The New York Times* (April 13, 1961).

39. Robert F. Kennedy, *Thirteen Days: A Memoir of the Cuban Missile Crisis* (New York, 1971) pp. 31–33.

40. *The New York Times* (October 23, 1962).

41. Kennedy, *Thirteen Days*, p. 53.

42. Ibid., p. 54.

43. Ibid.

44. Ibid., p. 55.

45. Prime Minister Ben-Gurion to President Kennedy, October 29, 1962, President's Office Files, 119, JFKL.

46. President John F. Kennedy to Ambassador Adlai E. Stevenson, October 29, 1962, The Adlai E. Stevenson Papers, Box 47, File 5, The Mudd Archives Library, Princeton University.

47. Memo from R. W. Komer to President Kennedy, December 22, 1962, *Foreign Relations of the United States 1961–1963*, XVIII, pp. 272–273.

48. Memo of Conversation between President Kennedy and Foreign Minister Golda Meir, December 27, 1962, JFK Presidential Papers, NSF 119, JFKL.

49. Memo from R. W. Komer to President Kennedy, December 22, 1962, *Foreign Relations 1961–1963*, XVIII, pp. 272–273.

50. Ibid.

51. Jeffrey Michaels, *Shifting Sands: John F. Kennedy and the Middle East* (Yale Univ. Ph.D., 2002).

52. Memo of Conversation between Kennedy and Foreign Minister Meir, December 27, 1962, *Foreign Relations of the United States 1961–1963*, XVIII, pp. 276–283.

53. Ibid.

54. Ibid.

55. Ibid.

56. Ibid.

57. Ibid.

58. Ibid.

59. Ibid.

60. Ibid.

61. Memo for the Record by Robert Komer, January 14, 1963, JFK Presidential Papers, NSF 119, JFKL.

62. Ibid.

63. Robert W. Komer Memo to President John F. Kennedy, February 12, 1963, JFK Presidential Papers, NSF 119, JFKL.

64. Memo for the Director from Sherman Kent Chairman, March 6, 1963; Consequences of Israeli Acquisition of Nuclear Capability, JFK Presidential Papers, NSF 119, JFKL, and President's Office Files, 119A, JFKL.

65. Ibid.

66. Ibid.

67. Ibid.

68. Ibid.

69. Ibid.

70. Ibid.

71. Ibid.

72. *Public Papers of the Presidents of the United States: John F. Kennedy, 1963* (Washington, D.C., 1964) p. 280.

73. Robert Komer Memo for President John F. Kennedy, March 22, 1963, JFK Presidential Papers, NSF 119, JFKL.

74. Ambassador Barbour to Dean Rusk, April 4, 1963, JFK Presidential Papers, NSF 119, JFKL.

75. Ibid.

76. McGeorge Bundy notation dated March 26, 1963, *Foreign Relations of the United States 1961–1963*, XVIII, p. 435.

77. Myer Feldman Interview, p. 476.

78. *Foreign Relations of the United States 1961–1963*, XVIII, pp. 449, 450–451.

79. Department of State Memo, April 2, 1963, JFK Presidential Papers, NSF 119, JFKL.

80. Memo of Conversation, April 8, 1963, President's Office Files, 118, JFKL.

81. Department of State Memo, April 2, 1963, JFK Presidential Papers, NSF 119, JFKL; Memo of Conversation, April 8, 1963, President's Office Files, 118, JFKL.
82. Ibid.
83. Ibid.; Memo of Conversation, Feldman phone call with Talbot, April 5, 1963, NSF 119A, JFKL; Ball telegram to Barbour, April 4, 1963, *Foreign Relations of the United States 1961–1963*, XVIII, pp. 449–450.
84. Shimon Peres, *Battling for Peace: Memoirs* (London, 1995) p. 258.
85. Ibid.
86. Ben-Gurion to President Kennedy, April 26, 1963, President's Office Files, 119A, JFKL.
87. Talbot-Feldman telephone conversation, April 4, 1963, *Foreign Relations of the United States 1962–1963*, XVIII, pp. 435, 449, 450–451.
88. Interview with Mordechai Gazit, August 3, 1997, Jerusalem, Israel.
89. U.S. Embassy Tel Aviv Circular, May 1, 1963, JFK Presidential Papers, NSF 119, JFKL.
90. Ibid.
91. Ambassador Barbour to Dean Rusk, April 5, 1963, JFK Presidential Papers, NSF 119, JFKL.
92. Feldman-Harman discussions, May 6, 1963, JFK Presidential Papers, NSF 119, JFKL.
93. *The New York Times* (April 6, 1963).
94. State Department circular, April 11, 1963, President's Office Files, 119, JFKL.
95. Ambassador Barbour to Secretary Rusk, April 4, 1963, President's Office Files, 119, JFKL.

CHAPTER 5

1. Ben-Gurion to JFK, April 26, 1963, JFK Presidential Papers, NSF 119, John F. Kennedy Library (JFKL), Boston.
2. Ambassador Barbour to Dean Rusk, April 5, 1963, JFK Presidential Papers, NSF 119, JFKL.
3. Feldman-Harman discussions, May 6, 1963, JFK Presidential Papers, NSF 119, JFKL.
4. Ben-Gurion to J.F.K., April 26, 1963, JFK Presidential Papers, NSF 119, JFKL.
5. Ibid.
6. Ibid.
7. Ibid.
8. Ibid.
9. Ibid.
10. Ibid.
11. Ibid.
12. Ibid.
13. George Balb to Robert McNamara, April 27, 1963, *Foreign Relations of the United States, 1961–1963*, XVIII, p. 483.
14. Meeting with the president on the issue of the UAR and Jordan, April 27, 1963, *Foreign Relations of the United States 1961–1963*, XVIII, p. 485.

15. Komer Memo, May 2, 1963, JFK Presidential Papers, NSF, Komer 322, JFKL.

16. Ibid.

17. Komer's Memo, May 2, 1963, JFK Presidential Papers, NSF, Komer 322, JFKL.

18. Ibid.

19. Ibid.

20. Hamilton to Rusk, May 1, 1963, JFK Presidential Papers, 119, JFKL.

21. *The New York Times* (May 1, 1963) pp. 1, 5.

22. Ibid.

23. Ibid.

24. Ibid.

25. Ibid.

26. Ibid.

27. Ibid.

28. President Kennedy to Prime Minister Ben-Gurion, May 4, 1963, JFK Presidential Papers, NSF 119, Komer 427, JFKL.

29. Ibid.

30. Ibid.

31. Ibid.

32. Ibid.

33. Ibid.

34. Ibid.

35. Ibid.

36. Barbour to Dean Rusk, May 5, 1963, JFK Presidential Papers, NSF 119, JFKL.

37. Ibid.

38. Barbour to Dean Rusk, May 5, 1963, JFK Presidential Papers, NSF 119, Israel, General, JFKL.

39. Feldman-Harman meeting, May 6, 1963, JFK Presidential Papers, NSF 119, Israel, General, JFKL.

40. *The New York Times* (May 6, 1963).

41. Memo of Conversation between Avraham Harman and Myer Feldman, May 6, 1963, JFK Presidential Papers, NSF 118, JFKL.

42. Ibid.

43. Ibid.

44. Ibid.

45. *The New York Times* (May 9, 1963).

46. Ibid.

47. Ibid., May 10, 1963.

48. Ibid.

49. Ibid.

50. *The New York Times* (May 9, 1963).

51. Ibid.

52. Dean Rusk to Ambassador Barbour, May 10, 1963, JFK Presidential Papers, NSF 119, JFKL.

53. Ben-Gurion to President Kennedy, May 14, 1963, JFK Presidential Papers, JFKL.

54. Ibid.

55. Ibid., Israel State Archives, May 8, 1963, 3377/9.

56. Ben-Gurion to President Kennedy, May 14, 1963, JFK Presidential Papers, JFKL.

57. Ibid.

58. Ibid.

59. Ibid.

60. Memo of Conversation, participants W. Averell Harriman, Ambassador Avraham Harman, Minister Mordechai Gazit and William R. Crawford Jr. of Near East division, May 10, 1963, JFK Presidential Papers, NSF 119, JFKL.

61. Ibid.

62. Ibid.

63. *The New York Times* (May 14, 1963).

64. Ibid.

65. Komer Memo, May 15, 1963, JFK Presidential Papers, NSF 119, JFKL.

66. Ibid.

67. Ibid.

68. Ibid.

69. Ibid.

70. Ibid.

71. Ibid.

72. Komer Memo to JFK, May 16, 1963, JFK Presidential Papers, NSF 119, JFKL.

73. Memo of Conversation, May 8, 1963, JFK Presidential Papers, NSF 119, JFKL.

74. Ibid.

75. Ibid.

76. Ibid.

77. Ibid.

78. Ibid.

79. Ambassador Barbour to Secretary Rusk, April 19, 1963, President's Office Files, 119, JFKL.

80. Memo of Conversation, May 15, 1963, President's Office Files, 119, JFKL.

81. Ambassador Barbour to Rusk, May 16, 1963, JFK Presidential Papers, NSF 119, JFKL.

82. Ibid.

83. Ibid.

84. Ibid.

85. Ibid.

86. Ibid.

87. Ibid.

88. Ibid.

89. Ibid.

90. Ibid.

91. Ibid.

92. Ibid.

93. Ibid.

94. Ibid.

95. Ibid.
96. Ibid.
97. Ibid.
98. Ibid.
99. Ibid.
100. Ibid.
101. Ibid.
102. John F. Kennedy to Ben-Gurion, May 18, 1963, JFK Presidential Papers, NSF 119, JFKL.
103. Ibid.
104. Ibid.
105. Ibid.
106. Ibid.
107. Ibid.
108. Barbour to Rusk, May 27,1963, JFK Presidential Papers, NSF 119, Israel, JFKL.
109. Ibid.
110. Ibid.
111. June 12, 1963, *Foreign Relations of the United States 1961–1963*, XVIII, pp. 575–576.
112. May 14, 1963, *Foreign Relations of the United States 1961–1963*, XVIII, pp. 529–535; June 15, 1963, *Foreign Relations of the United States 1961–1963*, XVIII, pp. 589–592.
113. Special Assistant to the President Arthur Schlesinger Jr. to Phillips Talbot, June 5, 1963, JFK Presidential Papers, NSF, Komer 427, JFKL.
114. Ibid.
115. Ibid.
116. Ibid.
117. JFK to Ben-Gurion, June 15, 1963, POF, 119A, Israel, Security, JFKL.
118. Ibid.
119. Ambassador Barbour to Secretary of State Dean Rusk, June 17, 1963, President's Office Files, 119, JFKL.

CHAPTER 6

1. *The New York Times* (June 25, 1963).
2. *Foreign Relations of the United States, 1961–1963*, XVIII, pp. 624–625; President's Office Files, 119A, Israel, John F. Kennedy Library (JFKL), Boston.
3. *The New York Times* (June 25, 1963).
4. *The New York Times* (June 27, 1963).
5. Ibid.
6. Ibid.
7. *The New York Times* (June 30, 1963).
8. *The New York Times* (July 16, 1963).
9. Ibid.
10. Prime Minister Eshkol to President Kennedy, July 17, 1963, in Ambassador Barbour's message to Secretary of State Rusk, July 17, 1963, JFK Presidential Papers, NSF, Komer 427, JFKL.

11. Ibid.
12. Ibid.
13. Ibid.
14. Ibid.
15. Robert Komer Memo to JFK, July 19, 1963, NSF 427, Israel, Nuclear Energy Program, 1963, White House Memo, JFKL; Robert Komer Memo to JFK, July 23, 1963, NSF 884A, UAR, UAR-Israel Arms Limitation, JFKL.
16. *The New York Times* (July 20, 1963).
17. Ibid.
18. Ibid.
19. Ibid.
20. *The New York Times* (July 18, 1963).
21. *The New York Times* (July 27, 1963).
22. Ibid.
23. *The New York Times* (July 26, 1963).
24. Ibid.; *President Papers, John F. Kennedy, 1963* (Washington, D.C., 1964) pp. 601–605.
25. *The New York Times* (July 27, 1963).
26. Robert Komer, Memo of Conversation, August 9, 1963, JFK Presidential Papers, NSF, Komer 427, JFKL.
27. Ibid.
28. Ibid.
29. Ibid.
30. Ambassador Barbour to Secretary Rusk, August 19, 1963, with Prime Minister Eshkol's letter to President Kennedy, August 19, 1963, JFK Presidential Papers, NSF, Komer 427, JFKL.
31. Ibid.
32. Ibid.
33. Ibid.
34. Ibid.
35. Rusk to U.S. Embassy, August 26, 1963, with letter from President Kennedy to Prime Minister Eshkol, August 26, 1963, JFK Presidential Papers, NSF, Komer 427, JFKL.
36. President Kennedy to Prime Minister Eshkol, August 26, 1963, JFK Presidential Papers, NSF, Komer 427, JFKL.
37. Ambassador Barbour to Dean Rusk, August 8, 1963, NSF 427, Robert Komer Papers, Israel, Nuclear Energy Program, 1963, JFKL.
38. *The New York Times* (August 11, 1963).
39. *The New York Times* (August 20, 1963).
40. *The New York Times* (August 21, 1963).
41. Ibid.

CHAPTER 7

1. Memorandum for the record, Gazit-Komer conversation, September 9, 1963, JFK Presidential Papers, NSF, Komer 427, John F. Kennedy Library (JFKL), Boston.
2. Ibid.

3. President Kennedy to President Nasser, September 12, 1963, NSF 884A, United Arab Republic, UAR-Israel, Arms Limitation, JFKL; *Foreign Relations of the United States, 1961–1963*, XVIII, pp. 717–719.

4. Komer Memorandum for the Record, September 24, 1963, JFK Presidential Papers, NSF, Komer 427, JFKL.

5. President Kennedy to P.M., draft September 26, 1963, JFK Presidential Papers, NSF, Komer 427, JFKL.

6. Komer Memo of October 2, 1963, JFK Presidential Papers, Komer 428, JFKL.

7. JFK to Eshkol, President's Office Files, September 26, 1963, 119A, Israel, Security, JFKL.

8. Dean Rusk circular, November 13, 1963, JFK Presidential Papers, NSF, Komer 428, JFKL.

9. President John F. Kennedy to Prime Minister Levi Eshkol, October 3, 1963, JFK Presidential Papers, NSF 119, JFKL.

10. Prime Minister Levi Eshkol to President Kennedy, November 4, 1963, JFK Presidential Papers, NSF 427, JFKL.

11. Ibid.

12. Memo of Conversation, Harman, Gazit, Talbot and Russell, October 28, 1963, JFK Presidential Papers, NSF, Komer 428, JFKL.

13. Memo of Conversation, A. Harman, M. Gazit, Alexis Johnson and E. Earle Russell, October 17, 1963, JFK Presidential Papers, NSF, Komer 428, JFKL.

14. Memo of Conversation, Counselor, Israel Embassy Shaul bar Haim and H. Russell Jr., October 29, 1963, JFK Presidential Papers, NSF, Komer 427, JFKL.

15. Memo of Conversation between Jacob Blaustein, W. A. Harriman, J. P. Grant, Rodger P. Davies, October 31, 1963, JFK Presidential Papers, NSF, Komer 427, JFKL.

16. Ibid.

17. Ibid.

18. Ibid.

19. Ibid.

20. Ibid.

21. Ibid.

22. Ibid.

23. Ibid.

24. Prime Minister Eshkol to President Kennedy, November 4, 1963, in Ambassador Barbour's letter to Rusk, November 4, 1963, JFK Presidential Papers, NSF, Komer 427, JFKL.

25. Ibid.

26. Ibid.

27. Ibid.

28. Ibid.

29. Prime Minister Eshkol to President Kennedy, November 11, 1963, NSF 119A, Israel, JFKL.

30. Talbot remarks November 12, 1963, JFK Presidential Papers, NSF 119, JFKL.

31. Ibid.

32. President Kennedy's conversation with Ambassador Barbour, August 27, 1962, Tape # 17, JFKL.

33. Ibid.
34. Ibid.
35. Ibid.
36. Robert Komer Memorandum for the Record, November 18, 1963, JFK Presidential Papers, NSF, Komer 428, JFKL.
37. Ibid.
38. Ibid.
39. Ibid.
40. Ibid.
41. Ibid.
42. Ibid.
43. Ibid.
44. Ibid.
45. Robert W. Komer Memorandum for the Record, November 18, 1963, JFK Presidential Papers, NSF, Komer 427, 428, JFKL.
46. Ibid.
47. Ibid.
48. Ibid.
49. Ibid.
50. Ibid.
51. Ibid.
52. Ibid.
53. Ibid.
54. Ibid.
55. Ibid.
56. Ibid.
57. Ibid.
58. Ibid.
59. Komer Memorandum for the record of conversation with Gazit, November 21, 1963, JFK Presidential Papers, NSF 119A, JFKL.
60. Ibid.
61. Ibid.
62. Ibid.
63. Ibid.
64. William Brubeck Memo for McGeorge Bundy regarding U.S. actions favorable to Israel, JFK Presidential Papers, NSF 119, JFKL.
65. JFK Memo of meeting with CIA Director McCone, Philipps Talbot and Robert Komer, *Foreign Relations of the United States 1961–1963*, XVIII, p. 590.
66. Ambassador Harman to Israel Foreign Office, December 25, 1963, Israel Foreign Office Papers, 3378/1, Israel State Archives, Jerusalem.
67. Ibid.
68. Ibid.
69. Ibid.
70. Prime Minister Eshkol to President Johnson, December 25, 1963, Israel Foreign Office to Ambassador Harman, Israel Foreign Office Papers, 3378/1, Israel State Archives, Jerusalem.
71. Ibid.

OBSERVATIONS AND CONCLUSIONS

1. Robert Komer Interview, JFKL.
2. Ibid.
3. Ibid.
4. Ibid.
5. Ibid.
6. Arthur M. Schlesinger, Jr. *A Thousand Days: John F. Kennedy in the White House* (Boston, 1965) pp. 566–567.

BIBLIOGRAPHY

GOVERNMENT ARCHIVES AND PAPERS

The Harry S Truman Papers, The Harry S Truman Library, Independence, Mo.
Israel Foreign Office Papers, Israel State Archives, Jerusalem.
Office of Strategic Services Papers, National Archives, Washington, D.C.
The John F. Kennedy Papers, The John F. Kennedy Library, Boston, Mass.
The Joseph P. Kennedy Papers, The John F. Kennedy Library, Boston, Mass.
The Papers of Franklin D. Roosevelt, The FDR Library, Hyde Park, N.Y.
The Papers of Lyndon B. Johnson, The Lyndon B. Johnson Library, Austin, Tex.
The Robert F. Kennedy Papers, The John F. Kennedy Library, Boston, Mass.
U.S. Department of State Papers, National Archives, Washington, D.C.

ORAL HISTORY INTERVIEWS AT THE JOHN F. KENNEDY LIBRARY

George Aiken

Carl Albert

Joseph Alsop

Robert Amory

John Badeau

Walworth Barbour

David Ben-Gurion

Adolf Berle

Sir Isaiah Berlin

Leonard Bernstein

Charles Bohlen

Habib Bourgiba

Chester Bowles

McGeorge Bundy

Arleigh Burke

James MacGregor Burns

Maurice Couve De Murville

Mary W. Davis

Eamon De Valera

William O. Douglas

Allen W. Dulles

Myer Feldman

Thomas Finletter

Philip M. Klutznick

Hirsch Freed

Robert Komer

J. W. Fulbright

Evelyn Lincoln

Fowler Hamilton

Walter Lippmann

Raymond Hare

Robert Lovett

W. Averell Harriman

Paul Nitze

Richard Helms

Hyman G. Rickover

Bourke B. Hickenlooper

Walt W. Rostow

Hubert H. Humphrey

Dean Rusk

Jacob K. Javits

Arthur M. Schlesinger

Carl Kaysen

Theodore C. Sorensen

Robert F. Kennedy

Maxwell Taylor

Rose F. Kennedy

Eugene M. Zuckert

Nikita Khrushchev

PAPERS AND PRIVATE COLLECTIONS

Dean Acheson Papers, Yale University, Manuscripts and Archives, New Haven, Conn.
Benjamin Akzin Papers, Zionist Archives, New York.
American Jewish Committee Papers.
American Zionist Emergency Committee Papers, Zionist Archives, New York.
W. Averell Harriman Papers, The Library of Congress, Washington, D.C.
Louis D. Brandeis Papers, Zionist Archives, New York.
Clark Clifford Papers, Harry S Truman Library, Independence, Mo.
Benjamin V. Cohen Papers, Zionist Archives, New York.
Levi Eshkol Papers, Israel State Archives, Jerusalem.
Nahum Goldmann Papers, Zionist Archives, Jerusalem.
Jewish Agency Papers, Zionist Archives, New York.
Admiral William D. Leahy Papers, Library of Congress, Washington, D.C.
Breckinridge Long Papers, Library of Congress, Washington, D.C.
Julian W. Mack Papers, Zionist Archives, New York.
James G. McDonald Papers, Columbia University, New York.
Henry Morgenthau Jr. Papers, Yale University, Manuscript and Archives, New Haven, Conn.
Samuel I. Rosenman Papers, Harry S Truman Library, Independence, Mo.
Charles Ross Papers, Harry S Truman Library, Independence, Mo.
Adlai E. Stevenson Papers, Seeley G. Mudd Library, Princeton Library, Princeton, N.J.
Henry L. Stimson Papers, Yale University, New Haven, Conn.
Robert Szold Papers, Zionist Archives, New York and The Robert Szold Home, New York.
Stephen S. Wise Papers, Brandeis University, Waltham, Mass.
Zionist Archives, New York. (All Zionist Archives Materials were transferred to Zionist Central Archives, Jerusalem. When I examined them they were in the Jewish Agency building at 515 Park Avenue, New York.)
Zionist Organization of American Files, Zionist Archives, New York.

Zionist Archives, Individuals Files:

Benjamin Akzin Papers

David Ben-Gurion Papers

Jacob DeHaas Papers

Abba Eban Papers

Albert Einstein Papers

Nahum Goldmann Papers

Rose Jacob Papers

Eddie Jacobson Papers

Judge Julian Mack Papers

George C. Marshall Papers

Robert Szold Papers

AUTOBIOGRAPHIES AND PERSONAL DOCUMENTARIES

Aaronsohn, Alexander. *With the Turks in Palestine* (Boston, 1916).

Abdullah, King of Jordan. *Memoirs* (New York, 1950).

Allon, Yigal. *The Making of Israel's Army* (New York, 1971).

Arens, Moshe. *Broken Covenant: American Foreign Policy and the Crisis between the U.S. and Israel* (New York, 1995).

Arlosoroff, Chaim. *K'tavin* (Tel Aviv, 1934).

Badeau, John S. *The Middle East Remembered* (Washington, D.C., 1982).

Barkley, Alben W. *That Reminds Me* (New York, 1951).

Begin, Menachem. *The Revolt* (New York, 1951).

Ben-Gurion, David. *Ben-Gurion Looks Back in Talks with Moshe Pearlman* (New York, 1965).

———. *Israel: A Personal History* (New York, 1972).

———. *Making Peace: A First-Hand Account of the Arab-Israeli Peace Process* (Westport, Conn., 2000).

Bentsur, Eytan. *Recollections* (London, 1970).

Bernadotte, Folke. *To Jerusalem* (London, 1951).

Byrnes, James F. *Speaking Frankly* (New York, 1947).

Carter, Jimmy. *Keeping Faith* (New York, 1982).

Crossman, Richard. *Palestine Mission* (New York, 1947).

Dayan, Moshe. *Story of My Life: An Autobiography* (New York, 1976).

———. *Breakthrough: A Personal Account of the Egypt-Israel Peace Negotiations* (New York, 1981).

Eban, Abba. *My Country* (New York, 1972).

Eden, Anthony. *Full Circle* (London, 1960).

Eisenhower, Dwight D. *The White House Years: Mandate for Change, 1953–1956* (New York, 1963).

———. *The White House Years: Waging Peace, 1956–1961* (New York, 1965).

Elath, Eliahu. *Israel and Elath: The Political Struggle for the Inclusion of Elath in the Jewish State* (London, 1966).

———. *Yoman San-Frantsisko* (Tel Aviv, 1971).

Goldmann, Nahum. *The Autobiography of Nahum Goldman: Sixty Years of Jewish Life* (New York, 1969).

Granados, Garcia. *The Birth of Israel: The Drama as I Saw It* (New York, 1948).

Jabotinsky, Vladimir. *The Story of the Jewish Legion* (New York, 1945).

Johnson, Lyndon B. *Vantage Point* (New York, 1971).

Joseph, Bernard. *British Rule in Palestine* (Washington, D.C., 1948).

Kenen, I. L. *Israel's Defense Line: Her Friends and Foes in Washington* (Buffalo, 1981).

Kennedy, Robert F. *Thirteen Days: A Memoir of the Cuban Missile Crisis* (New York, 1971).

Kissinger, Henry. *The White House Years* (Boston, 1979).

———. *Years of Upheaval* (Boston, 1982).

———. *Years of Renewal* (New York, 1999).

Kollek, Teddy. *For Jerusalem: A Life* (New York, 1978).

Macmillan, Harold. *At the End of the Day, 1961–1963* (New York, 1973).

McDonald, James G. *My Mission in Israel* (New York, 1951).

Meir, Golda. *A Land of Our Own* (Philadelphia, 1973).

———. *My Life* (New York, 1975).

Michaels, Jeffrey. *Shifting Sands: John F. Kennedy and the Middle East* (Yale University Ph.D., 2002).

Neumann, Emanuel. *In the Arena: An Autobiographical Memoir* (New York, 1976).

Nixon, Richard. *RN: The Memoirs of Richard Nixon* (New York, 1973).

Peres, Shimon. *David's Sling: The Armies of Israel* (London, 1970).

———. *Battling for Peace: Memoirs* (New York, 1995).

Phelby, H. St. John. *Arabian Jubilee* (London, 1953).

Rabin, Yitzhak. *The Rabin Memoirs* (Tel Aviv, 1994).

Rafael, Gideon. *Destination Peace: Three Decades of Israeli Foreign Policy* (London, 1981).

Reagan, Ronald. *An American Life: The Autobiography* (New York, 1990).

Roosevelt, Eleanor. *This I Remember* (New York, 1949).

Rosenman, Samuel. *Working with Roosevelt* (New York, 1952).

Shamir, Yitzhak. *Summing Up: An Autobiography* (Boston, 1994).

Smith, Amanda, ed. *Hostage to Fortune: The Letters of Joseph P. Kennedy* (New York, 2001).

Stettinius, Edward. *Roosevelt and the Russians* (New York, 1949).

Truman, Harry S. *Memoirs*, 2 vol. (New York, 1953–1955).

Weizman, Ezer. *The Battle for Peace* (New York, 1981).

Weizmann, Chaim. *Trial and Error* (New York, 1949).

Welles, Sumner. *We Need Not Fail* (Boston, 1948).

Wise, Stephen S. *Challenging Years* (New York, 1949).

Zionist Organization of America. *John F. Kennedy on Israel, Zionism and Jewish Issues* (New York, 1965).

PUBLISHED GOVERNMENT DOCUMENTS

Congressional Record, 1960–2000 (Washington, D.C.).

Documents on the Foreign Policy of Israel, 1947–1953, 1960, ed. by Yehoshua Freundlich (Jerusalem).

Public Papers of the Presidents of the United States:

Dwight D. Eisenhower   Richard M. Nixon

Lyndon B. Johnson   Franklin D. Roosevelt

John F. Kennedy

United Nations General Assembly and Security Council Official Records and Minutes, 1960–2000.

United States Department of State, *Foreign Relations of the United States 1961–1963* (Washington, D.C.).

NEWSPAPERS

Chicago Tribune   *Maariv*

Haaretz   *The New York Times*

Jerusalem Post   *Wall Street Journal*

Jewish Telegraphic Agency   *Washington Evening Star*

Jewish Week   *Washington Post*

Long Island Press

SECONDARY WORKS CONSULTED

Allon, Yigal. *The Making of Israel's Army* (London, 1970).

Alpher, Joseph, ed. *War in the Gulf: Implications for Israel: Report of Jaffee Center Study Group* (Boulder, Col., 1992).

Alroy, Gil Carl. *The Kissinger Experience, American Policy in the Middle East* (New York, 1975).

Avriel, Ehud. *Open the Gates! A Personal Story of 'Illegal' Immigration to Israel* (London, 1975).

Bar-On, Mordecai, ed. *Israel Defense Forces: The Six Day War* (Philadelphia, 1969).

———. *The Gates of Gaza, Israel's Road to Suez and Back, 1955–1957* (New York, 1994).

Bar-Siman-Tov, Yaacov. *Israel, the Superpowers, and the War in the Middle East* (New York, 1987).

Bar-Zohar, Michael. *Ben-Gurion: The Armed Prophet* (New Jersey, 1968).

———. *Embassies in Crisis: Diplomats and Demagogues behind the Six-Day War*, trans. Monroe Stearns (Englewood Cliffs, N.J., 1970).

Bass, Warren. *Support Any Friend: Kennedy's Middle East and the Making of the U.S.-Israel Alliance* (New York, 2003).

Bell, Coral. *The Diplomacy of Detente: The Kissinger Era* (London, 1977).

Ben-Porat, Yeshayahu. *Yom Kippur, An Account of Israel's October 1973 War* (Tel Aviv, 1973).

Ben-Zvi, Abraham. *The United States and Israel: The Limits of the Special Relationship* (New York, 1993).

————. *Decade of Transition: Eisenhower, Kennedy, and the Origins of the American-Israeli Alliance* (New York, 1998).

Brandon, Henry. *The Retreat of American Powers* (New York, 1973).

Brands, H. W. *Into the Labyrinth, The United States and the Middle East* (New York, 1994).

Brecher, Michael. *Decisions in Israel's Foreign Policy* (New Haven, Conn., 1975).

Burns, James MacGregor. *John F. Kennedy: A Political Profile* (New York, 1959, 1960, 1961).

Chafets, Zeev. *Double Vision: How the Press Distorts America's View of the Middle East* (New York, 1985).

Christman, Henry M., ed. *The State Papers of Levi Eshkol* (New York, 1969).

Churchill, Randolph S., and Winston Churchill. *The Six Day War* (New York, 1967).

Cline, Ray S. "Policy without Intelligence." *Foreign Policy* (Winter, 1974).

Cohen, Avner. *Israel and the Bomb* (New York, 1998).

Cohen, Michael J. *Truman and Israel* (Berkeley, Calif., 1990).

Cuneo, Ernest. "U.S. Saved Arab Army from a Rout." *Long Island Press* (November 7, 1973).

Curtis, Richard H. *A Changing Image: American Perceptions of the Arab-Israeli Peace Negotiations* (New York, 1981).

Dagan, Avigdor. *Moscow and Jerusalem: Twenty Years of Relations between Israel and the Soviet Union* (London, 1970).

Daniels, Jonathan. *The Man of Independence* (New York, 1950).

Dayan, Moshe. *Diary of the Sinai Campaign* (New York, 1966).

Druks, Herbert. *The U.S. and Israel, 1945–1973* (New York, 1979).

————. *Truman and the Russians* (New York, 1981).

————. *The Uncertain Alliance: The U.S. and Israel from Kennedy to the Peace Process* (Westport, Conn., 2001).

————. *The Uncertain Friendship: The U.S. and Israel from Roosevelt to Kennedy* (Westport, Conn., 2001).

Elath, Eliahu. *Israel and Elath: The Political Struggle for the Inclusion of Elath in the Jewish State* (London, 1966).

Fahmy, Ismail. *Negotiating for Peace in the Middle East* (Baltimore, Md., 1983).

Feinberg, Nathan. *The Arab-Israeli Conflict in International Law* (Jerusalem, 1970).

Finer, Herman. *Dulles over Suez, The Theory and Practice of His Diplomacy* (Chicago, 1964).

Freedman, Max. *Roosevelt and Frankfurter, Their Correspondence* (Boston, 1967).

Friedman, Isaiah. *The Question of Palestine, 1914–1918* (New York, 1973).

Friedman, Saul S. *No Haven for the Oppressed* (Detroit, 1973).

Gazit, Mordechai. *President Kennedy's Policy toward the Arab States and Israel, Analysis and Documents* (Tel Aviv, 1983).

Gilbert, Martin. *Israel, A History* (New York, 1998).

Golan, Galia. *Yom Kippur and after: The Soviet Union and the Middle East Crisis* (Cambridge, 1977).

Golan, Matti. *The Secret Conversations of Henry Kissinger* (New York, 1976).

————. *Shimon Peres: A Biography* (New York, 1982).

Grose, Peter. *Israel in the Mind of America* (New York, 1983).

Habas, Bracha. *The Gate Breakers* (New York, 1963).

Haber, Julius. *The Odyssey of an American Zionist: A Half-Century of Zionist History* (New York, 1958).

Halpern, Ben. *The Idea of the Jewish State* (Cambridge, 1961).

Hamilton, Nigel. *J.F.K Reckless Youth* (New York, 1992).

Harkabi, Yehoshafat. *Arab Attitudes to Israel* (Jerusalem, 1972).

Henriques, Robert. *100 Hours to Suez* (New York, 1957).

Hersh, Seymour M. *The Samson Option: Israel's Nuclear Arsenal and American Foreign Policy* (New York, 1991).

Hertzberg, Arthur, ed. *The Zionist Idea* (New York, 1959).

———. *A Jew in America: My Life and a People's Struggle for Identity* (San Francisco, 2003).

Herzog, Chaim. *The War of Atonement* (London, 1975).

Holly, David C. *Exodus 1947* (Boston, 1969).

Horowitz, David. *State in the Making* (New York, 1953).

Hyamson, Albert. *Palestine under the Mandate* (London, 1950).

The Jaffe Center for Strategic Studies. *Report of a Commission of Jurists of the Crimes of the PLO in Southern Lebanon* (Tel Aviv, 1982).

Kalb, Marvin L., and Bernard Kalb. *Kissinger* (Boston, 1974).

Katz, Samuel. *Days of Fire* (New York, 1966).

Kennedy, John F. *Why England Slept* (Greenwood, 1981).

———. *Profiles in Courage* (New York, 1956).

Kessler, Ronald. *The Sins of the Father: Joseph P. Kennedy and the Dynasty He Founded* (New York, 1996).

Kimche, Jon. *There Could Have Been Peace* (New York, 1973).

Kimche, Jon, and David Kimche. *The Secret Roads: The "Illegal" Migration of a People, 1938–1948* (London, 1954).

Kohler, Foy D. *The Soviet Union and the Other 1973, Middle East War: The Implications for Detente* (Miami, 1974).

Kurzman, Dan. *Genesis 1948, The First Arab-Israeli War* (New York, 1970).

———. *Ben-Gurion: Prophet of Fire* (New York, 1983).

Lacqueur, Walter Z. *The Struggle for the Middle East: The Soviet Union in the Mediterranean, 1958–1968* (New York, 1969).

———. *A History of Zionism* (New York, 1972).

Landau, Julian J., ed. "The War in Lebanon, 1982, a Case Study," in *The Media: Freedom of Responsibility* (Jerusalem, 1984).

Lash, Joseph P. *Eleanor: The Years Alone* (New York, 1972).

Learsi, Rufus. *Fulfillment: The Epic Story of Zionism* (Cleveland, Ohio, 1951).

Lenczowski, George. *American Presidents and the Middle East* (Durham, N.C., 1990).

Levey, Zach. *Israel and the Western Powers, 1952–1960* (Chapel Hill, N.C., 1997).

Livneh, Eliezer. *Yahadut Amerika* (Ramat Gan, Israel, 1967).

London Sunday Times. "Yom Kippur War" (New York, 1969).

Lorch, Netanel. *The Edge of the Sword: Israel's War of Independence* (New York, 1961).

Love, Kenneth. *Suez, Twice Fought War* (New York, 1969).

Manuel, Frank E. *The Realities of American-Palestine Relations* (Washington, D.C., 1949).

Mardor, Manya. *Haganah* (New York, 1957).

Marshall, S.L.A. *Sinai Victory* (New York, 1958).

Mason, Alpheus T. *Brandeis: A Free Man's Life* (New York, 1946).

Morse, Arthur D. *While Six Million Died: A Chronicle of American Apathy* (New York, 1967).

Nadich, Judah. *Eisenhower and the Jews* (New York, 1953).

O'Brien, Michael. *John F. Kennedy, A Biography* (New York, 2005).

Organsky, A.F.K. *The $36 Billion Bargain: Strategy and Politics in U.S. Assistance to Israel* (New York, 1990).

Painter, David S. *Oil and the American Century: The Political Economy of U.S. Foreign Oil Policy, 1941–1954* (London, 1986).

Parkes, James. *A History of Palestine from 135 A.D. to Modern Times* (London, 1949).

Pearlman, Moshe. *Ben Gurion Looks Back* (London, 1965).

Pollock, David. *The Politics of Pressure: American Arms and Israeli Policy Since the Six-Day War* (Westport, Conn., 1982).

Prittie, Terrence. *Eshkol: The Man and the Nation* (New York, 1969).

Quandt, William B. *Decade of Decisions: American Policy toward the Arab-Israeli Conflict, 1967–1976* (Berkeley, Calif., 1977).

———. *Camp David: Peacemaking and Politics* (Washington, D.C., 1986).

Rabinowitz, Ezekiel. *Justice Louis D. Brandeis: The Zionist Chapter of His Life* (New York, 1968).

Reeves, Richard. *President Kennedy: Profile of Power* (New York, 1994).

Reich, Bernard. *Quest for Peace: United States-Israel Relations and the Arab-Israeli Conflict* (New Brunswick, N.J., 1977).

Rosenne, Shabtai. *Israel's Armistice Agreement with the Arab States* (Tel Aviv, 1951).

Sachar, Howard M. *A History of Israel: From the Rise of Zionism to Our Time* (New York, 1979).

Safran, Nadav. *The United States and Israel* (Cambridge, 1963).

———. *From War to War: The Arab-Israeli Confrontation, 1948–1967* (Indianapolis, 1969).

———. *Israel, The Embattled Ally* (Cambridge, 1978).

Samuel, Viscount Herbert L.S. *Memoirs* (London, 1955).

Schechtman, Joseph B. *The U.S. and the Jewish State Movement, The Crucial Decade: 1939–1949* (New York, 1966).

Schiff, Zeev. "Green Light in Lebanon." *Foreign Policy* (Spring, 1983).

Schiff, Zeev, and Ehud Yaari. *Israel's Lebanon War* (New York, 1984).

Schiff, Zeev, and R. Rothstein. *Fedayeen* (London, 1972).

———. *October Earthquake: Yom Kippur 1973* (Tel Aviv, 1974).

Sheehan, Edward R.F. *The Arabs, the Israelis and Kissinger: A Secret History of American Diplomacy in the Middle East* (New York, 1976).

Schlesinger, Arthur M. Jr. *A Thousand Days John F. Kennedy in the White House* (Boston, 1965).

Sicherman, Harvey. *Broker or Advocate? The U.S. Role in the Arab-Israeli Dispute, 1973–1978* (Philadelphia, 1978).

Smith, Amanda. *Hostage to Fortune: The Letters of Joseph P. Kennedy* (New York, 2001).

Smith, Charles D. *Palestine and the Arab-Israeli Conflict* (New York, 1996).

Snetsinger, John. *Truman, the Jewish Vote and the Creation of Israel* (Stanford, 1974).

Sorenson, Theodore. *Kennedy* (New York, 1965).

Spiegel, Steven L. *The Other Arab-Israeli Conflict: Making American's Middle East Policy, From Truman to Reagan* (Chicago, 1985).

Stein, Leonard. *The Balfour Declaration* (London, 1961).

Steinberg, Alfred. *The Man from Missouri* (New York, 1962).

St. John, Robert. *Eban* (New York, 1972).

Sunday Times Correspondents. *Insight on the Middle East War* (London, 1974).

Thomas, Abel. *Comment Israel Fut Sauve, Les Secrets de L'Expedition de Suez* (Paris, 1978).

Thomas, Hugh. *Suez* (New York, 1967).

Tsur, Ya'akov. *Prelude a Suez: Journal d'une ambassade, 1953–1956* (Paris, 1968).

Urofsky, Melvin. *American Zionism from Herzl to the Holocaust* (New York, 1975).

———. *We Are One* (New York, 1978).

Urofsky, Melvin, and David W. Levy, eds. *Letters of Louis D. Brandeis* (New York, 1971).

Zaar, Isaac. *Rescue and Liberation: America's Part on the Birth of Israel* (New York, 1954).

INDEX

About the Author

HERBERT M. DRUKS is Professor of History and Politics in the Department of Judaic Studies at Brooklyn College. He has taught at Haifa University, The School of Visual Arts, and Yale University. His previous books include *The Uncertain Friendship: The U.S. and Israel, from F.D.R. to Kennedy* (Greenwood, 2001) and *The Uncertain Alliance: The U.S. and Israel from Kennedy to the Peace Process* (Greenwood, 2001).